Marriage Enrichment

Marriage Enrichment: Preparation, Mentoring, and Outreach

By
Richard A. Hunt, Ph.D.
Graduate School of Psychology
Fuller Theological Seminary
Pasadena, California

Larry Hof, M.Div.
Advanta Corporation
Spring House, Pennsylvania

Rita DeMaria, Ph.D.
Delaware Valley Relationship Center
Spring House, Pennsylvania

USA	Publishing Office:	BRUNNER/MAZEL *A member of the Taylor & Francis Group* 325 Chestnut Street Philadelphia, PA 19106 Tel: (215) 625-8900 Fax: (215) 625-2940
	Distribution Office:	BRUNNER/MAZEL *A member of the Taylor & Francis Group* 47 Runway Road Levitttown, PA 19057 Tel: (215) 269-0400 Fax: (215) 269-0363
UK		BRUNNER/MAZEL *A member of the Taylor & Francis Group* 1 Gunpowder Square London EC4A 3DE Tel: +44 171 583 0490 Fax: +44 171 583 0581

MARRIAGE ENRICHMENT: Preparation, Mentoring, and Outreach

1 2 3 4 5 6 7 8 9 0

Printed by Edwards Brothers, Ann Arbor, MI, 1998.

A CIP catalog record for this book is available from the British Library.
∞ The paper in this publication meets the requirements of the ANSI Standard Z39.48-1984 (Permanence of Paper)

Library of Congress Cataloging-in-Publication Data
Hunt, Richard A., 1931–
    Marriage enrichment: preparation, mentoring, and outreach/by
Richard A. Hunt, Larry Hof, Rita DeMaria.
      p.   cm.
    Rev. ed. of: Marriage enrichment / Larry Hof. c1981.
    Includes bibliographical references and index.
    ISBN 0-87630-913-9 (case: alk. paper). — ISBN 0-87630-914-7
(pbk.: alk. paper)
      1. Marriage counseling—United States.   2. Family—United States.
3. Interpersonal relations—United States.   I. Hof, Larry.
II. DeMaria, Rita.   III. Hof, Larry.   Marriage enrichment.
IV. Title.
HQ10.H855   1998
306.8—dc21   98-25594
                                     CIP

ISBN 0-87630-913-9 (case)
ISBN 0-87630-914-7 (paper)

Contents

Part Three
Research on Marriage Enrichment

Part Four
Strengthening Marriages: Treatment, Enrichment,
Mentoring, and Outreach

Preface

This book provides an overview of the principles and programs for strengthening and enriching marriage. It updates and expands the pivotal work of Larry Hof and William R. Miller, published in 1981 as *Marriage Enrichment: Philosophy, Process, and Program*. Building on their solid foundation, we also describe some of the expanding possibilities for delivering accurate information and teaching useful skills to couples.

For practitioners, students, and others who are new to this field, this volume will introduce the principles, history, programs, and possibilities of marriage enrichment. For practitioners who are already acquainted with marriage enrichment and are trained in one or more programs, this book will update basic principles for assisting couples. However, this book is not intended to provide an in-depth coverage of all of the rapidly increasing varieties of marriage, couple, and family enrichment programs. Information on locating current information about programs, training, and their availability is noted in chapter 5.

For both the novice and experienced in this field, we hope this book will stimulate more involvement in providing preventive and wellness services to marriages in support of families. For all readers, we hope to present the great benefits that marriage enrichment programs can provide to couples, and through them to families, children, business, health, society, and the world.

We focus on sustaining, nurturing, enriching, and strengthening marriages for many reasons. First and foremost, healthy marriages are the foundation and backbone of healthy families and healthy societies. Through society's sanctioning, marriage structures how men and women will satisfy their most intimate sexual desires; provides for mutual support and nurture around life's most essential transitions (such as births, deaths, crises, illnesses); forms the basis for establishing a home/residence; is the basis for identifying parental responsibilities for children; and provides for the transmission of property, money, and other real resources of life. Healthy and successful marriages are built-in models for the next generation as they in turn respond to their own adult life journeys. In equally powerful ways, dysfunctional or broken marriages model negatives for the next generation.

Second, as David Mace proclaimed years ago, we can have better marriages if we really want them. Recent research demonstrates that marriage skills are learned and can be learned. No couple needs to be stuck in dysfunctional patterns, yet finding better ways to reach the hearts of spouses and free them to decide to change is one of the central challenges facing those who envision successful marriages for all couples.

Third, we focus almost exclusively on marriage enrichment, rather than family enrichment and alternate couple relationships, because we believe that the most effective and efficient way to enrich families is to focus on the husband-wife relationship. The quality of that marriage greatly influences and determines the quality of all family relationships, both within the home residence and among the extended and in-law families. This does not negate the value of enriching the family as an integrated system, yet we must leave that challenge to others. It does emphasize the central importance of the marriage subsystem in the larger system of the family. A stronger marriage is very likely to motivate family enrichment as well.

Fourth, there is no other human relationship like a man-woman dyad sanctioned by their society. There is a depth of human knowing that can only be found in a long-term relationship with another person who is similar enough to make contact yet different enough to bring growth-producing challenges in the context of unconditional regard and affirmation. In studying marriages, both healthy and unhealthy, we will newly discover the wisdom of the woman-man dyad that cannot be fully matched by other arrangements. We seek to find what is right, joyful, and wonderful about marriages and, through marriage enrichment, to make these findings available to all couples around the world.

Marriage is here to stay. Marriage appears in some form in every culture and society. In every generation, the vast majority of adults do marry (at least once), which points to the powerful place of marriage in the networks of every society. Since marriage is so powerful, everyone, whether married or not, has a vital stake in enabling marriage to succeed. So we hope that an increased understanding of what makes marriage work well will enable decision-makers in business, government, education, religion, entertainment, and all other areas of society to support marriage preparation, education, and enrichment efforts such as those presented in this book. We also hope it will enable them to create and develop new marriage supports that are more effective, efficient, economical, and widely available than those in current use.

We do not address the varieties of couple situations that in some ways seem similar to marriage, such as gay and lesbian couples, unmarried cohabitants, never-married singles, and single parent families. We applaud those who are addressing these populations, but marriage enrichment is so vast a topic we do not have space for those additional fields. However, all of the alternatives to marriage (and/or to family) begin with persons who, for one reason or another, have been unable or unwilling to find satisfaction and success in a woman-man marriage. We must leave to others the tasks of finding how the marriage enrichment principles and programs can apply to situations other than marriage. Undoubtedly mutual agreement, common values, respect, cooperation, equality, shared power, and other social relations skills will still apply.

We view marriage enrichment programs as part of a cooperative range of aids to couples and families, not as a substitute for marital or other types of therapy nor as the only panacea for the world's problems and challenges. We have great interest in expanding the types of effective education and support that can enable married couples to find satisfaction, fullfillment, and joy, which they in turn can express through better parenting, work, and community living. As a by-product, these gains will demonstrate that the "institution" of marriage can be truly alive and healthy. We are clearly committed to equalitarian woman-man marriage and know that other types of marriages are less desirable. We are convinced that where millions of couples find genuine joy, growth, and fulfillment in healthy marriages, the future of marriage is easily assured through these models of marriage, family, and community enrichment.

We believe that couples who adopt the marriage enrichment philosophy, who are involved in the ongoing process of marriage enrichment, and who participate in marriage enrichment programs that meet their specific needs, will be better able to maximize their potential as individuals and as a married couple. These couples will be able to cope with the stresses and problems that emerge when two persons live together in an intimate relationship. We also believe that marital therapy may be enhanced by marriage enrichment programming. Although further research will give increasing support for these statements, we offer this book as a step toward applying current knowledge to the needs of couples, families, and societies, and encouraging the continual expansion of research and its application to the urgent needs of couples and families for marriage preparation, education, and enhancement.

PART ONE

MARRIAGE ENRICHMENT PHILOSOPHY AND CONCEPTS

Marriage enrichment (ME) is an expanding frontier in many ways. It is coming of age as a subdiscipline of marriage and family education and therapy. The need for ME and support efforts is greater than ever. Marriage assessment, treatment, enrichment, and outreach are interrelated facets of our concern to strengthen families by strengthening marriages. In chapter 1, we summarize some of these basic foundations and assumptions of ME.

In chapter 2 we summarize the history of ME; describe its theoretical foundations, nature, and positive emphases; and attend to the use of confrontation, communication, and self-disclosure in enrichment settings. Our emphasis on marriage as a major key to the quality of families and society is the focus of chapter 3.

Chapter 1

An Expanding Frontier

You have probably seen many couples like Meg and Bill:

Meg: Just look at all the stars . . . and to think that they have been there millions of years.

Bill: That's a long time . . . we hardly know what's going to happen in five years.

Meg: If things keep going like they are now, we'll be broken up by then, just like all our friends.

Bill: Yeah, and it's all your fault! I wish we were half as happy as we were at our wedding.

Meg: It's just as much your fault as mine. If it weren't for the kids, I would be out of here now.

Bill: Nobody knows how to make marriage work these days.

Now, suppose you could rewrite this brief exchange in the spirit of Nan and Matt:

Nan: Just look at all the stars . . . and to think that they have been there millions of years.

Matt: That's a long time . . . and I want us to be together just as long.

Nan: If things keep going like they are now, we'll make it. We do face some problems, but we're learning how to cope with them.

Matt: Yeah, it helps to have friends who stick together, like those we met at the marriage enrichment weekend.

Nan: It meant a lot to me to talk with other couples like us who are balancing kids, work, and money, and still love each other.

Matt: It's encouraging to know there are still so many couples who are making marriage work these days.

There is little doubt which couple would have added a warm embrace to their conversation.

Most professionals and couples can recognize the difference between successful and unsuccessful couples, between couples who care for each other, their children, and society, and couples who hurt and destroy themselves and others. In their search for ways to prevent distress in marriage and family before it is too late, many are turning to a variety of psychoeducational programs that can move couples like Meg and Bill to be more mutually caring, supportive, nurturing, and successful.

Marriage enrichment (ME)[1] and outreach are major tools for practitioners to use with couples as part of their care and treatment. Many professionals predict that, in the coming years, ME increasingly will become a major dimension of work with couples and families (Goldberg, 1993). Some see ME as being where parent training was 20 years ago.

ME expresses the fundamental assumption that couples can create better marriages (Mace & Mace, 1974). ME is an educational and preventive approach to couple relationship enhancement. It is both a philosophy and a process that is expressed in a variety of programs and techniques. Although ME is not a magic solution that can cure all ills of couples, it is a major tool for therapists to use with couples as part of their care and treatment.

Even in the short conversations of Meg and Bill and of Nan and Matt, there are many reminders of basics that ME shares with other types of couple improvement. The religious foundation of ME has produced several assumptions about marriage that are part of most ME programs and approaches. Some of these are such basic assumptions that ME programs may not articulate them. Among these implicit assumptions are

1. Permanent marriage between one man and one woman is the preferred norm for couples.
2. A legalized marriage, sanctioned by both a religious institution and the state, is the preferred lifestyle for couples.
3. In a formal ceremony with witnesses, usually a wedding, the woman and the man commit to a long-term permanent relationship.
4. The wedding vows and commitment as spouses are set in the context of the faith of both partners and the community.
5. Others are expected to respect the integrity and boundary of the married couple.

---

[1]The acronym ME is used throughout this book. Although it looks like the word "me," please remember that the capitalized ME stands for marriage enrichment, a generic term not referring to any specific program.

6. Although common-law marriages usually are treated the same as registered marriages for the purposes of ME, couples "living together" may not have the same level of commitment, plans, and so forth.
7. Engaged and other prewedding couples are planning to be married.

Some ME programs, such as Marriage Encounter, are sponsored officially by several Christian or Jewish groups, and most of the remaining ME programs, such as Association of Couples for Marriage Enrichment (ACME), have been developed and continued by persons who have some type of religious heritage or are actively involved in a religious faith group.

THE QUADRANGLE OF HELPING COUPLES: ASSESSMENT, TREATMENT, ENRICHMENT, OUTREACH

Mace (1987) differentiated education, therapy, and enrichment as three basic ways of helping married couples, a set also used by Stahmann and Salts (1993). Education is the dimension through which professionals reach out to couples at any stage with information about how to make couple relationships successful. Therapy includes both assessment and treatment, and ME is the enrichment dimension.

Like Mace, we emphasize enrichment as a preventive approach that attempts to reach couples before they become mired in dysfunctional patterns and while they are still motivated to seek improvement. Mace argues that each approach should be retained, yet it is the preventive perspective of ME that offers the most hope for widespread use because ME retreat programs enable couples to gain new perspectives and discover any marital problems early. Support groups, therapy, and education can be used in relation to ME programs as appropriate for each couple.

In rearranging Mace's basics, we see professionals as having four major types of approaches or tools for couple improvement: couple assessment, treatment, enrichment, and outreach (CATEO). All involve direct personal contact with one or both partners.

Although our primary focus is on how ME can be used by practitioners and couples, seeing ME in the context of these related types of marriage improvement gives a much broader perspective on the professional's work. These four overlapping face-to-face approaches to marriage are interrelated yet distinct. Each focuses directly on couples and includes issues of training, research, and support.

1. *Assessment* is the systematic process of identifying the strengths and growth areas (or dysfunctions) of a couple and deciding (diagnosing) what should

be done, what may be ruled out, and what related guidance should be applied for intervention in a dysfunctional situation.

2. *Treatment* is intervention with the goal of correcting existing marital dysfunctions. Therapy always has implicit assessment procedures and increasingly includes assessment and diagnostic tools.

3. *Enrichment* typically refers to weekend retreat and other group settings in which reasonably healthy married couples learn how to improve their marriage and increase pleasure and success. Enrichment uses psychoeducational methods that address affective, behavioral, cognitive, and intentional dimensions.

4. *Outreach* includes informational and educational efforts that seek to establish contact with couples who are in need of intervention, support, and nurture. Outreach seeks to offer as much help as possible and to open avenues through which couples can connect to assessment, therapy, and enrichment services and programs that can improve their relationships.

In outreach, a professional works in large group formats with the following types of institutions, media, and structures of society to assist couples:

Institutions include schools, churches, synagogues, and community agencies that offer high school, college, or community-level courses in relationships, marriage, and family living.

Media refers to all the communication channels including television, movies, musicals, audio- and videotape, drama, music, art, and other portrayals of women and men interacting in couple relationships.

Society denotes the range of laws, customs, mores, and traditions that affect marriage in many ways, as especially noted by Popenoe, Elshtain, and Blankenhorn (1996).

Marriage improvement services to couples are set in the context of these structures that affect marriage directly or indirectly. These larger contexts are very important, but we limit our focus to ME, with some attention to the other three direct services that professionals provide to couples.

NEED FOR MARRIAGE ENRICHMENT

The quality of marriage is the fundamental key to the quality of the family because the wife and husband are the leaders in their family with the power to influence what happens to their children and others in their household, thus affecting the next generation and all of us in society (Blankenhorn, 1995; Brody, Arias, & Fincham, 1996; Glendon & Blankenhorn, 1995; Gottman, 1994, p. 4; Reagan, 1996).

By some estimates, approximately 40 to 50% of all marriages end in divorce, with the exact percentage varying considerably with socioeconomic status, personal commitment, faith involvement, and other factors (Gottman, 1994; Larson, Swyers, & Larson, 1997). In addition, some estimates are that half of the remaining couples who stay married continue in unsatisfying marriages.

Most of the major problems in society, such as crime, violence, drug abuse, and declines in educational quality, are rooted in dysfunctional family situations that fail to build acceptance and self-esteem in family members and fail to teach children and adolescents to respect persons and property. These basic patterns for good citizenship in turn are controlled by the quality of the relationship between the woman and man who procreated and/or adopted these children (Glendon & Blankenhorn, 1995; Larson, Swyers, & Larson, 1997).

The adults in the family (parents and other caregivers) shape the family atmosphere. These adults control in large measure the ways that respect for persons and property, self-identity, self-esteem, sexuality, and related basic life dimensions are laid in the foundation years of childhood and adolescence. Because marriage is the fundamental relationship in the family, the quality of the relationship between the parents as husband and wife has pervasive effects—for good or ill—on the couple, their children and relatives, and the community.

The Council on Families in America (1995, pp. 1, 4; Popenoe et al., 1996, chap. 13) expressed its concern for improving marriage, especially in relation to the effect of marriage dysfunction on children.

> The divorce revolution—the steady displacement of a marriage culture by a culture of divorce and unwed parenthood—has failed. It has created terrible hardships for children, incurred unsupportable social costs, and failed to deliver on its promise of greater adult happiness. . . .
>
> The weight of evidence points to a most disturbing reality. Child well-being is deteriorating. Almost all of the key indicators point toward this conclusion: rates of delinquency and crime, . . . drug and alcohol abuse, suicide, depression, the growing number of children in poverty, and others. Some experts have suggested that the current generation of children and youth is the first in our nation's history to be less well-off—psychologically, socially, economically, and morally—than their parents were at the same age.
>
> To reverse the current deterioration of child and societal well-being in the United States, we must strengthen the institution of marriage. . . . Unless we reverse the decline of marriage, no other achievements—no tax cut, no new government program, no new idea—will be powerful enough to reverse the trend of declining child well-being.

The crises in marriages and families challenge us to find more effective and efficient ways to reach couples earlier, before they become locked into dysfunctional patterns that not only destroy their relationships but seriously affect their children and others about them (McManus, 1995).

Over the past 35 or more years, the ME movement has emerged in response to the serious problems facing marriage and families today. ME leaders and participants recognize the importance of marriage for adults and families and see ME programs as a major resource for changing this dim prediction to positive action. These hundreds of thousands of couples affirm and demonstrate that people can create and develop personal fulfillment and interpersonal intimacy within the marital relationship. They have committed themselves to affirming and stabilizing marriage in our society by challenging and helping people to develop their marital relationship continually, mutually, and reciprocally, in a disciplined, committed, and responsible way.

NEED FOR MARRIAGE OUTREACH

More recent research and discussion indicates that four facets—assessment, treatment, enrichment, and outreach—interact in many ways. A couple or professional may begin at any point and get to the other elements, often moving between focal points according to a couple's needs, progress, skills, interests, and opportunities.

As the "new kid on the block" of marriage improvement, outreach needs further explanation. The term *outreach* is intended to include all of the many activities that seek to reach couples with some type of marriage improvement message. Books, videos, television, movies, and other media that portray ways to improve marriage and that are directed at the general population can be considered outreach efforts. Usually, the motivation of the authors and creators of these products is to help couples improve their marriages, families, and other human relationships, and to do this in an entertaining, attractive, and (it is hoped) profitable format.

Laws, regulations, and government agencies that structure marriage and family relationships (through enforcement of regulations) are also, in a sense, outreach because their aim usually is to support healthy well functioning couple and family relationships or to intervene in dysfunctional harmful situations, such as domestic violence, or attain equitable distribution of property in cases of divorce.

The primary meaning of outreach as used here is to focus on specific activities that seek to reach couples in need and link them to assessment, therapy, and enrichment. The Caring Couple Team model and the Marriage Savers programs (described later in this volume) are clear examples of intentional outreach to other couples.

The primary reason for specific outreach programs and strategies is that the majority of couples in greatest need of assessment, treatment, and enrichment are probably least likely to know about marriage resources, less likely to use marriage media, and more likely to be surrounded by a higher percentage of dysfunctional marriage models among their relatives and friends.

Outreach means that those who do have more healthy marriages and do see the positive possibilities for couples are the persons who must find appropriate ways to carry the message to others, especially those who are less likely to know or utilize the other three types of marriage improvement. Greeley (1991), drawing data from Gallop polls, demonstrates that the percentage of happy, successful marriages is much higher than often is assumed, suggesting that there are many healthy married couples who could be mobilized to share their stories of success with others.

Couples who have participated in treatment or enrichment services can become the primary outreach agents on behalf of healthy marriages. This usually has happened in a haphazard, serendipitous manner as one couple tells their friends about the help and growth they found in an enrichment program or through treatment by a professional.

As described in chapter 12, a more organized outreach movement could use these couples, especially many who have experienced successful ME, as "minutemen and -women," ready to go to one or both members of a hurting couple and provide support, hope, and a vision of possibilities to link the needy couple to available resources.

TOWARD A DEFINITION OF MARRIAGE AND COUPLES

What Is a Couple?

Couples may be dating, engaged, unmarried and living together, or married and living together. Partners may be married yet living apart or living together but not legally married. Persons may consider themselves to be temporarily together as a couple or committed to a long-term relationship ended only by death or divorce. Thus married couples are a subset of all couples.

Although marriage has always existed in some form in human societies, its focus usually has been either to produce children and train them to fit that society or to give continuity to family tradition and property (Mace & Mace, 1986, p. 12). There typically was little attention to the quality of the man-woman relationship itself in marriages. However, Browning et al. (1997) and Regan (1996) trace how the modern understanding of the family as an emotional haven from the pressures of society emerged from earlier eras, with individuals having a positive status in the family.

The importance of marriage and family for the stability of society long has been recognized among human societies (Murstein, 1974). Across the centuries interpretations of marriage have emphasized at different times the person, couple, family, or household. Religious interpretations of marriage have been guided by the metaphors of sacrament, vocation, covenant, and communion (W. E. Johnson, 1990, pp. 1–10, 35–55).

Most ME programs usually have assumed that the couples who participate are married, or intend to be married (currently engaged). The assumption that exactly two persons constitute the couple unit is so widespread that it seldom is questioned, although in some areas of the world a two-person couple would not be assumed. Couples usually are understood to be one woman and one man, although some enrichment programs are now available for same-sex couples.

Although other arrangements may be possible (or advocated), such as polygamy (polyandry and polygyny) and same-sex (gay or lesbian) marriage, the focus of most ME is usually upon long-term, man-woman marriages. In actual practice, however, some ME programs probably include a few couples in which the partners are living together as a common-law marriage, but the usual ethos of the event is that these couples have made, or will make, their relationship into a long-term marriage.

Many programs, such as Miller's Interpersonal Communication Programs ([ICP] Miller, Nunnally, & Wackman, 1976; Miller, Wackman, Nunnally, & Miller, 1988) and Guerney's Relationship Enhancement ([RE] Guerney, 1977, 1987), also have been applied to single persons. Some growth and enrichment programs, such as Hendrix's (1992) Keeping the Love You Find, are designed for single persons. These programs usually assume that participants want to form a couple relationship with a partner, even if they are not currently in such a couple relationship.

Among ME programs, some would disapprove strongly of any nontraditional type of couple situation, some would tolerate alternative couple lifestyles but not assume that they are in all ways equivalent to legal marriage, and a few would openly welcome same-sex and other nonmarried couples. Because gay and lesbian couples face many of the same issues as do heterosexual couples, some of the better known ME programs openly invite same-sex couples to participate. For example, Hendrix's (1988) Getting the Love You Want has a version designed for same-sex couples with long-term commitments between the partners.

Within these definitions of married couple, most ME programs intend to be available to couples from any socioeconomic level, any ethnic group, and any type of interethnic, interracial, or international combination. In practice, however, some ME events may be more limited in scope because of the cost of the program, its location and scheduling, its sponsorship, the type of program and leadership, and other factors.

The terms "spouses" and "partners" usually are used interchangeably here, recognizing that all spouses are partners but some partners may not be legal spouses.

Living Together or Married: Couple or Marriage?

In every couple, each partner has a guiding image of the future. Every couple has dreams, goals, hopes, fears—both immediate and long-term. These assumptions guide them as they make basic decisions about their future. Every couple defines their relationship in their own way as they create a life together that seems to fit their own needs best.

Often ME and couple enrichment are used interchangeably, but there are important distinctions. Marriage includes some type of vow of permanence, or at least a decision to be seen in society as a unit for legal and social advantages. Although nonmarried couples may feel just as closely bonded as married couples, for their own reasons they choose not to make this official or public. This may make their commitment to a future together much less clear and certain. It also may result in much less support from others for working on continuing a relationship. The vows of marriage close many of the exits from the relationship, making the challenges of marriage into incentives to grow as individuals and as a unit (Hendrix, 1988).

The term "marriage" in ME also implies a major set of assumptions about what constitutes marriage and married couples. Fundamental is that marriage is a two-person system consisting of the commitments, goals, and interactions of a woman and a man, set in the networks of larger systems such as family, community, and society. The following definition of marriage tries to capture this in a general way that fits any society.

> In the context of society, marriage is a comprehensive system consisting of persons bound together by voluntary mutual commitment as spouses sanctioned by society, and who are continually interacting in order to achieve individual and mutual goals (Hunt & Rydman, 1979, p. 13).

In a more interpersonal and subjective description, David and Vera Mace (1986, p. 13) summarize marriage as

> an ongoing task achieved by a mutual process of joint personality growth and behavior change, in which differences are as important as similarities, and possession of the appropriate skills to interact creatively is the decisive factor. Building a marriage is, therefore, a task very similar to building a house or cultivating a garden. Our new expectation of marriage as a deeply satisfying interpersonal relationship, combined with our almost total failure to train couples in the use of the necessary skills to

achieve this goal, is all the explanation we need for the devastating breakdown of family life which we witness today.

Common Elements That Make Marriages Succeed Can Be Taught

In the major theoretical approaches to marital therapy, there is agreement that couples learn the patterns they use (Jacobson & Gurman, 1986; Stuart, 1980). Because conflictual or inadequate patterns were learned, they can be replaced with new skills and more effective patterns. Thus communication and problem-solving techniques (e.g., Miller, Miller, Nunnally, & Wackman, 1991) often have been a major focus of ME programs. These skills foster insight and behavioral change. Couple are taught to express respect, commitment, affirmation, awareness of links of past to present, and ways to network with others for support.

ME emphasizes especially the interaction between the two partners in the couple relationship. It is couple education in the best sense of psychoeducation, including both information and guided practice in an atmosphere that supports and encourages growth toward individual and marital wellness.

Key skills needed to achieve marital success are commitment, an effective communication system, and creative use of conflict (Mace & Mace, 1986, pp. 14–15). Giblin (1993) and Robinson and Blanton (1993) expand these to five key characteristics associated with enduring marriages: intimacy balanced with autonomy, commitment (bonding, affection), communication and conflict resolution, religious orientation, and congruent perceptions of the relationship (similarity of values). Olson (Lavee & Olson, 1993; Olson, Russell, & Sprenkle, 1988) emphasizes his circumplex model in which combinations of cohesion and flexibility produce five to seven types of marriages.

In line with the emphasis on relationship commitment, attitudes, skills, and patterns, the aim of ME is to assist couples in achieving goals such as the following:

1. To increase each person's self-awareness and the awareness of his or her partner, especially regarding the positive aspects, strengths, and growth potential of the individuals and the marriage;
2. To provide a safe setting in which partners can increase exploration and self-disclosure of their thoughts and feelings;
3. To increase mutual sensitivity, empathy, and other strengths that improve intimacy, love, care, concern, and support for each other;
4. To develop and encourage the use of skills needed by the partners for effective communication, problem solving, and conflict resolution.

Zimpfer (1988, p. 44) summarizes these ME objectives as awareness of each person's own needs and expectations, awareness of the partner's needs and expectations, communication (including empathy and self-disclosure), enhanced problem-solving and negotiating skills, and satisfaction with the marriage.

The best-known programs have been those designed for couples who want to improve an already well-functioning marriage (Garland, 1983; Otto, 1976). However, an increasing number of practitioners are offering ME programs to couples identified as troubled, dysfunctional, or clinical (Guerney & Maxson, 1990; Zimpfer, 1988). Some programs, such as Retrouvaille (McManus, 1995; B. Zwann & P. Zwann, personal communication, April 15, 1997), are designed specifically for couples who are in distress or in process of divorce.

Creating Marriage: Many Different Models

There are many ways to have a healthy marital relationship. Gottman (1994, pp. 189, 413) describes three general types of couple interaction—volatile, validating, and avoiding—which express high, moderate, and low levels of regulating the balance between positives and negatives in the marriage to achieve a ratio of at least five positives for each negative.

When there are more negatives than can be balanced by positives, the "four horsemen of the apocalypse" (Gottman, 1994, p. 414) appear: complaining/criticizing, contempt, withdrawal, and stonewalling. This need for partners to use their power (skills, resources, choices) to increase the ratio of positive affect (love, care) to negative affect (fear, hate) has been recognized in various ways by many writers (e.g., Hunt & Hunt, 1994; Lederer & Jackson, 1968; Gottman, 1994, pp. 14–19).

The Future Begins Now, With the Next Step, the Next Statement

The importance of clear, specific, immediate changes in shaping the future is emphasized in folk wisdom (such as "today is the first day of the rest of your life" and "a journey of a thousand miles begins with the next step") and in many couple treatment programs (e.g., Hendrix, 1988; Markman, Stanley, & Blumberg, 1994; Miller et al., 1991).

In the first couple's dialogue, Meg and Bill could have gone in a different direction at any point in their conversation. Most professionals repeatedly see this confirmed in their work with couples and families, and any couple can test this assumption by selecting any statement of either Bill or Meg and creating an alternative response that would move them toward a more positive resolution. These changes can be termed "first-order" because they are made within the context of the current assumptions about the relationship.

Second-order changes address the context and assumptions about a relationship, such as each partner's perception of whether change is possible, how much it will cost them, and motivation to change. Perhaps the major second-order change that professionals and couples most need is the couple's awareness that they can change and that they have the desire to do so. The assumption that change *is* possible, can be learned, and can become part of each partner's repertoire of positive skills and affects is central to all couple improvement.

WHAT IS BEING ENRICHED?

ME "can be described as a systematic effort to improve the functioning of marital couples through educational and preventive means" (Zimpfer, 1988, p. 44). Diskin (1986) sees the goal of ME as providing support to couples in search of a deeper, more intimate relationship. ME provides training in spouse relationship skills and support for couples in their continuing journey and growth toward increasing wellness.

The banner of ME includes many types of theoretical perspectives, programs, and formats. The common elements in ME are an emphasis on increasing couples' marital health, satisfaction, and positive functioning. Ideally, to do this requires direct involvement of both spouses in settings with other couples who provide healthy marriage models, in which skills can be taught and practiced, and spouses renew their commitments to continue working on their own marriages.

The exact origin of the term marriage enrichment is unclear, but other terms, such as marital enrichment, marital growth, communication training, and preventive marital health, frequently have been used as synonyms. Early surveys of marriage improvement approaches other than therapy described them as "skill training" programs (L'Abate, 1981). ME continues to include much skill training along with a broader understanding of both intrapsychic and interpersonal processes and of holistic spiritual development.

Enrichment means that something that originally had worth and value is improved further in some way. Persons may be enriched by increasing their financial worth, obtaining more education, expanding their awareness of cultural differences and similarities, or adding artistic and cultural decoration. Bread and other foods are enriched by adding vitamins and other compounds that are considered to be helpful to health.

The usual assumptions about ME are that good marriages can be strengthened, improved, and made more satisfying, more successful, and healthier for the spouses involved. The Maces prefer to emphasize marital wellness rather than health "because wellness is unambiguously positive. You can have either good health—or bad health, but you can't have bad wellness!" (Mace & Mace, 1986, p. 7).

To enrich a marriage means to improve and strengthen a couple (i.e., both spouses and the relationship they share) so that they can function with each other in ways that are more constructive, healthier, and more satisfying to both persons. Because marriage is a system comprising two persons "espoused" to each other, the enrichment of that marriage involves both the interpersonal relationship between the two partners and the intrapsychic (or biopsychosocial) system of each individual.

ENRICHMENT ASSUMPTIONS ABOUT MARRIAGE

ME involves several fundamental assumptions, beliefs, and concepts (Guerney & Maxson, 1990; Hof & Miller, 1981; Mace & Mace, 1978b, 1986).

1. A positive growth orientation for each partner as a person and for their relationship to the other partner.
2. A systemic, dynamic relationship between the partners who are willing to change as an open system.
3. A goal of enabling spouses to have an intentional companionship.
4. An educational, experiential approach to couples that teaches attitudes and specific skills in a structured, orderly fashion.
5. A preventive approach that seeks to support couples in ways that reduce the emergence, development, or recurrence of interpersonal dysfunction.
6. A balance between relational and individual growth in which the focus on the relationship interacts with helping spouses to reach their own individual potentials.
7. Development of intimacy and nurture.
8. ME and growth as a lifelong process.
9. Mutual support between couples through group experiences.

Positive Growth Orientation

At the core of ME is a positive, growth-oriented, and potential-oriented philosophy of the individual. Proponents of ME frequently verbalize this positive aspect to program participants, encouraging them to see change as possible and to accept continuing responsibility for the growth and development of their personal and interpersonal life.

The keystone of ME is growth and human potential, based on the premise that all persons and relationships have a great many untapped strengths and resources that can be developed (Mace & Mace, 1975, 1976; Otto, 1976). People are viewed as having a natural drive toward growth, health, and personal development.

Given the appropriate environment, people can learn how to choose and change behaviors and attitudes that will improve their interpersonal relationships and allow them to experience increased satisfaction in life and in relationships with other people. Problems and conflicts are not ignored but are faced with the affirmation that people can learn how to cope with them in a creative and positive way and develop a more fulfilling life.

Dynamic View of Marriage

Proponents of ME view marriage as positive and growth oriented. The marital relationship can provide opportunities for individual and couple growth and fulfillment, and for acceptance and love, as each partner is known and loved by the other in an interdependent way (Mace & Mace, 1974). Marriage is seen as a growing, dynamic, constantly changing relationship, based on "the dynamic interplay of the unique and changing needs, expectations, and skills of the two partners themselves" (Sherwood & Scherer, 1975, p. 14).

Luthman and Kirschenbaum (1974) have described the marital system as a dynamic complex of patterns of behaviors, ways of function, attitudes, feelings, and norms that exist between two married partners. Each believes these aspects are necessary for the relationship to function effectively and to maintain a satisfactory equilibrium. A change in one aspect of the system is seen as having effects upon other aspects of the system.

Marital systems can be open or closed. An open system is receptive to change, able to change, and open to alternative ways of responding to various life situations. It respects and affirms the worth and value of differences, permits a wide range of feeling responses, and can make flexible adaptations to new inputs. A closed system resists change, has rigid qualities, values conformity, sees differences as a threat, does not value the expression of the full range of feelings such as anger, tenderness, and sadness, and is relatively incapable of making flexible adaptations to new input.

A marital system tends to maintain a homeostatic balance between the two partners that permits the stability needed for the accomplishment of necessary tasks and the addressing of relationship needs. However, too rigid a balance does not permit change to occur when it is needed for an individual or the relationship to grow.

Luthman and Kirschenbaum (1974) also have identified important aspects of growth within an open system and well-functioning marital or family relationship:

1. There is appropriate feedback.
2. Personal differences among family members are viewed as challenges, rather than threatening.

3. Conflict and disagreement are valued as learning opportunities.
4. Internal intent is separated from external manifestations.
5. There is the ability to express feelings and perceptions.
6. Channels are kept open for communication, intimacy, and growth.

Such an open system, which the proponents of ME value, does not happen by chance. Continued efforts are always needed on the parts of both partners to keep the relationship viable over time. Partners are their own active agents of change rather than victims of the change that occurs continually, and are able to develop the necessary interpersonal skills to make continued viability and creative change possible (Lederer & Jackson, 1968; Mace & Mace, 1975, 1977; Miller et al., 1991; Otto, 1969). Gordon (1993) and others emphasize the I-Thou (Buber, 1923) spiritual nature of marriage as well.

The Intentional Companionship Marriage

For many people, there has been a change from the concept of marriage as a rigid and hierarchical institution to the concept of companionship marriage, which is a relationship based on intimacy, equality, and flexibility in interpersonal relationships (Mace & Mace, 1974, 1975). The ultimate goal and underlying value of most ME programs is the attainment and maintenance of such a relationship. Hof and Miller (1981) refer to it as "*intentional companionship marriage*." Hendrix (1988) uses "conscious marriage" to refer to a similar concept.

Intentional companionship marriage is a relationship in which there is a strong commitment to an enduring marital dyad in which each person experiences increasing fulfillment and satisfaction. There is a strong emphasis on developing effective interpersonal relationships and on establishing and maintaining an open communication system. There is the ability to give and accept affection in an unconditional way, to accept the full range of feelings toward each other, to appreciate common interests and differences, to affirm each other's uniqueness, and to see each other as having equal status in the relationship.

In this quality marriage, there is a commitment to expanding and deepening the emotional aspects of the relationship, including the sexual dimension, and to developing and reinforcing marital strengths. This relationship is characterized by mutual affection, honesty, true intimacy, love, empathy, and understanding. There is an awareness of changing needs, desires, and aspirations and appropriate responses to them. There is also a sense of self-worth in each partner and a balance between autonomy and interdependence, with each partner accepting equal responsibility for the success of the relationship. This commitment to grow in love is based on the concept of "permanent love" as the basis for long-term woman-man marriage (Conner, 1988; Ford & Englund, 1979).

The intentional companionship marriage is imbued with a conscious realization that marriage is not a static system with inflexible roles, but rather a dynamic, changing relationship, calling for continued commitment to openness, creative use of differences and conflict, negotiation and renegotiation of roles and norms, and continued individual and couple awareness and growth. In other words, there is an intentional commitment by both partners to work on the process of relationship, and to obtain skills needed to ensure the continued growth and vitality of the relationship.

ME practitioners use a variety of methods to help couples develop the acceptance, trust, and skills needed to achieve such a relationship. Even if one considers the intentional companionship marriage as more an ideal than a reality, this higher view of marriage calls couples to growth and achievement across their lifetime journey. It is a continually developing and expanding goal to which the ME movement has committed itself. In a real sense, the process of working toward the goal is the fulfillment of it!

Educational Nature of Marriage Enrichment

Proponents of ME emphasize its dynamic, experiential, and educational nature (Clinebell, 1976; Gordon, 1988, 1993; Guerney, 1977; Hendrix, 1988; Mace & Mace, 1978a; Otto, 1976; Sherwood & Scherer, 1975).

Guerney (1977) describes an educational model as one in which attitudes and specific skills are taught in a structured and systematic fashion. Behavioral objectives are stated clearly and appropriate evaluative measures are included in the program. A rationale is provided for what is to be learned, along with practice and supervision in developing skills and teaching participants to generalize beyond the learning situation to their everyday life experiences.

The focus of this educational model is on setting goals and reaching them, increasing understanding, and creating a climate of growth and development. There is an emphasis on individual and relationship strengths rather than on what is wrong with the relationship or how the relationship got to be where it is. There is a conscious avoidance of references to sickness or labels that have become associated to a greater or lesser degree with a medical model; virtually all ME programs follow such an educational model.

Harrell and Guerney (1976) note that research has shown that educational models can provide a successful structure for increasing interpersonal functioning. There is some agreement among professionals in the field of marital and family therapy that one of the goals of therapy is the education and reeducation of the couple to facilitate their ability to relate interpersonally in a mutually satisfying way (e.g., Hendrix, 1988; Markman et al., 1994; Hunt & Hunt, 1994).

There is also an increasing tendency to use cognitive and experiential educational models in therapy (Jacobson & Addis, 1993). Such models include the identification of strengths as well as the learning of new skills in areas such as communication, problem solving, and conflict resolution. These models support the rationale for using an educational approach in the ME programs (Worthington, Buston, & Hammonds, 1989).

The educational nature and growth orientation of most ME programs may appeal to a broader segment of the population than programs identified with counseling or therapy. Because of the stigma attached to these terms, people may shy away from programs associated with them. However, education and skill training have positive connotations that could apply to any couple, and thus may have a broader appeal (Jacobson & Addis, 1993; Schauble & Hill, 1976).

Preventive Nature of Marriage Enrichment

Although the program design is primary preventive, couples in need of secondary and tertiary prevention also participate (see part 4). Proponents of ME long have emphasized its preventive nature (Clinebell, 1976; Guerney, 1977; Hendrix, 1988; Mace & Mace, 1975; Otto, 1976; Markman et al., 1994). That is, one aim is to prevent the emergence, development, or recurrence of interpersonal dysfunction. It is believed that by dealing with people in marriages that are basically functional, and by developing the potential and strengths that are there, growth and satisfaction can occur. As a positive, growth-oriented base develops, deterioration in the relationship can be halted or prevented. The parties learn how to recognize problems early, and how to cope with change and conflict. Of course, along with the preventive emphasis, there is a primary emphasis on increasing emotional and interpersonal satisfaction and on strengthening marriage and family life.

L'Abate (1981) and Sauber (1974) make reference to three possible levels of prevention. These levels involve feedback loops between them that inform each level. They are

primary prevention, which consists of promoting health, providing specific protection, and building specific skills;
secondary prevention, which focuses on early diagnosis and intervention to block further development of the dysfunction within the couple or family system;
tertiary prevention, where there is apparently irreversible dysfunction, and the focus is on limiting the spread of the dysfunction and promoting rehabilitation.

The majority of ME programs tend to fall into the primary prevention category (e.g., Hendrix, 1988; Mace & Mace, 1975; Markman et al., 1994; Otto, 1976; Sauber, 1974). However, Guerney (1977) and L'Abate (1981), among others (e.g., Gottman, Notarius, Gonso, & Markman, 1976; Hendrix, 1988; Hof & Miller, 1981; Schauble and Hill, 1976), have expanded into the areas of secondary prevention by using enrichment programming as an adjunct to intensive marital and family therapy. The program developed by Hof (Hof & Miller, 1981) has been used at the Penn Council for Relationships (formerly, the Marriage Council of Philadelphia) with clinical as well as nonclinical couples from 1977 to 1995. More recently, programs such as Retrouvaille (B. Zwann & P. Zwann, personal communication, April 15, 1997) are demonstrating that major causes of distress and divorce can be treated and reversed more often than has been formerly assumed. In addition, ME and therapy increasingly are seen as parts of systemic treatment for couples and individuals, not as a question of which treatment to use.

The need for mental health services far exceeds the number of qualified professionals available to give such services. In addition, the cost of such services is frequently prohibitive for couples and families in need. Like many professionals, David and Vera Mace (1975) expressed the need for preventive mental health services to make a shift away from a pathological remedial orientation to a preventive, experiential approach, emphasizing positive growth. They believe that such a shift will provide a better balance between the need and the availability of mental health services because fewer people will be in need of such services. It is hoped that ME will provide a needed and valuable service in the area of preventive marital health, and indeed, that is one of its major aims.

Balance Between Relational and Individual Growth

Herbert Otto (1976, p. 14) defines ME in terms of the "development of marriage and individual potential while maintaining a consistent and primal focus on the relationship of the couple." His definition indicates the balance that most ME programs try to provide between relational and marital growth on the one hand, and individual growth on the other.

Mace and Mace (1977) state that ME programs need to focus on the simultaneous growth and development of the individual and of the marital relationship, with each aspect supporting the other. Such a focus contributes to the development of a growing, flexible, mutually satisfying relationship. Miller et al. (1991) note that one goal of the Couples Communication Program is increased self-awareness, partner-awareness, and couple-awareness, and increased self- and other-esteem. Otto (1969) speaks of actualizing the potential of the couple in relationship to each other and the personal potential of each individual in the relationship. Travis and Travis (1975) stress that self-actualization is needed along with relationship actualization.

Most ME programs emphasize improvement of the marital relationship, devoting the majority of time to couple interaction, improving couple communication, deepening the mutual acceptance and emotional life of the couple, fostering marriage strengths, and developing marriage potential.

At the same time, acceptance, esteem, actualization, and expression of the self are crucial aspects of growth and development in the marriage and other relationships and need to be addressed as well. Luthman and Kirschenbaum (1974, p. 110) state that the "ideal base for a marital relationship is that each partner have a strong sense of himself as a separate, whole person, whose survival is attached to himself and to his own growth." They also stress the ability to be parents, children, and friends to each other as necessary to actualize the potential of the individual and the couple. Travis and Travis (1975) speak of the need to grow individually together, which implies personal growth, individuality, self-identity, and self-love as the bases for relationship enhancement.

Some developers of ME programs believe that the ME process should begin with the individual sense of fulfillment and worth. Others focus immediately on enhancement of the relationship and do not address the intrapsychic concerns of the individuals who form the participating dyad. Of course, in the latter instance, the climate of sharing, trust, empathy, and support contribute to personal growth anyway. In either case the primary focus is on the relationship between participating partners.

ME programs must respond to both individual and couple needs for growth and development. This can occur whether the program focuses equally on individual and couple growth, or just on enhancing the relationship. A problem emerges only when one or the other is virtually excluded or ignored.

Many ME practitioners emphasize the inevitability of conflict and the legitimacy of appropriately managed conflict within the marital relationship. They also stress that emerging conflict within a dynamic system is not always easily managed solely through dialogue, and they frequently provide skill training in conflict management. Constructive conflict management and problem solving is much needed as the application and practice of what is stated verbally.

Development of Intimacy and Nurture

Within this general paradigm, a specific ME program may emphasize communication skills, conflict resolution, family-of-origin influences, or other factors. To enrich a marriage means that the agent of enrichment, such as ME leaders and materials, addresses in a beneficial way some combination of the elements that enable marriages to be healthier. Obviously, "healthy" and similar terms involve a major set of values and images concerning what constitutes marital health and wellness, as noted above in our definition of marriage and the goals of ME.

Improving couple communication skills seems to increase self-esteem, better use of verbal interactions, and more agreement on goals and roles in the marriages (Hill, 1991). Important cognitive processes affect functioning and satisfaction in the relationship by activating attention, controlling perceptual processes, and evoking behavioral and affective responses from both partners (Lopez, 1993), which contribute to the enrichment of both spouses and their relationships with each other.

Improved intimacy is also part of ME. Rampage (1994) notes that intimacy depends upon equality between partners, empathy for each other's experience, and a willingness to collaborate around both meaning and action. A couple will interpret their interactions as intimate and satisfying when they are experienced as collaborative, empathic, accepting, intense, and validating of the relationship as well as of the self. Rampage's observations about marital power and process, meanings and obstacles to intimacy, and ways to increase intimacy provide a valuable feminist perspective on enrichment.

Intimacy is improved when couples have an opportunity to talk about their own concerns, which in turn increases their awareness and gives examples of ways to improve their marital interactions. Worthington et al. (1989) compared couples under each of four conditions: assessment, information, group discussion, and information plus group discussion. They found that information had little apparent effect on couples, but group discussion improved couples' marriage satisfaction and their sexual and intellectual intimacy.

Oliver and Miller (1994) see caring and skilled communication processes as prerequisites to effective problem solving, conflict resolution, and the ability to communicate affection effectively. These processes and skills need to be based in systems-theory properties and principles that provide a framework for examining and understanding relationship development and dysfunction.

Marriage Enrichment and Growth as a Lifelong Process

Every stage of the couple's journey needs a variety of specific programs and events available as appropriate to the marital stage of each couple. A conceptual framework for enrichment and prevention efforts is provided by Markman et al. (1986) who emphasize the transitions involved in moving from single life to a marital relationship.

A focus on the positive aspects of the relationship gives the partners confidence and hope that they will continue to be together. As this becomes clearer and more dependable, each person can be open to making changes that will increase mutual satisfaction. This is another way to emphasize the need for enough positives to balance the negatives and to give assurance that the work of change is worthwhile and productive.

Many authors (e.g., Augsburger, 1988; Campbell, 1981; Hendrix, 1988; Hunt & Hunt, 1994; Levinson, 1978; Romney and Harrison, 1983) emphasize the lifetime journey of marriage as a major dimension of life development. ME programs are increasingly aware of the changing needs of couples across their lifetimes, with the possibility of new growth occurring at every stage of life and in every situational challenge. This sense of a stable history and future also encourages both security and flexibility as essential for growth.

Mutual Support Between Couples Through Group Experiences

All forms of ME have had couples meeting together in group settings, although the amount of contact between couples varies among programs. Much positive support arises out of the informal friendships that develop among couples who participate in the same event. Some programs, such as Marriage Encounter, minimize disclosure by couples in the group setting, whereas others, such as ACME, encourage leaders to be self-disclosing as one model of openness about the realities of marriage. Even with these variations, the common theme is to encourage honesty about the full range of marital issues and concerns. Within a strong respect for the privacy of each couple, discussions among couples allow them to compare notes about marriage and to encourage and support each other in their marriage relationships.

This overview of assumptions and principles presents a positive view of ME principles and assumptions that can be part of the services that practitioners can provide. The next chapter describes valuable opportunities for practitioners to expand their services to couples and families.

Chapter 2

Threat or Promise for Practitioners?

ME is a field whose time has come. In the past three decades the ME field has expanded greatly, a wider variety of programs is available, research supports the value of ME, and there are major exchanges of theory and techniques between marriage assessment, therapy, and enrichment.

ME offers many promising possibilities for professionals who are concerned for couples and families and want to expand their practice. ME is a threat only to practitioners who still focus only on individuals, with little or no attention to the systemic nature of individual, marriage, family, and community interactions and relationships.

ME in its many variations is being utilized more today than ever before. The general climate favoring healthy marriage as the central key to family wellness is increasing. Religious groups as well as community agencies increasingly recognize and support early tertiary preventive programs that enable marriages to succeed. Although primary and secondary treatments are still essential, preventive treatments offer much greater gains at much less cost. The professional who is able to participate in networks that provide ME not only will help more families but also has a ready-made source of referrals.

In the early 1970s, Otto (1975, 1976) surveyed various marriage and family enrichment programs in the United States and Canada and concluded that at least 420,000 couples have been participants—over 3,500 in the Couples Communication Program (CCP), over 7,000 in the United Methodist Communication Labs, and over 400,000 in the various expressions of Marriage Encounter—with almost 60,000 couples being added each year to the total (Gallagher, 1975). Otto (1976) estimated that at least twice that number had participated in enrichment programs based on the increasing number of facilitators and programs that had come to his attention since his initial survey.

Estimates are that 2 million to 3 million couples have participated in the programs in the United States and Canada since the early 1960s, when ME programs began. In addition, if each couple who has participated in an enrichment event favorably influences one or two other couples, the ripple effects of ME are doubled or tripled. Such numbers, if anywhere near accurate, indicate that the ME movement is touching the lives of enormous numbers of people and therefore deserves careful examination. Nevertheless, even with the growth of enrichment programs, the number of couples who participate in some type of ME event in any one year is still probably between 100,000 and 200,000 (McManus, 1995).

One way of obtaining estimates is to assume that, in the United States alone, an average of 50 to 100 ME events (one or two per state) of all types occur each week, and that about 20 couples attend per event. If approximately 1,000 to 2,000 couples are being reached each week, then, projected across 50 weeks (one year), 50,000 to 100,000 couples directly participate in enrichment events each year. Because most events have fewer than 20 couples attending, the occasional large event of 50 or more couples probably would not change this estimate much.

With some 48 million marriages among a U.S. population of 250 million, even if ME events have several hundred thousand participating couples each year, at best fewer than 1% of all marriages are reached in any one year by any type of ME program. Because many ME programs require that couples make a full weekend commitment, pay housing and program costs, and often make their own child care arrangements, it is likely that few couples at the lower end of the socioeconomic spectrum are reached by any marriage improvement program.

BRIEF HISTORY OF MARRIAGE ENRICHMENT

The ME movement originated from a variety of sources. The Roman Catholic Marriage Encounter program began in Spain in January 1962 under the initiative and leadership of Father Gabriel Calvo. It grew out of a desire to help families to relate more effectively together, and Father Calvo's belief that it was necessary to start with the relationship of the marital dyad to address the needs of families (Demarest et al., 1977). A helpful account of personal growth through Marriage Encounter is provided by McManus (1995, pp. 175–192).

Marriage Encounter reached the United States in 1965 through initial leadership of Father Chuck Gallagher, who helped to organize Worldwide Marriage Encounter in 1968 (McManus, 1995, p. 175). In 1975 alone, 105,000 couples attended a Marriage Encounter event (McManus, 1995, p. 176), and over 200,000 couples had participated in Marriage Encounter since its beginning (Genovese, 1975). Although Marriage Encounter originated in the Roman Catholic Church, several Protestant and Jewish versions of Marriage Encounter have developed and continue in widespread use today. Counting both Roman Catholic and other denominational Marriage Encounter expressions, by 1980, well over 1 million couples had attended some type of Marriage Encounter weekend event. In addition, thousands of couples have participated in some form of Engaged Encounter.

In 1975, Marriage Encounter (800-795-LOVE) attendance had dropped to around 15,000 per year. In addition, National Marriage Encounter (405-672-0177) annually involved some 2,100 couples, and United Marriage Encounter (800-334-8920) added another 1,000 per year (McManus, 1995, p. 172).

David and Vera Mace began their work with retreats for the Quakers in October 1962 (Mace & Mace, 1974, 1978a). As early as 1961, Herbert Otto was conducting a variety of experimental programs in the area of marital and family enrichment (Mace & Mace, 1978a; Otto, 1969). Leon and Antoinette Smith were conducting Marriage Communication Labs for United Methodist and other groups in the mid 1960s. They initiated the first leadership training program for couples in 1966 (Mace & Mace, 1978a).

In the late 1960s, Sherod Miller and his associates began conducting their studies in marital communication from which they developed the Minnesota Couples Communication Program, which evolved into the CCP. Undoubtedly, many other people were doing concurrent exploratory work in the areas of ME and marital communication. By the early 1970s, the movement had begun to expand. In a survey of 30 professionals, Otto (1975, 1976) found that 90% had conducted their first program in 1973 or later.

ME programs originally were designed for married couples who had no major conflicts and perceived their relationship as basically healthy, but who wanted to further enrich and add spark to it (Garland, 1983; Zimpfer, 1988a). However, ME soon was expanded to include various specialized groups. Among these are pre-marital and dating couples (e.g., Markman's Prevention and Relationship Enhancement Program [PREP], Guerney's Relationship Enhancement [RE]), wife batterers (e.g., Waldo), dual-career couples (Avis, 1986), remarried couples (Heitland, 1986), couples at different stages of the family life cycle (L'Abate, 1975; Garland, 1983), and those experiencing severe difficulty and dysfunction in their marriage (Guerney, 1977). Attitudes toward couples have shifted from looking at individuals and their relationships in isolation to treating the married couple and their relationship together (Zimpfer, 1988a). Family life education and enrichment programs, such as Gordon's Parent Effectiveness Training and related effectiveness programs (Gordon, 1970), also were being developed during this same period.

In 1973, the Association of Couples for Marriage Enrichment (ACME) was founded by David and Vera Mace with the following four purposes:

1. to encourage and help member couples to seek growth and enrichment in their own marriages,

2. to organize activities through which member couples can help each other in their quest for marital growth and enrichment,
3. to promote and support effective community services designed to foster successful marriages,
4. to seek to improve the public image of marriage as a relationship capable of fostering both personal growth and mutual fulfillment (Hopkins et al., 1978, p. 21).

ACME is made up of couples representing many different programs. By 1979 the membership included approximately 1,800 lay and professional couples, with members in all 50 states, 6 Canadian provinces, and 13 other countries (Hopkins et al., 1978). As of May 1996, there were 2,300 members and 78 local chapters ("energy cells") in North America, with many state, regional, and North American Conferences on Marriage Enrichment being held at various places in the United States. Many ACME members are trained as leader couples, most of whom conduct one or more enrichment weekends each year, with each event involving 5 to 20 couples.

In 1975, ACME joined other enrichment groups to form the Council of Affiliated ME Organizations (CAMEO), which concerned itself primarily with developing leadership and training standards.

By 1979, there were at least 50 different programs known to Hof and Miller (1981), attended by as few as 10 couples to as many as thousands of couples (Mace & Mace, 1978a; Otto, 1976). Included in that group of 50 are several educational therapy programs developed and conducted by marital therapists and counselors (e.g., Bolte, 1975; Smith & Alexander, 1973).

ME programs are not limited to the United States, but this country led the field in the 1970s (Otto, 1976). The human-potential movement and the encounter- and small-group movement clearly have been the forerunners of the ME movement in America, contributing breadth to the philosophy, process, and design of most programs (Otto, 1976).

The movement in America, since its inception, also has had strong roots in many religious or faith systems because of their keen interest in the family and their concern for the future of marriage and the family (Hopkins & Hopkins, 1975). There are at least 14 ME programs that are national in scope and connected directly to an established religious organization. However, there are many other programs that do not have religious affiliations, such as the CCP, Family Service Association of America, Marriage Effectiveness Training, and the Relationship Enhancement programs.

Most ME programs have been created by spiritually committed persons from Christian or Jewish religious groups or traditions. Some of these programs, such as

Marriage Encounter, are officially sponsored by a specific Christian denomination, whereas most of the programs, such as ACME, have been developed and continued by persons who come out of a religious faith group.

Many ME programs are local in scope, in that they have been developed and are used, for the most part, by particular individuals or couples and their associates within a small geographical area. The Pairing Enrichment Program (Travis & Travis, 1975) and the Marriage Diagnostic Laboratory (MARDILAB) (Stein, 1975) are examples of such programs.

Many programs that are national in scope, in terms of organization, leadership training, location, and contact information, are described in detail in part 2 of this volume. Some of the earlier programs included in this category are Marriage Encounter (Bosco, 1973; Demarest et al., 1977; Genovese, 1975), Relationship Enhancement programs (Guerney, 1977), CCP (Miller et al., 1991), ACME (Hopkins et al., 1978), Getting the Love You Want (Hendrix, 1988), the PREP (Markman et al., 1994), PAIRS (1984), and the Celebrating Marriage program of the United Methodist Church (General Board of Discipleship, 1981).

In the most recent two decades, many additional expressions of ME have been created by concerned professionals and trained couples. In the 1970s, Harville Hendrix began his Love or Illusion couples weekend workshops that he developed into the Getting the Love You Want weekend workshops for couples (Hendrix, 1988) and Keeping the Love You Find weekend workshops for singles (Hendrix, 1992). Hendrix has carefully developed his Imago Relationship theory and therapy to show linkages between the interactions of marriage partners and each partner's childhood history of positive and negative nurturing experiences. Through the Institute for Imago Relationship Training, over 1,100 therapists have been trained in Imago theory and therapy, many of whom are certified to offer couples and singles workshops. Over one million copies of Hendrix's 1988 book have been sold.

Hof developed his Creative ME program in the 1970s (Hof & Miller, 1981). The impact of this program has been widespread because he has allowed others to adapt and utilize it in other settings that may not carry its name.

In the late 1970s, Howard Markman, who did his dissertation under John Gottman, began his longitudinal research on factors in the relationship of premarital couples that predicted their marital quality several years later. Markman and his associates teach the principles of communication and commitment and then coach individual couples to apply these principles in their interactions. They make good use of videotaped vignettes of couple interaction to teach communication and commitment. Markman and his associates have produced many technical research reports on PREP and have made their approach available through a book

(Markman et al., 1994) and video series and programs for training leaders of PREP workshops.

McManus (1995) provides excellent summaries of marriage preparation, enrichment, and support programs with contact addresses and telephone numbers. A video series illustrating many of these programs is also available from McManus through his Marriage Savers Institute. McManus challenges religious groups, including independent, conservative, mainline, and liberal churches, to join in support of marriage rather than passively to allow a divorce culture to continue to destroy marriages and families.

H. Norman Wright (1990) created his Christian Marriage Enrichment series of programs of couple workshops, leader training, and marriage and family books and resources. These have been especially well received among evangelical Christian groups.

For many decades several mainstream Christian denominations have developed marriage support and enrichment programs. In the Roman Catholic Church, in addition to Marriage Encounter, Pre-Cana conferences, Couple-to-Couple League, and other marriage support programs have been widely used.

In the United Methodist Church during the 1960s and 1970s, Leon Smith created his Marriage Communication Labs and was instrumental in leading the denomination to provide "Celebrating Marriage," a ME weekend program. In 1981 the *Growing Love in Christian Marriage* couples book (Hunt & Hunt, 1981) and pastors book (Smith & Smith, 1981) with many elements based on ME principles were available as resources. In 1982 the denomination established the Celebrating Marriage ME weekend, which incorporated leadership training guidelines similar to those of ACME.

In 1987, Father Dick McGinnis started Marriage Ministry at St. David's Episcopal Church in Jacksonville, Florida (McManus, 1995, p. 203). That program adapted the Twelve Steps Alcoholics Anonymous program to form 17 action statements (nicknamed M&Ms) for marriages. As a lay ministry of couples to other couples, there is considerable interest in this type of program, yet few churches have actually established it in their parishes (McManus, 1995, p. 215). Dick Dunn at Roswell, Georgia, developed Stepfamily Support Groups (Dunn, 1993) with specific attention to couples who form stepfamilies.

The Caring Couples Network was initiated in 1996 by the United Methodist Church to enable couples to network with each other for support, enrichment, nurture, and encouragement and to bring together resources for three major types of couples: premarital and newly married or recently married couples, couples who are parenting children, and couples facing serious difficulties, dysfunctions, or divorce. A handbook and video describe how to organize a Caring Couples Network Team in any local church, ecumenical as well as United Methodist (Hunt

& Hunt, 1996a,b). Updated versions of the Growing Love in Christian Marriage and Celebrating ME programs are included as part of this umbrella network that emphasizes couples reaching out to other couples and families.

Several specialized ME programs have been developed for couples who are facing divorce. Among these are Recovery of Hope and Retrouvaille programs for couples who are considering divorce (McManus, 1995).

Using concepts from Marriage Encounter, the Recovery of Hope program was adapted to the needs of couples in serious difficulty. It is sponsored primarily by the Mennonite Hospitals. The basic format is a Saturday morning program consisting of three parts. Participating couples first hear three couples describe serious diffi-culties (such as alcoholism, extramarital affairs, or divorce) that they have faced and then, in the second part, how they overcame those difficulties. Participating couples are asked to make notes about how they see their own relationship and what each partner wants from the relationship. In the third part, each participating couple has the opportunity to consult with a professional therapist about goals and the next steps that the couple can take to reach those goals. Most couples who attend do follow through with therapy and other interventions.

The Retrouvaille (French, meaning "rediscovery") intensive recovery program, in many ways similar to the Recovery of Hope program, is intended for couples who are separated and considering divorce or are "on the brink" of ending their marriage. It was developed by the Roman Catholic Church but has been extended to any couple seriously facing divorce.

The basic principle of Retrouvaille is mentoring from couples who have been through major difficulties to couples currently in difficulties. The program has four primary phases:

1. Initial separate interviews with each spouse to determine that both persons want to make the marriage work;
2. A weekend event with presentations by three couples who have overcome serious difficulties and by a pastor or priest;
3. A postweekend series of meetings, usually every other Saturday for three months, in which couples work on changes and receive positive support for each other;
4. A support group for attending couples, called CORE for Continuing Our Retrouvaille Experience. Meetings usually involve socializing, presenta-tions, and finding ways to reach out to help others.

The Third Option (Ennis, 1989; McManus, 1995, pp. 249ff.) is a 14-week course developed in the Catholic Diocese of Syracuse for couples facing serious difficul-ties. The central principle of this program is that couples who have successfully come back from the brink of divorce can support and encourage other couples by telling their own story and how they have made changes in themselves to replace dysfunctional relationships with a healthy marriage.

Another enrichment variation is in utilizing couple group formats to give feedback on premarital and marriage assessment inventory information to couples. One example is the Prepare/Enrich Growing Together program that uses a structured group process of six to eight sessions in which individualized results from their Prepare or Enrich inventory are considered by a group of couples. Sherod Miller and David Olson are cooperating to bring couple communication skills and couple assessment instruments to couples (Miller, 1997).

For example, Miller has focused more recently on providing training to persons who then will initiate and lead couple communication or their own related programs for couples. Because the number of couples involved in these groups is seldom reported, the influence of Miller's communication work may extend more widely than is known.

The many developments and adaptations of ME in the past two decades have involved influences from both ME and marriage or couple therapy and assessment. Many exercises and other therapeutic elements that were developed for ME programs also are being used by marital therapists in sessions and as homework (Luquet, 1996). ME has emerged out of both the visions and the frustrations of therapists who have worked with couples from several theoretical approaches. This suggests that the ME movement extends well beyond the couples who have participated in enrichment events to indirectly influence marital therapy and psychoeducation.

In contrast to marital or couples therapy, it is helpful to think of ME as being a structured psychoeducational program in a group setting, and marriage therapy as being more focused on individual couples therapy with a flexible agenda guided by both the needs of the couple and the goals of the therapist. Couples group therapy, led by a trained professional therapist, may incorporate exercises and activities that originated in ME. According to their training, ME leaders may at times and in limited ways utilize therapeutic techniques with couples in ME settings.

Several major ME programs cooperated in the International ME Conference in 1992 in Atlanta, Georgia, and in 1996 in Fort Worth, Texas. Key sponsors in 1996 were ACME, CCP, PREP, and Prepare/Enrich.

In 1996, these sponsors expanded to form the Coalition for Marriage, Family, and Couple Education (CMFCE) with an advisory board of 17 leaders in ME. Under the leadership of Diane Sollee, CMFCE sponsored the Smart Marriages— Successful Families conference in Washington, D.C., in May 1997, which included over 50 additional ME programs and leaders. CMFCE has a World Wide Web site (see Selected Resources at the end of this volume), a directory of providers of ME programs, and plans for an annual ME conference.

HISTORICAL PERSPECTIVE ON MARITAL INTERVENTION

The foundations of contemporary marital intervention emerged in the 1930s when marriage counselors moved beyond their initial short-term focus on sexual difficulties to providing counseling for marital distress. At that time, marriage counseling was seen as an emerging new service that would be offered to the relatively few people who might need it. As this shift toward counseling took place through the 1940s, psychoanalysts began to consider the concurrent analysis of marital partners. Ackerman (1954) was one of the first to examine the marital relationship as an entity in itself. The early discussions focused primarily on variation in the technique and method of marital intervention, rather than on theories of marital quality and adjustment. Concomitant treatment—one therapist treating both spouses individually—was extremely controversial, but conjoint treatment—one therapist treating both spouses simultaneously—was regarded as heretical. There was considerable change in attitudes about family relationships during the 1950s. In particular, systems theories began to be applied to understanding the marital bond. Communication styles and processes were being studied closely. However, it not until the late 1960s, with the emergence of family therapy, that conjoint marital therapy as we know it today began to be practiced. In particular, it was the influence of family communication theory, and pioneering family therapists such as Virginia Satir (1967), that validated the practice of conjoint treatment.

During the 1960s, there was also wider recognition of the interdisciplinary nature of the field, and marriage counseling became established as a profession with the formation of the American Association for Marriage Counseling (later to become the American Association for Marriage and Family Counseling, now known as the American Association for Marriage and Family Therapy). Behavioral approaches gained steam through the 1970s and were conducive to research. By the end of the 1960s, behavioral methods had been added to the marital intervention repertoire. For the first time, marriage counseling was able to draw on a body of knowledge based on research.

The roots of ME are entwined in the evolution of marital therapy practice. In 1943, David Mace opened the first marriage counseling clinic in Europe, but when Mace returned to the United States, he and his wife Vera were becoming convinced that remedial services needed to be supplemented with preventive services. In 1962 in Kirkridge, Pennsylvania, David and Vera Mace led their first weekend program for a group of married couples. As their enrichment work expanded and evolved, marital theory was advancing, and intervention strategies based on these emerging frameworks were being put into practice.

During this era, the publication of *Marital Tensions* (Dicks, 1967) expanded the practice of psychodynamic marital therapy. The integration of marital, sex, and psychoanalytic theory, first advocated by Kaplan (1974), became the hallmark of marital and sex therapy practice. Various approaches to family therapy began to focus on marital dynamics, and schools of marital therapy began to emerge as the family therapy models consolidated their theoretical positions (Jacobson & Gurman, 1995).

During the 1970s, practice models for marital therapy proliferated. This was also a time of expansion for ME. ACME, CAMEO, Retrouvaille, CCP Relationship Enhancement, Creative ME, PAIRS, Training in Marital Enrichment (TIME), and many other programs were being developed and taught throughout the United States. Gottman had detailed the early framework for his Marriage Lab; behavioral research was beginning in earnest. Olson was pioneering the development of an assessment tool that would be reliable, valid, and clinically practical.

In the 1980s, greater theoretical emphasis was placed on integrating divergent theories. *Helping Couples Change* (Stuart, 1980) led the way. Marriage Encounter was now reaching over 250,000 couples per year. Yet, despite a growing body of research pointing to the effectiveness of behavioral marital therapies, most marital therapists emphasized eclectic and integrative models of practice. ME was considered a premarital intervention. With the emergence of a new generation of ME and education programs such as PAIRS, Getting the Love You Want, and PREP, the field of marital therapy not only reconnected with its early roots in education for marriage but combined behavioral methods with psychodynamic, developmental, affective, and systems theory.

Current marital theory, practice, and research encompass divergent viewpoints. Piercy and Sprenkle (1986) point out that each school of family therapy has its own approach to marital therapy, and they differentiate premarital therapy, divorce therapy, and ME as fields separate from marital therapy. Theoretical frameworks for couples therapy include behavioral models (Hahlweg & Markman, 1988); experiential models incorporating systemic, gestalt, and affective theories (Johnson & Greenberg, 1984); strategic approaches (Jacobson & Addis, 1993); insight-oriented system models (Hendrix, 1988); and developmental models (Bader et al., 1981). The intersystem model (Weeks, 1989) integrated intrapsychic, interpersonal, and intergenerational models. Models are evolving that incorporate biological aspects of intimate interpersonal relationships (Gottman, 1994). There are increasing efforts to integrate sex therapy and marital therapy (Schnarch, 1997; Weeks, 1989).

As early as the 1970s, the overlaps between ME programs and marital therapy were noted. In particular, Schauble and Hill (1976) called for a marriage lab to supplement traditional marriage counseling. Rather than distinguish enrichment as a separate service, they said that marital treatment would take a variety of forms and considered communication skills training as a laboratory approach to treatment in marriage counseling. They suggested that the laboratory approach could be used either in lieu of, or in conjunction with, more traditional marital counseling. Similarly, L'Abate and McHenry (1983) suggested that marital interventions take place along a continuum, ranging in degree of structure from preventive, skill-training programs to unstructured remedial therapies.

THEORETICAL FOUNDATIONS OF MARRIAGE ENRICHMENT

Although there is no one widely accepted metatheory that guides marital interventions, research and practice wisdom have facilitated the evolution of theories that attempt to explain marital satisfaction. Not a silent partner, ME has contributed to this body of knowledge through emphasis on empathic environments, skill building, and use of group process. Marital theory is a complex conglomeration of intrapsychic, interpersonal, intergenerational, and sociocultural models. Intrapsychic models emphasize the role of object relations theory and the healing nature of marriage. These models emphasize the developmental advantages of commitment to marriage in fostering individuation, differentiation, and attachment as well as personal satisfaction and meaning in adulthood. Interpersonal models address the importance of communication and conflict resolution as key processes that minimize the likelihood of divorce. Intergenerational theories underscore the influence of family legacies, patterns of accommodation and affiliation, and the emotional architecture of the marital subsystem. Sociocultural patterns in mating describe historical, anthropological, and social influences on the couple relationship.

We now take a closer look at the philosophical foundation of ME and examine some of the common elements of this movement that has touched the lives of so many people.

An examination of the process of ME needs to be preceded by a discussion of the theoretical foundation on which both the process and the programs are built. Many of the early ME programs were eclectic, in that they drew from a variety of contributors and theoretical frameworks, such as those outlined by Satir, Perls, Frankl, Rogers, and Berne (Hof & Miller, 1981). However, some practitioners use "eclectic" synonymously with "hodgepodge" or "smorgasbord," or to cover for, or rationalize away, the lack of a well-developed theoretical framework.

Humanistic psychology, which emerged and flourished in the 1960s, can be seen as one precursor to the ME movement. This psychology, which espouses the expression of feelings, the creation of effective relationships, and the fulfillment of personal potential, was one of the early inspirations for ME because it saw marriage as a major area in which each person can enact his or her inherent tendency toward growth and self-actualization, with respect to self and others. The human potential movement also helped to make our society aware of the benefits of group experiences and techniques, an important aspect of the ME process.

Building on these basic concepts, Bernard Guerney established a clear and specific theoretical base for his Relationship Enhancement programs. He carefully developed the elements of Rogerian psychotherapy, behavior modification (operant learning theory), and social learning theory. These same elements, as well as group process theory, expressed or not, appear to form the foundation of virtually all ME programs, as well as group process theory.

Rogerian psychotherapy affirms the importance of the emotional life and self-concept of the individual, as well as the important effects that interpersonal relations have upon these intrapsychic dimensions. Complete acceptance and respect for the participants is emphasized as is acceptance of negative as well as positive feelings (Guerney, 1977). In ME programming, there is an emphasis on providing an empathic environment in which participants can freely express their feelings and experience increased self-acceptance and knowledge, and increased acceptance of others and from others, especially their marital partner. Leader congruence and modeling of empathic behavior also are stressed. The assumption is made that all of this will contribute to changes in cognition and the attitudes that underlie behavior (Guerney, 1977) and will lead the participants to change their behavior.

Behavior modification approaches that incorporate social learning theory with modeling and behavior rehearsal, and that recognize the importance of reeducation in the area of cognitive functions as well as the more traditional behavioral functions, also are utilized (Hendrix, 1988). ME frequently is less specific than traditional behavior modification and has more general goals, such as increased interpersonal effectiveness, increased intimacy, and relationship enhancement. However, along with these general goals, many programs also have very specific behavioral goals, such as the Relationship Enhancement program (Guerney, 1977), CCP (Miller, Nunnally, & Wackman et al., 1976), and Marriage Encounter (Bosco, 1973).

Although some program developers do not clearly state their specific behavioral objectives, they still employ a variety of behavioral methods and techniques within the program. To a greater or lesser degree, virtually all ME programs use techniques such as modeling, behavior rehearsal, prompting, and reinforcement. In some programs, they are systematically employed as instructional methods, as in the programs of Guerney and of Miller, whereas in others they are employed in less systematic ways.

Most ME experiences appear to be designed to accelerate behaviors perceived to be desirable and rewarding in the marriage relationship (e.g., positive statements, ownership and expression of feelings, effective negotiation skills). Some programs virtually prohibit the expression of negative statements or feelings, apparently with the belief that a deceleration of negative verbal and affective exchanges, plus an acceleration of positive verbal, behavioral, and affective exchanges, will lead to the elimination of undesirable and dysfunctional behaviors.

ME clearly is indebted to Skinner (1953, 1969) for his emphasis on social reinforcement, an important aspect of behavior modification approaches. However, proponents view the significance of such reinforcement in the learning process as secondary to repeated practice and modeled demonstrations. In ME, the main contribution of social reinforcement may be the increase in positive feelings that participants have about themselves, which thus keeps motivation high to improve and develop effective relationship skills (Guerney, 1977).

Proponents of ME believe that people can learn new interaction skills and can correct deficiencies in social learning. For example, people who have never learned how to manage conflict can be taught to do so. Deficiencies in social learning thus are viewed as important components in relationship discord, and the learning and continued practice of appropriate skills is viewed as an important component in marital and relationship health and in family systems contribution.

In addition to Rogerian psychotherapy, behavior modification, and social learning theory, group process theory also is one of the foundation blocks of ME. The group experience is seen as providing a temporary and safe learning environment through which trust can grow, and from which support can be drawn. In such an environment, couples can observe alternative models of relating as they observe other couples interacting. They learn and practice interactional skills, and how to give and receive positive feedback among peers (Miller et al., 1976).

In group settings, participants have the opportunity to consult with and help other couples (altruism) and to experience a sense of universality. More specifically, Irvin Yalom (1970) has identified the following as primary categories of curative factors in group therapy:

1. Imparting information;
2. Instillation of hope;
3. Universality (sense of "I am not alone with this problem");
4. Altruism (helping other group members through support, reassurance, etc.);
5. Corrective recapitulation of the primary family group;
6. Development of socializing techniques (social learning);
7. Imitative behavior (modeling);
8. Interpersonal learning;
9. Group cohesiveness (sense of solidarity, wellness, experiencing the group as a source of strength and encouragement);
10. Catharsis (ventilation of positive and negative feelings).

These curative factors are interdependently operative in every type of therapy group, including couples groups, but they have varying degrees of importance depending on the nature, goals, and composition of the specific group.

More recently, several proponents of ME have responded to the need to develop a clearer theoretical base for their programs. Among these are Gordon (1993); Guerney (1977); Hendrix (1988, 1992); Markman et al. (1994); and Miller et al. (1991).

Mace (1975a, p. 171) reminds us that a ME event is not just a group of unrelated individuals, but a group of subgroups (couples), "each of which is a preexisting and ongoing social unit," making for a more complex group process. He further reminds us that enrichment groups are different from therapy groups and comparisons between the two require careful analysis. A proper comparison awaits appropriate empirical research. However, virtually these same curative factors have been identified by Egan (1986) as being operative in all growth-oriented group experiences (with the exception of the corrective recapitulation of the primary family group):

1. Opportunity to reveal the way a participant sees things, feels, etc.;
2. Climate of experimentation;
3. Feedback;
4. Supportive atmosphere;
5. Cognitive map;
6. Practice;
7. Planning application of new yearnings to everyday life;
8. Relearning how to learn;
9. Emphasis on effective communication and emotional or affective learning;
10. Participative leadership;
11. Normal populations;
12. Use of structured experiences.

To a greater or lesser degree, these curative factors and common elements are present in ME groups as well. The curative factors provide the rationale for the use of group experiences in ME programming. However, as Yalom (1970) noted, the curative factors will have varying degrees of importance depending on the nature, goals, and composition of a specific group or program. For example, at one end of the continuum would be the Marriage Encounter program, which focuses almost entirely on dyadic interaction, with group process being limited to the experiencing of several presentations by the leadership team in the total group setting, shared meals, and a religious service. In such a group setting, many of the curative factors are not overtly operative, but the sense of universality and vicarious support that the participants can experience, as they realize that everyone has gathered for the same purpose, has been reported by many couples. In addition, follow-up sharing groups, which meet on a regular basis after the initial weekend experience, provide the opportunity for more of the curative factors to be experienced.

On the other end of the continuum is the program model used by Mace and Mace (1976). This model involves a minimum of organization and structure, and the group of couples meeting for a weekend experience decide for themselves what the agenda and goals will be. Needless to say, in such an unstructured group setting, more of the curative factors will be overtly operative. Mace (1975b, p. 40) even suggests that leaders in such groups serve as models and surrogate parents, which, in this case, suggests Yalom's idea of corrective recapitulation of the primary family group.

Another major element in ME programs is a set of shared beliefs about the importance of persons, their marriages, and the value of encouragement from others. Programs that are identified with a religious institution, such as Marriage Encounter and Christian ME, have assumptions about the value of commitment between spouses in the context of their commitment to God. There is a built-in community that shares these values and provides a structure for a variety of follow-up and ongoing supports for couples and their families.

In summary, the theoretical bases of the process of ME are the broad base of humanistic psychology, Rogerian psychotherapy, behavior modification and social learning theory, group process theory, object-relations and family systems principles, and shared values. These form the foundation from which all other aspects of the process of ME emerge. The essential particulars of this process are its ongoing nature and positive emphasis, the use of confrontation with support, the emphasis on developing communication skills, and the experience of self-disclosure, all which are developed in the following sections of this chapter.

THE ONGOING NATURE OF MARRIAGE ENRICHMENT

ME usually is identified with weekend-long programs, or time-limited, marital growth groups, which meet, for example, once a week for six to eight weeks, two to four hours each meeting. Many couples initially experience enrichment through such a program and come to view that experience as an important part of their growth. However, the process of ME must be ongoing and not restricted to participation in weekend experiences or time-limited groups. At best, these groups can give couples visions of new possibilities and encourage them to continue growing in their relationship. Many practitioners and participants emphasize that such participation is the beginning, not the end, of the process of marital and relationship growth and enhancement (Mace and Mace, 1976, 1978a). Couples participating in a basic program can be introduced to certain skills. They can gain a sense of the potential of their relationship and can perceive the need for change and growth.

More and more leaders are emphasizing the need for an ongoing support system or time-limited group, with continued growth experiences after the initial experience (deGuzman, 1996; Hendrix, 1988; Hopkins et al., 1978; Mace, 1975b; Otto, 1976; Rappaport, 1976). Such follow-up groups provide support, encouragement, and positive reinforcement and feedback. There are further opportunities to learn and practice interactional skills, and opportunities to give and receive help. Without such a support system, gains from the initial experience quickly fade.

Clinebell (1976) noted that a variety of ME programs are needed for different points in the life span, and it is clear that he sees ME as a lifelong process. The variety of programs now available demonstrates the validity of his early observation.

Emphasis on the ongoing process of ME reflects the idea that established and entrenched patterns of marital interaction do not change overnight or by participation in one program. It also is based on the belief that self-help programs, by themselves, are not sufficient to produce enduring change. A couple must make a commitment to work continually to enhance their relationship.

Couples also must decide to become involved with other couples who are committed to the same goal by joining an ongoing program of growth, be it a growth group or special-interest group in areas such as decision making, parenting, or sexuality. The process may even include the use of regular, preventive, marital checkups (even if nothing seems to be wrong in the relationship) as a means of identifying assets and strengths as well as areas where improvement is needed. Competent third-party consultation can be helpful, but individuals, couples, or groups of couples could do their own checkups as well.

It is also likely that marriage or relationship counseling will be needed when individual, couple, or support group resources are insufficient to enable a couple to move through a blockage in the relationship. Practitioners who provide assessment and therapy services and also are involved in leading ME events are more likely to be sought when therapy is needed.

POSITIVE EMPHASIS OF MARRIAGE ENRICHMENT

A review of several programs shows that ME has a major emphasis upon the positive aspects of the marital relationship (Clinebell, 1976; Durana, 1994; Hendrix, 1988; Mace & Mace, 1978b; Markman et al., 1994; Otto, 1972, 1976). Identifying and sharing positive aspects with each other can generate a highly satisfying emotional experience for both partners and make it possible for negative feelings to be expressed in ways that can lead to goal-setting behavior (Clarke, 1970; Mace & Mace, 1976). Among the long-term benefits that can accrue to the couple after such a highly satisfying emotional experience are a sense of hope based on remembrances of loving, positive exchanges that can be drawn upon in times of pain or distress, perhaps serving as a motivation to overcome current difficulties. Those memories of what was once experienced may help a couple to believe that they can achieve better levels of desired intimacy.

The positive emphasis provides a base for moving to more sensitive and difficult issues, such as those involving conflict or anger (Liberman et al., 1976). The teaching of specific skills, which makes the expression and constructive resolution of negative feelings possible, is also a part of many programs (Guerney, 1977; Miller et al., 1991).

Although positive affirmation skills are essential, it is also necessary for a program to enable couples to cope effectively with potential areas of conflict such as unfulfilled wants and needs. Couples who receive training only in the expression of positive feelings and thoughts cannot be expected to express themselves effectively when negative feelings and thoughts in conflicted situations arise (Gottman, 1994). Couples need practice in both areas, and this assumption has led many facilitators to include components that deal with the expression of negative feelings and conflict resolution in their programs (e.g., Gordon, 1970; Guerney, 1977; Mace & Mace, 1976; Sherwood & Scherer, 1975; Hendrix, 1988; Miller et al., 1991; Markman et al., 1994).

CONFRONTATION IN MARRIAGE ENRICHMENT PROGRAMS

Mace and Mace (1974) and Otto (1976) note that most ME program leaders do not utilize, encourage, or even permit pressure to elicit sharing or self-disclosure. Nor is confrontation utilized, encouraged, or permitted to expose behavior or to attempt to force a change in behavior. ME programs operating from a Gestalt perspective (e.g., Pinker and Leon, 1976) appear to be the one consistent exception to this rule or norm. These programs incorporate criticism as well as strong confrontation.

Program leaders do well to prevent irresponsible confrontation (e.g., telling people off), which can be destructive to relationship and individual growth. However, responsible confrontation can have beneficial results (Egan, 1986; Hendrix, 1988). Responsible confrontation involves a caring invitation to the person to examine, and if appropriate, modify his or her behavior, to improve the ability to relax with others. Needless to say, this is quite different from what many people have learned through their experiences with confrontation. The concept of nondemanding requests for behavioral change is an idea foreign to some programs. The concept of care as an element of responsible confrontation is also alien. The idea of confronting behavior, and not motivation, is new for many people, as is Egan's idea of confronting strengths, or potential strengths, as well as weaknesses. (An example of a confrontation of unused potential would be the following: "You rarely share your feelings directly with me, but when you do, I feel closer to you. I wish you would do it more often.")

Responsible confrontation (Egan, 1986) requires that the confronter consider, in advance, the following:

1. Motives of the confrontation;
2. The potential impact upon the confronted at this point in time;
3. The needs, sensitivity, and capabilities of the person being confronted as well as the person offering the confrontation;
4. The confrontation occurs only if there is a genuine desire to work toward creative change, as opposed to a desire to punish.

Most ME program designers and leaders now realize that responsible confrontation is not antithetical to support, caring, and warmth. They also must be careful not to ignore the very real need that people have to learn effective confrontation skills as part of effective conflict utilization. If this need is ignored, gains from increasing positive expressions may be offset when the inevitable negative expressions occur. By contrast, individuals and couples may move to a position of denying the reality of conflict and avoiding requests for behavioral change in order to avoid irresponsible confrontation and the feared expression of negative feelings. It would be better to teach couples how to rechannel conflict and confrontation into a positive experience, albeit one that is frequently painful. This positive approach to conflict utilization and confrontation is addressed by several ME programs (e.g., Gordon, 1970; Guerney, 1977; Hendrix, 1988; Markman et al., 1994; Miller et al., 1991).

EMPHASIS ON COMMUNICATION

The content of ME programs varies greatly, but most programs emphasize the need to communicate effectively (L'Abate, 1977; Mace & Mace, 1974, 1975; Miller et al., 1991; Otto, 1976). Seventy-seven percent of enrichment leaders surveyed by Otto (1975, 1976) indicated that an average of more than half of the time spent in the program was devoted to the development of communication skills. Many participants have indicated that the training they received in effective communication and emotional expression has been extremely valuable to them as individuals and as a couple.

It can be said that the heart of ME is couple communication or dialogue (Mace & Mace, 1977; Regula, 1975). Specifically, that means effective, deep sharing of feelings, thoughts, wants, needs, and intentions between partners.

This is a learned process that is cultivated intentionally, and practiced with discipline, rather than a one-time-only experience. In some programs, this dialogue takes place between partners in total privacy (e.g., Marriage Encounter [Bosco, 1973]). In other programs, couple dialogue in a group setting is considered essential (e.g., ACME model [Mace & Mace, 1976]). The aim is for couples to be able to experience "total human expression" with each other (Egan, 1986) and to be more fully aware of how past influences contribute to current patterns (Hendrix, 1988). ME seeks to teach partners how to communicate fully on intellectual and emotional levels, both verbally and nonverbally, in a way that permits emotions to be appropriately allied with rational expression.

Another goal is for couples to learn how to give and receive supportive behavior. An atmosphere that encourages growth is helpful and needed for that growth to occur. In other words, people must feel supported in their efforts to grow. Egan (1986) strongly believes the prerequisite of supportive behavior is total listening, one of the core concepts of communications training (Gordon, 1970; Miller, Nunnally, & Wackman, 1975). Total listening involves becoming aware of all of the cues emitted by the other person, listening with one's ears, eyes, mind, heart, imagination, and even one's touch. It involves listening to words and feelings, and being alert to hidden or coded messages. It involves listening to one's self as well as the other person, and it is an objective and subjective process. As Lief (1977, p. 289) has suggested, total listening includes self-awareness, or sensitivity to one's own feelings and thoughts and behaviors; empathy, or sensitivity to the other person; "recipathy, or sensitivity to one's own feelings in response to the behaviors or words of the other person"; and impact awareness, a "sensitivity to the impact of one's own words or behavior on the other person."

Miller's "awareness wheel" (Miller, Nunnally, & Wackman, 1975) provides a very helpful structure for such listening. He emphasizes being aware of sense (perceptual) data, interpretations, feelings (emotional reactions), intentions, and actions. The three-part process of message–feedback–confirmation, along with encoding and decoding (Hunt & Rydman, 1979), usually is assumed in most ME programs. One helpful standard for accurate communication is when the effect of the message on the receiver matches the intent of the sender (Markman, 1984).

Egan (1986) believes that reinforcement for growth-producing behavior also involves the following:

1. A necessary degree of warmth;
2. Unconditional positive regard, with genuine, nonjudgmental acceptance (not necessarily approval) of the other person;

3. Affirmation of the universality of our human experience (feelings, successes, failures, etc.);
4. Physical and psychological availability to each other;
5. Congruent interactions;
6. Trust in one's self and in the other person;
7. Appropriate recognition of the contributions and behavior of others and appropriate responses to them.

Total human expression and supportive behavior thus are seen as integral parts of effective communication. And, clearly, effective communication is linked positively with marital adjustment and satisfaction, as well as increased self- and other-acceptance (Jackson, 1968a, 1968b; Alexander, 1973; Collins, 1977; Epstein & Jackson, 1978; Jacobson & Martin, 1976; Olson, 1976; Rappaport, 1976).

The positive relation of communication quality and marital quality has been supported repeatedly in research (Jacobson & Addis, 1993). Navran (1967) showed a positive correlation between marital adjustment and the ability to communicate, suggesting that couples can improve their relationship by focusing on how they communicate and by improving their skills in this area. He also attempted to clarify the often fuzzy term "open communication." He found that happily married couples talked more to each other, conveyed the feeling that they understood what was being said to them, had a wide range of subjects available to them, preserved communication channels, showed more sensitivity to each other's feelings, personalized their language symbols, and made more use of supplementary nonverbal techniques of communication.

In view of the increasing evidence that relates effective communication to effective marital functioning and satisfaction, it is easy to see why ME programs place such a heavy emphasis upon communications training. The emphasis is based on several assumptions: that individuals and couples need to learn how to communicate effectively; that they can learn new skills and make needed changes through practice and feedback in a supportive, experimental, and experiential setting; that they then can transfer their yearnings to everyday situations; and that such a joint effort builds self- and couple esteem and relationship satisfaction (Bolte, 1975; Miller et al., 1975; Stuart, 1980).

Early ME programs relied on the communications theories of Satir (1967, 1972); Watzlawick et al. (1967); Berne (1968); Gordon (1970); and Miller, Nunnally, and Wackman (1975, 1976). This emphasis continues in programs today, with additional theoretical support from many sources, such as Hendrix (1988) and Gottman (1994). In virtually all programs, the focus is on the present process of communication and interaction as well as the content. Leaders model the skills to be learned. These skills and concepts are taught in a supportive atmosphere with emphasis on awareness of interaction patterns. Skills are developed and practiced in a dyad, while focusing on important issues and using supportive feedback from other participants. Some programs make use of homework assignments to facilitate the integration of new skills and the transfer of learning to everyday situations (Miller, Corrales, & Wackman, 1975). The research of Goldstein (1973), Jacobson and Martin (1976), and McLeish et al. (1973), among others, suggests that such a combination of experiential, didactic-cognitive, and modeling techniques is the most effective way to teach couples new communication skills (L'Abate, 1977, 1990).

Some enrichment programs are oriented specifically toward skill training. That is, they focus on the development of a particular set of communication and interaction skills (e.g., CCP [Miller et al., 1976]; Relationship Enhancement program [Guerney, 1977]). It has been suggested that participation in such a program is a helpful precursor or adjunct to participation in one of the more broadly based, open-ended, or issue-oriented ME programs (Guerney, 1977; Hopkins et al., 1978; Mace & Mace, 1976). These skill-training programs can teach participants how to develop basic skills that are needed to explore other areas and content issues. Basically, the skills focus on honest, open communication the ability to express feelings, desires, and thoughts, and the ability to respond in an empathic manner. PAIRS has attempted to incorporate skill training and attention to attitudinal changes, as couples are taught ways to include and develop more bonding in their relationships.

In the more broadly based programs, the specific skill-training emphasis often is absent or less heavily emphasized. In such programs, the content of what is shared appears to be valued as highly as the process, and there is emphasis on attitudinal changes in the relationship. In the Marriage Encounter program, a specific, but limited, method of dialogue is practiced (Genovese, 1975). In the model suggested by ACME (Mace & Mace, 1976), there is a minimum of organization and structure; the skills that are taught and practiced emerge from the expressed needs of the group of couples meeting for that particular period of time.

Obviously, there is much overlap among the various programs in the area of communications. The ME emphasis on communication skills also is used often by therapists who are treating couples and families. The details and distinctions in emphases on communication is a matter of emphasis on the type of training, the specific skills to be learned, and the degree of structure within which the skills are taught. Proponents of each method are able to defend their approach, some with more research support than others (e.g., Guerney, 1977; Miller et al., 1976). Some of the more broadly based and more popular programs have not yet been researched adequately and, overall, the number of relevant studies on ME still needs to be expanded (see part III, this volume).

Epstein and Jackson (1978), reporting on a specific and systematic communication training program that they developed, suggest that it may be easier to implement behavioral rather than attitudinal changes in close interpersonal relationships. Their suggestion leads us to raise a series of questions. Should participation in a sharply focused communication training program precede a more broadly based, issue-oriented ME program? Would this enable the participants to gain more from the latter experience by having already increased their basic communication skills? Or, should participation in the more broadly based program precede the communication-skill training? Would this sequence generate a high level of positive feeling that might increase the commitment to a sharply focused communication training program? Or, is the sequence irrelevant? Or, do both have to occur, perhaps even simultaneously, for stable, enduring, positive behavioral and attitudinal change to occur between partners? Recent research (Verseveldt, 1993) suggests that the sequence makes little difference if both are done well.

In conclusion, proponents of ME view training in communication skills as an important part of programming, though they implement such training in various ways. The mastering of communication skills of itself is not viewed as a panacea. However, in combination with a spirit of good will and a commitment to the goals of ME, communication training stands out as an important contribution to relationship enhancement.

SELF-DISCLOSURE

Self-disclosure—the revealing of one's thoughts and feelings to another person— is of central significance to the philosophy and process of ME. Several studies have been conduced which show that self-disclosure is most effective when it is appropriate, honest, direct, explicit, and congruent. In addition, when there is a balance between the expression of thoughts and feelings, the disclosure takes on an even greater meaning (Egan, 1986; Gilbert, 1976; Jourard, 1964, 1971; Luft, 1969).

According to Lief (1977), self-disclosure is appropriate and most helpful when the following criteria are met:

1. When it is a function of the ongoing relationship,
2. When it occurs reciprocally,
3. When it is timely,
4. When it is pertinent,
5. When it moves by relatively small increments,
6. When it can be confirmed by the other person,

7. When account is taken of the effect that disclosure has on the other person,
8. When it creates a reasonable risk,
9. When it accelerates during a crisis,
10. When the content is mutually shared (Lief, 1977, pp. 132–133).

Self-disclosure exerts its influence on relationships in several ways. First, one gains a greater awareness of true self through successful disclosure (Jourard, 1964, 1971). Second, self-disclosure helps an individual discern similarities and differences between his or her perceptions and feelings and those of others. It also makes it possible for people to learn directly from each other what their specific needs, expectations, and intentions are. Thus, self-disclosure encourages people to redirect their perceptions of others from roles such as husband, wife, mother, or father to unique sensitive individuals. Third, self-disclosure and self-esteem apparently are positively related (Gilbert, 1976). In other words, the higher the self-esteem, the higher the level of self-disclosure. Finally, disclosure begets more disclosure (Jourard and Richman, 1963), but a climate of trust and acceptance is needed to initiate and maintain the reciprocating cycle.

Although the benefits of self-disclosure cannot be disputed, the philosophy of ME does not endorse unlimited disclosure. It is limited to the extent that it is positive and voluntary and not the result of confrontation. These limitations are supported by research. Evidence suggests that the valence of a disclosure (its positiveness or negativeness) may be more important than the level of intimacy achieved (Gilbert, 1976). That means that high levels of disclosure actually may be destructive if the thoughts and feelings disclosed are highly negative (Gottman, 1994).

The research also suggests that there is a point at which further disclosure reduces satisfaction within a relationship (Cozby, 1973; Gilbert, 1976). Therefore, it is important to match couples with varying self-disclosure needs and abilities to the appropriate program. For example, if a relatively low-disclosing couple participates in a program where the norm is for high disclosure in a group setting, that couple may feel pressured to disclose themselves beyond the point that is optimal for their growth and development. Or, the couple may emotionally withdraw from the experience out of anxiety and the need to maintain their defenses.

A fact of life for some couples is that security needs may outweigh their needs for relationship depth. If pressured too much, the potential benefits of the ME program may be reduced or lost accordingly. In fact, negative results often may occur. But, if couples participate in a program with disclosure norms that match or slightly exceed their own, their security needs probably would be met. Within this trusting environment, they also would be encouraged to work at the growing edges of their relationship, increasing self-disclosure at their own rate, thereby experiencing new depths of intimacy. Conversely, a relatively high-disclosing couple participating in a program that has a norm of low disclosure may be extremely frustrated in their growth by the rigidness and inflexibility of the structure, the low level of disclosure, and the inability to share and disclose with other couples.

Another argument for limited disclosure in ME programs is that, at the high-risk end of the continuum, some couples are not able to survive in-depth examination and disclosure regarding information, disappointments, and conflicts (Gilbert, 1976). For some couples, the desire for intimate commitment and the ability to risk are such that they will go to great lengths to achieve their potential in this area. Other couples, however, may desire a different degree of intimate commitment, or may not have the same capacity for risk. These couples may need to avoid certain or most aspects of disclosure at the high-risk end of the continuum. This does not mean that they are less competent or open than other couples. They are simply different in this respect and will need to be encouraged to discover and develop their own kind of intimacy (Gottman, 1994).

What is needed in ME programming is a response to the varying disclosure needs of all couples. There is also a need for clear, public expression of disclosure norms and possibilities that are likely to occur within the framework of a particular program model. Such a statement of norms would make it easier, and less a matter of chance, for a particular couple to select or be referred to a program that could suitably address their perceived needs and risk-level.

These needs have been met in varying degrees in recent ME programs. As shown in the research section of this book, careful and flexible structure is vital to enable couples to feel secure and be able to gain maximum benefit from participation in a program. Descriptions of programs such as those provided in chapter 5 and by authors such as Berger and Hannah (1998) can help couples to select programs that more closely fit their needs.

In summary, ME emphasizes certain key aspects of self-disclosure and sees them as integral parts of a mutually satisfying and growing relationship. They are that the disclosure be voluntary, positive, not the result of confrontation, and accented on the building of self-esteem. These attitudes are theoretically sound and supported by the research literature on self-disclosure. In other words, if disclosure occurs within this framework, which also emphasizes commitment, intimacy, and acceptance of each other, it appears that it serves the function of deepening the relationship between the persons involved.

ME is a philosophy, a process, and a variety of programs. As part of the continuum of services to couples, these programs are an important resource for interventions with couples and families. In chapter 3, we see the important ways that ME contributes to family and other systems.

Chapter 3

Marriage Keys to Family and Society

Gloria and Greg are typical of many couples who have strengthened their marriage relationship through both therapy and enrichment. Listen to some of their reflections about their families and their own marital journey.

Gloria: I'm glad we have learned how to use time-outs, "I" messages, and conflict resolution methods. My parents seldom used these skills. They just tried to out-shout each other until one gave in. Now I see how much joy they missed.

Greg: Yeah. Being in the enrichment weekend helped me to believe that these do work. When we tried these in our couple therapy sessions, it gave me opportunity to practice with some private coaching from our therapist.

Gloria: It helps to find other couples who really believe in marriage. So often the media make it seem like the values we hold are weird or old-fashioned.

Greg: Just as others support and encourage us to learn how to improve our marriage, we are now trying to share these perspectives and suggest changes where we can. Through therapy and our own discussions, I now realize how much my parents' divorce affected me as a teenager. Because my brothers also divorced, I was thinking that having a long-term healthy marriage was impossible in today's society. Now I know we can do marriage well because we have experienced it for ourselves and are learning new skills for doing it.

Gloria: It takes two. Thanks for being willing to try, to forgive, and to renew our romance. And thanks to our friends who are also trying and succeeding.

Greg: Thanks to you also for being open and supportive. That's another reason I'm pushing our company to support programs for marriage and family enrichment and for all kinds of therapy. Prevention makes good sense in so many ways.

Greg and Gloria illustrate how marriage both depends on family models and relationships as well as shapes those relationships. Earlier distinctions between enrichment and treatment were based on differentiating methods and focus. For example, marriage enrichment (ME) typically uses group, educational, and experiential methods with a focus on skills whereas marital therapy has been practiced using conjoint methods with an interactional and intrapsychic focus. Although still somewhat useful, these distinctions are increasingly less helpful. From a systems perspective, both ME and couple therapy must be examined within the context of family and other systems. Practitioners' values and theories concerning marriage, marital adjustment, and models of treatment influence both couples and programs for intervention, enrichment, and education. Both ME and marital therapy literature contain many descriptions of and research about experiential, affective, behavioral, and cognitive approaches to helping couples. The setting, such as individual, couple, family, or group, is secondary to achieving positive results from techniques.

Marriage health and well-being as well as prevention of marital dysfunctions, distress, and divorce are grounded in some type of value system. Popenoe et al. (1996) trace in detail the interconnections between marriage and society. When the first ME programs originated in the 1960s, marriage was still generally valued in the United States and most western societies as the only acceptable relationship for sexual activities, male-female cohabitation, and procreation of children. Although some segments of society still hold to these values, in the 1990s there has been a plurality of views that either isolate marriage as merely a private matter between two partners or separate marriage as being unnecessary for full sexual activities, cohabitation, and children. Some emphases on families and family enrichment make little mention of marriage and its role in family systems.

The fundamental rationale for marriage in society is the foundation for examining the rationale for all types of marriage preparation, enrichment, mentoring, and outreach. We recognize that there are many conflicting views on the values and importance of marriage, yet we want to encourage open discussion of the role of marriage in society. Often, the emphasis of enrichment on couples has given little attention to the larger effects of marriage quality on parenting, education, work and family interactions, and social problems.

In this chapter we consider marriage from the largest perspectives of society and family to see why good marriages are so vital to all persons, married or not, and to all children in any type of home. The perspectives offered here are to invite critical inspection of assumptions and applications as well as to forge better links between ME, family enrichment, and other dimensions of society. Agreement with our perspectives is not expected, yet we hope that this chapter will encourage readers to join in some variation of these views or to search for better answers that compel our society to take marriage more joyfully and seriously. Our intent is not to impose answers but to raise issues with the hope that wider consensus on the ways that marriage, including both well-being and dysfunctions, affects all persons in a society, whether they are married or not.

We think that marriage is essential to family and to society (Glendon & Blankenhorn, 1996; Popenoe et al., 1996). To recognize the ways in which marriage is essential to society and to family greatly expands the role of marriage preparation, enrichment, and outreach from a pleasant option to an essential requirement for all couples (as explored further in chapter 13, this volume). If marriage is essential to society and its next generation—our children—then we face enormous challenges to support and improve the quality of marriages. This view confronts professionals to find ways to make existing programs and techniques available to all couples. It also awakens all citizens to examine and reshape cultural values and norms that support marriage.

MARRIAGE IN RELATION TO FAMILY AND SOCIETY

Marriage is both a part of larger family networks of blood relatives and in-laws as well as the defining relationship of a family. The interaction between marriage and family is itself very complex and beyond the scope of this book. To simplify and focus on ME, our systemic assumption is that the quality of a marriage directly affects these family networks in many ways, just as these family networks also affect the marriage.

The majority assumption is that the primary family structure consists of wife and husband and their children, although a married couple may or may not have children. Other variations of family, such as one-parent families and blended families, arise because something has happened to the marriage (or primary bond) of the woman and man who procreated the children. Society usually accepts these variations of family composition as the best available answer (when the marriage is not intact), not as the preferred answer over marriage. Children who lose their birth parents through divorce, death, or other factors must be cared for by relatives, foster parents, children's homes, or other agencies.

When there are three generations living in the same household, the adults involved must determine how the power structure and role responsibilities will be distributed among family members. Depending on the culture and circumstances, these adult household leaders may be from either the middle or the oldest generation, usually as the parents or grandparents.

The emphasis of this book is upon enrichment programs for married couples. Some ME programs have been extended and adapted to address couples who plan to marry and other unmarried couples who intend to continue in a long-term committed relationship. Some (e.g., Zimpfer, 1988a, p. 45) prefer a broader term, such as relationship enrichment or couple enrichment, to include all other couples who are not currently married. This expanded focus is essential because increasing numbers of couples live together for longer periods of time with no intention or desire to have a wedding or to obtain marriage license, yet often wanting to guarantee legal rights equivalent to those usually associated with marriage.

The rationale for using "couple" rather than "marriage" in phrases such as marriage therapy and ME is that the term couple is a broader inclusive term because not all couples are necessarily legally married (Jacobson & Gurman, 1995). However, this also can signify a subtle shift in the value given to marriage, inferring that being legally married may be a relatively minor consideration. Blankenhorn (1995, p. 314) shows how this subtle shift often has minimized marriage as old-fashioned and outdated, thus crowding it out of professional and educational circles and minimizing the role of commitment to making a relationship work well.

Our focus upon ME does not give equal consideration to family enrichment because of our belief that the most effective and efficient way to enrich families is to focus on the husband-wife relationship. The quality of the husband-wife relationship greatly influences and often determines the quality of the total family relationship. This does not negate the value of looking upon the family as an integrated system, but rather emphasizes the central importance of the subsystem of the marital dyad in the larger system of the family.

Because ME can result in a motivation for, and actualization of, family enrichment (Zimpfer, 1988a; L'Abate, 1990), we have chosen to focus on ME.

MARRIAGE AND OTHER SYSTEMS

Systems may be conceptualized either as concentric rings or as layers in relation to each other (Jackson, 1968a; von Bertalanffy, 1968). Each partner as a system has many subsystems such as physiological, sensory, memory, cognitive, emotional, volitional, and other components that enable each individual to have talents, skills, attitudes, and values. The two individuals who marry form a larger system (the marriage) that involves many interpersonal aspects such as communication skills, mutual rewards, common and mutually exclusive goals, and conflict resolution. The marriage as a system then becomes a key part of other systems from parent-child to extended intergenerational and in-law family relationships. Because of the interactions between marriage, family, and society, ME interventions need to be designed to address marriage in relation to these family and other systems.

These individual, marriage, and family systems are set in the context of larger neighborhood, work, community, society, and world systems that both support and interfere with successful marriage. Changes through ME both affect and are affected by larger systems of family, neighborhood, and society. Whitehead & Whitehead (1981) give a comprehensive description of the history and contexts of marriage, lifetime individual and couple development or passages, virtues and lifestyles, and spiritual and service implications of marriage. These are part of the lifelong marital journey (Bowen, 1991; Campbell, 1981) and family systems (Bowen, 1978; McGoldrick & Gerson, 1985).

Although they primarily address marriage and family therapy issues, Breunlin et al. (1992) identify essential foundation issues that also apply to ME and outreach. Their six core "metaframeworks" or domains are internal process, sequences, organization, development, culture, and gender. For each couple, these patterns underlie the partners' treatment of each other as they continue along their lifelong journey.

Karney and Bradbury (1995) have proposed an integrated theory of how marriage quality changes, based on their meta-analysis of 115 longitudinal studies representing over 45,000 marriages. They describe four major treatment theories of marriage—social exchange, behavioral, attachment, and crisis—and the advantages and limitations of each theoretical perspective. Their vulnerability–stress–adaptation model of marriage focuses on how the partners apply their adaptive processes to cope with enduring vulnerability and stressful events to improve marital quality, which in turn controls marital stability (continuing marriage vs. divorce or other dissolution).

In addition, in many practical ways, ME programs typically involve other systems, such as arranging schedules to enable couples to participate and discussion of couple issues such as finances, work, and parenting.

WHY FOCUS ON MARRIAGE RATHER THAN COUPLES OR FAMILIES?

Let's begin with the fundamental issue that every society must address—how to survive (Glendon & Blankenhorn, 1995). The answer becomes the basis for the visions on which all societies are built, namely, how to order the society and its members to ensure the continuation of the society. Although food, clothing, and shelter are the basic essentials for physical survival of individuals, in the long run, dependable sources for food, clothing, and shelter require cooperation among individuals.

Our entry into the third millennium A.D. increasingly places all of us in a world society that has expanded the question of survival beyond tribes, states, or nations to the world level. Among the many issues and questions that society faces are four that point to the vision of marriage in the culture:

1. What is our vision for society, whether it is our community, state, region, nation, or the world?
2. Why is marriage essential to this vision?
3. What agencies support marriage as the way to implement this vision?
4. What can we do for marriage that will achieve the vision?

The answers to these questions are directly relevant to our cultural context for marriage outreach and enrichment. They will guide ME leaders and participants as they formulate their assumptions and programs.

What Is Our Vision for Society?

Every society has a vision, whether it is explicit in a constitution or other written document or implicit in its mythologies, folklore, and epics. Societies vanish because they are overpowered by stronger societies through war or competition, bringing a different vision for the people. Every society also must deal with those who do not share the vision held by the majority.

The vision of what society is (or should be) shapes the society's childrearing practices, which then are implemented by parents, teachers, and other caregivers who nurture and care for the next generation. A society in its current form survives only to the extent that this vision is both "taught and caught" by its emerging generation. When the external rules become the internal motivations for enough people, they become the majority who shape the society for the next generation.

There are three fundamental paradigms for ordering society: laissez-faire, authoritarian, and democratic. Eventually, laissez-faire becomes authoritarian or autocratic because, when left without constraints, some person or group will become the dominant force that controls others, resulting in some type of autocracy. Even a theocracy eventually becomes either an autocracy (with religious leaders making the rules) or a democracy (with the voters deciding the rules, often through their elected officials).

Although the concepts and practice of democracy are rooted in the ancient Greco-Roman world, which was greatly influenced by religion, the emergence of the United States in the 18th century became the clearest modern attempt to replace authoritarian governments with democratic processes.

Two basic values are required for any democracy: respect for all persons and respect for all property. These values transcend laws, yet rules and laws are the specific guides to these values so that individuals may freely make these values their own. Social codes (e.g., the Ten Commandments, Code of Hammurabi) and constitutions (e.g., Greek, Roman, Magna Carta, United States) express to a considerable extent the value of persons and property, even when these values may not be distributed equally to all persons because of the way that citizenship is defined. In this century, the U.N. Charter and other documents continue to deepen and expand this basic understanding of respect for persons and property.

The vision of a society in which every person has equal right to "life, liberty, and the pursuit of happiness" (Preamble to U.S. Constitution) is continually tested, expanded, and renewed as each succeeding generation has sought to make this vision more completely implemented in every aspect of society. Similar processes operate in other nations as well as at world levels.

In this very brief and limited summary, we can only establish the central principle of value and respect for all persons (and by implication, their property) as the vision that guides (however incomplete and limited) our nations and our world in structuring society. This vision can happen only if we convey it to the next generation (our children), which means that those who influence our children truly have our individual and collective futures in their hands (Browning et al., 1997).

Our individual futures are in the hands of the children who soon will be mobile enough and strong enough (i.e., grown up) either to rob and kill us (if they have no respect for persons) or to improve the quality of our lives (if they do respect persons and property). There are many ways that these children (the next generation) can rob and kill, such as driving while drunk, drive-by shootings, muggings, home invasions. In addition, their destructive behaviors rob us by forcing higher insurance premiums, higher taxes for more policing and crime control, more prisons, increased security, and substance abuse prevention and treatment; higher prices because of shoplifting; and lowered work productivity and other indirect costs.

By contrast, there are many ways that these children can improve the quality of our individual lives, such as through acts of kindness, good manners, use of creative talents, and scholastic achievements, as well as acting in ways that benefit their parents, relatives, and friends. These children will become the persons who will find better ways to prevent disease, improve health, care for the environment, cooperate in multinational corporations, lead governments in peace, and enable all persons to have higher standards of living.

The children of our society have our collective future in their hands because they will become the leaders and citizens of the future. They will teach the generation after them (our grandchildren), control the corporations, make the laws, provide the entertainment, and control all other society functions that we currently control. Respect for persons and property is the cornerstone of democracy. Unless all citizens personally hold to these values, democratic society will either be destroyed or become an autocratic police state.

Why Is Marriage Essential to This Vision?

Marriage is essential to the democratic society's vision of value and respect for all people, property, and the environment because marriage is the most efficient method for ensuring the care of children.

> Marriage is a relationship within which a community socially approves and encourages sexual intercourse and the birth of children. It is society's way of signaling to would-be parents that their long-term relationship together is socially important—a public concern, not simply a private affair. . . .
>
> The institution of marriage was designed less for the accommodation of adults in love than for the proper functioning of society, especially regarding the care of children. . . .
>
> Marriage is society's most important contrivance for protecting child well-being, turning children into good citizens, and fostering good behavior among adults—a "social good" worthy of strong support. . . .
>
> Our message to young Americans is simple and challenging. As a foundation for family life and raising children, marriage is better than its fast-growing alternatives. It is our society's most important institution for bringing up children, for fostering high parental investment in children, and for helping men and women find a common life of mutual affection, care, and sexual intimacy (Popenoe et al., 1996, p. 303ff.)

Society, family, and marriage are linked in a system of mutual support for achieving and maintaining respect for person and property (e.g., Mace & Mace, 1977). By beginning at any point we will reach the other two as well. The assumption that marriage is essential to democratic society requires a systemic view of society, child rearing, and marriage.

Society. We have started by assuming that we prefer a democratic society rather than an autocratic society, although the difficulties of true democracy often push us into authoritarian operations. Nevertheless, our vision is a society in which there is mutual and equal respect for every person and for all property. Although many seek to maintain this vision in adult relationships, the wellspring for adult attitudes and values begins in childhood, which leads us to the quality of care, education, and nurture that children receive as well as what we received when we were children (Glendon & Blankenhorn, 1995).

Child rearing. The essential step in achieving this vision is child rearing that expresses respect for persons and property in everyday life. In a more formal sense this is socializing the child into the values of society. Because all child rearing socializes children into some type of value system, it is vital for parents, teachers, and others to be aware of the vision and values that they demonstrate to and reinforce in the children under their care. Nurturing and shaping a child is a constant task that requires much energy, dedication, concern, and love—a major investment of time and effort by caregivers. However, personal investments in specific children depend upon many factors, especially the extent to which the nurturing persons feel personally responsible for a specific child over other children or competing responsibilities.

Marriage. Marriage is the third essential element in this system of society, child care, and couples. In very critical ways that may not be obvious at first glance, marriage is the primary mechanism for achieving parental investment in specific children. The rationale and dynamics are described by contributors to the symposia supported by the Council on Families in America (Blankenhorn, 1995; Popenoe et al., 1996).

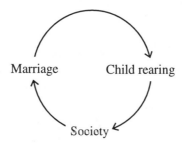

For society, marriage is the mechanism for achieving the stable investment of adults in the rearing of children who will be the next generation of society, thus enabling the survival of the society. This applies to all marriages, whether they have children or not, because the women and men in all marriages are the adults who structure society and, both directly and indirectly, affect the lives of the children in society. This connection is obvious for couples with children in their household but must be clear even for childless couples.

Asserting the importance of marriage requires that marriage be defined. Most ME programs define marriage as an egalitarian relationship between one man and one woman across their lifetimes (see chapter 1, this volume; also see Blankenhorn, 1995; Popenoe et al., 1996).

Browning (1996) provides a careful account of how marriage arises out of inclusive fitness, kin altruism, and parental certainty to ensure parental investment in children. Marriage addresses what he terms the "male problematic" and encourages men as well as women to invest their lives in their offspring. By male problematic, Browning (1996, p. 122) refers to the central question of whether men will concentrate their resources in a few children who will grow to responsible adulthood (the K-strategy as described by evolutionary theorists) or freely procreate and spread their resources thinly (or not at all) over many children with the possibility that a few of them will survive to adulthood (the R-strategy). Among humans (and among most other primates and a few other species) the K-strategy is the choice for species survival.

Blankenhorn (1995, chap. 12) emphasizes this point in practical ways for our society:

> The most urgent domestic challenge facing the United States at the close of the twentieth century is the re-creation of fatherhood as a vital social role for men. At stake is nothing less than the success of the American experiment. For unless we reverse the trend of fatherlessness, no other set of accomplishments—not economic growth or private construction or welfare reform or better schools—will succeed in arresting the decline of child well-being and the spread of male violence. To tolerate the trend of fatherlessness is to accept the inevitability of continued societal recession (Blankenhorn, 1995, p. 223).

According to Blankenhorn, more than anything else the quality of marriage—that is, the quality of the relationship between the man and the woman in the household—determines whether each parent, especially the man as father, not only continues to stay physically but in many more subtle ways provides a continuing presence of nurture and strength for the woman as mother. Through these two adults comes the first and primary source of love, nurture, stability, socialization, and shaping toward the values of respect for persons and property.

Some may argue that marriage is not essential to child rearing, because children can grow up in other child-care models, such as institutions, one-parent families, extended families, or other state-operated systems. Such were envisioned in ancient times by Plato in *The Republic*, but opposed by Aristotle on the grounds that "that which is common to the greatest number has the least care bestowed upon it" (Browning, 1996, p. 126, quoting from Aristotle's *Politics*).

Browning (1996, p. 127) traces how Thomas Aquinas followed Aristotle and in many ways anticipated current evolutionary theorists:

> In short, Thomas believed—as human ecologists Martin Daly, Margo Wilson, Donald Symons, and Robert Trivers do today—that paternal investment in children, paternal certainty, and monogamy tend to go together. Contemporary evolutionary ecologists are clearer than Aquinas about how paternal certainty is supplemented by two other conditions, as we say above, before paternal investment occurs (that is, sexual exchange and general reciprocal altruism between the couple). From the perspective of

the modern discussion, however, Aquinas was playing in the right ball park and, for his time, batting rather well.

If the vision of having respect for persons and property is essential to society, then those who care for children must learn this themselves, consistently practice it, and demonstrate this to, and nurture it in hundreds of specific ways in, the children under their care. As any parent and teacher often has experienced, being sure that each child feels respected and valued becomes much more difficult as the number of children under their care increases. This is further complicated by factors such as age, gender, economics, class, ethnicity, abilities, and time available with each child.

Marriage is the primary relationship in which two adults (one female, one male) live out their respect for each other in the most extremely free voluntary relationships, namely, what they do in private away from the view and judgment of others. What a couple does in private (sexual intercourse that conceives a child, whether intended or not) eventually affects us all in the birth of a child. Neither sex nor marriage is ever an absolutely private affair. What these two adults experience in private, they then express in public through child rearing as well as their other adult relationships of work, friendship, and citizenship.

Marriage connects so many aspects of living—career, leisure, finances, real estate, values, sexual activities, religious involvement, two sets of extended families, values, daily living patterns, names—in a grand balancing act. Every person, including spouses, is constantly challenged to make choices that have real consequences. Because marriage is such a fundamental building block in society, the quality of marriages eventually affects all of society in one way or another.

Marriage can never be isolated from parenting, family, and some type of community (church, synagogue, mosque, neighborhood, or other community). Marriage is a journey across the spouses' lifetimes. Along this journey, wife and husband affect each other, and in turn make major impacts, for good or ill, on others—their children, relatives, friends, work colleagues, neighborhood, and more.

The marital journey assumes that across the partners' lifetimes change will occur. Their common task is to be concerned about the next generation, both their own children and the children of society or the world. The quality of marriage is the fundamental key to the quality of the family, because the wife and husband are the leaders in their family with the power to influence what happens to their children and others in their household, thus affecting the next generation and all of us in society.

Up to this point, we have attempted to make two points about the essential role of marriage for society and children: *First, our democratic vision is fundamentally*

that every person and their property deserves and is entitled to value and respect.
Second, respect for persons and property is rooted in the child-rearing process
through which persons bring a set of values to their lives as adults and to the
survival and quality of their society.

Marriage is essential to society because it is the primary, most efficient way to
provide the care that every child needs.

There are many more details of how we arrive at this assertion about marriage
as essential to society, and therefore why society (i.e., all of us) must support
marriage, defined as the type of marriage that engenders respect for persons and
property, beginning with the spouses and extending to others—children, neighborhood, society, and world. These details have been well developed by others (e.g.,
Hendrix, 1988; Popenoe et al., 1996; Browning et al., 1997). On the assumption
that these points are fundamental to democratic society, but that our society is not
doing a very good job of implementing them, we now turn to how we can enable
marriages to achieve this vision of respect for persons and property.

What Agencies Support Marriage as the Way
to Implement This Vision?

Religious communities (e.g., churches, synagogues) provide the clearest and most
consistent support for marriage as the basis for forming a family (Greeley, 1991).
Although religious communities may differ on the details of marriage, they agree on
having some type of wedding to mark the change in life status and its implications
for all other relationships. Directly or indirectly, many of the ME and other efforts
to improve the quality of marriage have their roots in some faith perspective that
values persons in families. Sadly, there are far too many instances of dysfunctional
marriages and families who also are involved in a religious community. Happily,
there are also many instances of healthy marriages and families that have no current
active affiliation with any religious community, although usually these families are
involved in some other caring community based around common interests (e.g.,
the arts, crafts, outdoors, sports, recreation, community service, profession).

Educational communities (day care, preschool, public and private schools, colleges, etc.) function better when students and teachers come from stable families,
both two-parent and one-parent or other type of household. Especially in public
institutions, a wider range of views with less consensus is typical, yet most schools
support marriage, even if only for pragmatic reasons.

In addition to schools, other agencies have opportunities to support healthy
marriage as the major key to stable families. Among these are the court system,
police, and community assistance programs. The level of support, however, depends heavily upon the leaders of these groups. These leaders, in turn, have created

their views and values about marriage out of their own personal experiences of family, church, school, and other groups.

Learning respect for persons, property, and environment begins in infancy and continues throughout life. Each person is born with a very intense motivation to survive as an individual, regardless of what achieving that personal survival does to others. The infant's demands for food (such as loud and continuous crying) eventually will cause any parent to do something to quiet the baby. When caregivers are pushed beyond their own limits of respect for the child, they may abuse or even murder the struggling infant. The infant must learn early that his or her personal survival depends upon cooperation with others, and there are limits (boundaries) to his or her desires and demands. How this fundamental need is met lays the foundation for a dysfunctional or healthy adult.

Smiles or other affectionate responses from the infant reinforces the caregiver's positive response to the child as well as helps to expand the caregiver's own patience, insights, and skills in responding with respect to the child and to others. To the extent that both child and adult identify and stabilize identities and boundaries—initially expressed in positive and negative consequences of actions, later in rules, and finally in commitment to principles—the basis for community and society is laid.

When those in authority allow one child to hurt another child or to take toys from another child, the child who perpetrates the hurt learns that he or she can get away with it. The stakes become higher each time the consequences to the perpetrator are less than the gain from the causing the hurt or taking the property— a social learning view of socialization. In this process the perpetrating child learns to disrespect other persons and their property. This easily evolves to disrespect for the environment, both the natural world and public or private property.

When caregivers enable children to perform activities that require cooperation (such as games) and bring positive results to each participant, all involved discover that respecting other persons and their property is desirable because only when others respect us and our property can we be safe and secure.

Learning and practicing this principle is a lifelong task for all persons. How to guarantee equality and mutual respect for each other is the constant work of democracy, set against the basic tendency of each person to put himself or herself first at the expense of others. In the long run we can guarantee our own "rights to life, liberty, and the pursuit of happiness" (U.S. Constitution) only to the extent that we join together to guarantee these same rights to others, regardless of their power or prestige.

We learn this principle through years of experience in which respect for persons, property, and environment consistently and repeatedly results in positive consequences, whereas disrespect has correspondingly negative consequences. This is a 24-hour per day, seven-day per week process. Adults must work closely and carefully with each child to enable the child to have a socialization experience that will be the basis on which the adolescent as emerging adult can make positive decisions, regardless of pressures from others, about respecting persons, property, and the environment in all circumstances. Add to this the complication of coming to common agreement on what constitutes appropriate values and respect for each person when we are so diverse in age, gender, ethnicity, ability, opportunity, and so forth.

Marriage is the single most important means to socialize children into the values of respect for persons, property, and environment. The ways that men and women interact with each other, both in marriage and in other settings, set the standards and norms for adult behaviors as well as being models for children to observe and imitate. All marriages affect the next generation regardless of whether a couple has children in their own household. This is obvious with married couples who have children in their homes. The care that these spouses as parents give to their own children benefits the children involved in many ways. In addition, these families benefit us all by reducing the load of care that others must give (such as teachers, police, child advocacy agencies) and thus reducing the taxes and personal involvement that we all must share in trying to achieve the democratic vision.

Although less obvious, married couples who no longer have children at home or who never have had children also make equally vital contributions to children. All children are "our children." Through their marriages, adults are supported in their work efforts, both paid and volunteer, that benefit children. The encouragement of one's spouse for one's career objectives can be a powerful motivator to continue. Most careers contain decision points about how much good one is doing for others through one's job. For example, deciding whether to use one's marketing or service skills to make a lot of money from a product that harms others or to be content with less money from a product that helps children can be greatly influenced by which values and options one's spouse supports.

Every successfully married couple, with children or not, models for others, including children, how a woman and a man live out marriage. Couples who are involved with children and adolescents, as teachers, coaches, activity sponsors, aunts, uncles, godparents, chaperons, tutors, and other roles, demonstrate marriage for these children and their caregivers. Having the support of one's spouse makes it much easier for the other spouse to give time and effort in these activities.

Persons who have never married, or who have had negative experiences of marriage, still may be effective as caregivers for children and adolescents, yet they are hampered in describing and demonstrating positive marriage. Married spouses can support each other while one (or both) is directly or indirectly involved in giving care to others, from infancy through old age.

What Can We Do for Marriage That Will Achieve the Vision?

Because marriage is the most efficient and effective way to socialize the next generation, the challenge facing us is to find ways to enhance marriage as the primary channel for giving good care to children.

Marriage is a natural, sacramental, economic, social, psychological, emotional, and legal institution (Hunt & Rydman, 1979, p. 29; Popenoe et al., 1996, p. 304). As such, persons who have contact with marriage from each of these institutional perspectives also have opportunities to work toward strengthening marriage as the basis for socializing the next generation into the vision and values of respect for persons, property, and environment.

Without denying the serious challenges to marriage, the report of Greeley (1991) shows that there are many more potential allies of marriage and of efforts to improve the quality of marriages and families than may be assumed. On the basis of two Gallup polls of random samples of 657 married couples (1,314 respondents), Greeley gives empirical evidence to show that most married people are sexually faithful. He found that 96% of those surveyed said they were faithful to their spouses in the past year.

"There is no stronger predictor of marital happiness than religious devotion. . . . warmth of religious images has a powerful impact on marital satisfaction" (Greeley, 1991, p. 183). "Religious denomination—Catholic or Protestant—as such has less impact on marriage than the fact of denominational difference" between spouses (p. 187). In Greeley's surveys, 55% of married people go to church at least two or three times a month, and of those who attend, 70% reported being very happy in their marriages.

Greeley notes that spouses' images of God are highly correlated with the quality of their marriage. "Religion also plays another role in marriage: it relates to the two loves of which St. Paul wrote, the love of husband and wife and the love of humans and God. This is an empirical and not a theological statement. Whether there be a God or not, the images humans have of Her/Him profoundly affect their marital relationships. Warm and intense images of God correlate with a warm and intense relationship with the spouse" (Greeley, 1991, p. 193).

Greeley argues that religion is "experience, images, and story before it becomes creed, code, and cult. The latter are the necessary cognitive reflections on the former, but religion originates and derives its raw and primordial power from the former. Images of God ordinarily encode the experiences a person believes she/he has had with the Deity and explain on the symbolic and narrative level the meaning and purpose of human life. . . . The experiences of love in one's marriage should correlate with the experiences of love one has from one's encounter with the sacred: the warmer and more passionate one's religious images, the warmer and more passionate will be one's marriage relationships, and vice versa" (Greeley, 1991, p. 193).

One explanation of the mechanisms of how experiences, images, and stories impact marriage is provided by Hendrix in his Imago approach to marriage. Hendrix (1988, 1992) describes the ways in which each spouse's past family experiences contribute to their patterns of marital interaction, and places this in the context of both personal and societal history.

The report of Greeley (1991) indicates that the majority of married couples in the United States have positive experiences, images, and stories of marriage. These millions of couples provide a vast resource for demonstrating the essential value of marriage. Their experiences need to be more easily and widely available to all couples. They can become mentors to other couples as described in part III (Hunt & Hunt, 1996a; McManus, 1995). Because they want to continue to grow in their marriages, these couples are often most likely to participate in ME events. Through ME they can be better prepared not only to enjoy their own marriages but by their example to encourage other couples to grow.

The Council on Families in America (Popenoe et al., 1996, chap. 13) gives a wake-up call to action to counter the deterioration of marriage in America and the resulting disintegration of families.

> Many factors have contributed to the deteriorating well-being of children. But what ranks as the most fundamental factor of all, in our judgment, is *the weakening of marriage as an institution.* . . .
>
> Making marriage stronger will require a fundamental shift in cultural values and in public policy. . . . No one sector of society is responsible for the decline of marriage. We are all part of the problem, and therefore we all must be part of the solution. (Popenoe et al., p. 308).

In this chapter we have considered some of the ways that marriage is interconnected with family and with society in order to broaden perspectives on marriage. We consider in more detail several of the strategies and recommendations to major sectors of society by the Council on Marriage in America in chapter 13 of this volume. Part II examines how these principles are expressed in ME programs.

PART TWO

MARRIAGE ENRICHMENT
PROGRAMS

The philosophy and assumptions about marriage and its enrichment are embedded in the variety of marriage enrichment (ME) programs that are available today.

Chapter 4 describes major dimensions of ME programs and suggests strengths and needs relating to each dimension. These qualities form a template for examining any enrichment program.

This general format guides the organization of the descriptions of selected ME programs in chapter 5. Chapter 5 provides brief descriptions of some of the better known programs. Leaders in over 50 of these programs presented at the initial national conference in Washington, D.C., in May 1997, sponsored by the Coalition for Marriage, Family, and Couple Education (CMFCE). This conference has become an annual event at which program updates and new programs are presented. Current information on programs is also available on the CMFCE World Wide Web site (see Contact Information for Specific Programs, this volume). Several of the leaders in these programs were also active in producing two international conferences on ME in 1992 in Atlanta, Georgia, and in 1996 in Fort Worth, Texas.

ME programs have produced many tools and techniques, such as "I" and "You" messages, reflecting and paraphrasing, time-outs, and conflict resolution steps. As these tools have been shown to be effective through research and clinical experience, they have been adapted and modified by other programs and by clinicians in therapy situations. Some of these tools are summarized in chapter 6.

Chapter 4

Dimensions of Successful Programs

Marriage enrichment (ME) programs vary across several important dimensions that have emerged in the more than 35-year history of enrichment. In this chapter these elements are clustered under general program qualities, event characteristics, leader qualities, leader training, program elements and content, schedule and format, follow-up, and program settings.

PROGRAM QUALITIES

History

Although every enrichment program has a developmental history, how readily that is available depends upon whether the developers and leaders have provided written documentation, descriptions, and training procedures.

Sponsorship

Programs may be based in an independent professional institute or sponsored by a church, educational or community agency, or other organization. Some couples may be intimidated by a psychlogically oriented program and would rather choose one that is associated with a religious group. Conversely, other couples prefer to avoid some of the religious-based programs. Even where an explicit value system is not stated, programs still have implicit assumptions and values that are expressed in the program content and structure.

Cost

Most weekend programs charge registration and workshop fees that may range from a nominal amount to several hundred dollars. Lodging and meals are usually in addition to this charge. Expenses of leaders usually are paid from registration fees or other sources. Because couples programs do not include children, participants must make arrangements for child care for the weekend. This may add to the cost of the event for the couple.

Some leaders give their time and receive no remuneration for their services because they consider enrichment as important preventive work that is part of their practice or service. Many leaders receive remuneration according to the number of couples who attend. Some may receive a fixed fee of a few hundred dollars per leader or leader couple. A few professionals may receive well over $1,000 for leading a weekend program.

The cost for multiweek programs usually ranges in proportion to weekend programs, and couples are charged a one-time fee for the course. Multiweek programs sponsored by agencies or religious groups may be at reduced cost or free. Either way, Guerney (1977) and L'Abate (1977) have noted that enrichment, for the most part, is relatively inexpensive when compared to therapy, especially if the programs are led by trained nonprofessionals or paraprofessionals.

Outcome Assumptions

The primary goal is renewing and refreshing each couple's commitment and enjoyment of marriage. Most ME programs assume that couples will increase their skills for communication, problem solving, and nurturing their relationship. To maintain competence, couples must continue to practice to incorporate new skills into their daily interactions.

Many events plan for ways that couples can continue practicing skills and for periodic reunion/booster times every six months to a year. Some programs now schedule regular postevent booster sessions at three- to six-month intervals. In addition, some specialized programs, such as Retrouvaille and Recovery of Hope, focus on reconsidering divorce and participating in support groups or therapy to address factors that were leading toward divorce.

Some professionals offer ME programs and couples group therapy as part of their professional services and integrate these with couple and individual therapy. For ME events that are not directly related to marriage therapy, leaders usually receive inquiries from some participants about follow-up therapeutic work or referrals for therapy.

Research on Programs

Some programs, such as Couples Communication Program ([CCP], Miller et al., 1991), Prevention and Relationship Enhancement Program ([PREP], Markman et al., 1994), and Relationship Enhancement (Guerney, 1987), have maintained a continuing series of studies of their program effectiveness and outcome. More programs, such as PAIRS, are initiating studies, and many programs benefit from research overviews and meta-analyses (Giblin, 1986; Guerney & Maxson, 1990; Zimpfer, 1988). Many leaders obtain some type of pre- and postevent evaluations to guide them in modifying their program, some of which are described in chapters 7–9.

Chapter 5 provides summary information about representative major enrichment programs. Information about specific programs may be obtained from the Practitioners Directory available through the Coalition for Marriage, Family, and Couples Education (CMFCE).

EVENT CHARACTERISTICS

Types of Programs

In efforts to reach as many participants as possible, most programs offer ME experiential workshops that emphasize communication skills, problem solving, conflict resolution, personal development, sexuality, intimacy enhancement, and values clarification. Some programs may be available or limited to specific couple populations, such as engaged couples, couples considering divorce, single persons, or gay or lesbian couples.

In addition to ME programs that focus on couples, family enrichment and psychoeducational models (L'Abate, 1981; McFarlane, 1991) may reach couples as part of their concern for family well-being. Programs such as Promise Keepers for men and Women of Faith for women (Clairmont et al., 1997a,b) may further motivate men and women to participate in ME and family enrichment in relation to individual, marriage, and family growth as a follow-up.

Size of Event

Some well-known programs will be attended by 75 or more couples. In most enrichment programs, however, 5 to 15 couples typically participate in a given weekend or a multiweek experience, with one or two leaders or leader couples. For larger events that include small-group practice with feedback, additional leaders are necessary to assist in coaching and facilitating individual couple practice.

Much of the appeal of ME continues to be to middle-class persons. The cognitive and theoretical emphasis and the emphasis on verbal skills may more easily fit most programs to middle-class and upper-class couples who value and comprehend the intellectual material. The cost and time involved in leaving the home environment for a weekend experience might be prohibitive for lower-income couples. Guerney (1987) and L'Abate (1977) insist that their models can be used appropriately and effectively with various socioeconomic classes.

Although more research on which program elements are most effective with specific types of couples is needed (Worthington, 1992), it seems that most couples who are committed to growth and willing to participate in a program can benefit from it. Most leaders make some adaptations for couples who have difficulty with some parts of the program. Where the mismatch is too great, the leader can help the couple to find other programs. Where the couple's difficulty is due to more complicated dynamics that may be dysfunctional, the leader can help the couple find appropriate therapeutic interventions.

Perhaps the major barriers of most programs to reaching the full range of couples are the event costs and schedules. Some couples cannot attend Friday evening through Sunday weekend (or Saturday-Sunday) events because of work schedules or child-care needs. For these couples, weeknight and one-day enrichment formats are available. Churches, synagogues, and community agencies can arrange or provide child care for participating couples. Sponsoring agencies can pay some or all of the leaders', meal, and other expenses, or can provide subsidies for couples who cannot afford the full price of enrichment events.

Issues of cost and schedules may mask a deeper dimension of the reluctance of many men and women to participate in any group that encourages the exploration of personal and relationship matters. Mace (1987) has described a pervasive intermarital taboo that assumes that couples should not disclose the more negative and troublesome sides of their relationship. Thus many couples try to put up a good public image that tries to say that they are so in love and everything is just fine. This mask may hide not only the times when the partners disagree but also prevent disclosure of severe emotional, physical, or sexual abuse in the marriage and family. Replacing this taboo with honesty about both the work and the joy of marriage is the aim of slogans such as the Association of Couples for Marriage Enrichment (ACME) "better marriages, beginning with our own."

Another block to participation in enrichment programs is the "myth of naturalism" (Fincham & Bradbury, 1990; Vincent, 1973), which assumes that everyone naturally will have a satisfying marriage without any assistance or difficulty. This myth infers that seeking help for one's marriage is admitting failure and inadequacy, and it is embarrassing to ask for help or direction. Thus the initial factors that produce distress are complicated by closing one's eyes to the problems and not talking about them, perhaps with the illusionary hope that they will go away. If they don't, then divorce is seen as an easy way out, with a failure to realize that these same attitudes and behavior patterns will be carried into any future relationship.

PROGRAM LEADER QUALITIES

ME programs are led by people with varying professional backgrounds, degrees of training, and styles of leadership. Programs are conducted by

1. Nonprofessionally trained married couples working alone who are trained for the specific program model they are leading (e.g., ACME [Hopkins et al., 1978]). However, many of the couples who are ACME leaders have one or both partners who are trained in one of the helping professions.
2. Nonprofessionally trained married couples, working together with a trained professional from one of the helping professions, trained in the particular model they are using (e.g., Marriage Encounter [Demarest et al., 1977]).
3. A male-female leadership team, but not necessarily married to each other or to someone else, trained in the particular model they are using (e.g., Relationship Enhancement program [Guerney, 1977], PAIRS [Gordon, 1988]).
4. An individual of either gender, trained in the particular model he or she is using (e.g., CCP [Miller, Nunnally, & Wackman, 1975], Relationship Enhancement program [Guerney, 1977], PAIRS [Gordon, 1988]).
5. A professionally trained individual with additional training and certification in the specific program model (Hendrix, 1992, PAIRS [Gordon, 1988, 1990]).

Some programs permit a variety of these leadership options, but others do not. A fundamental principle involved in choosing a leadership option concerns issues of role modeling. To what extent are the leaders assumed to model or illustrate good marriage skills in the ways that they conduct the group? Some theorists describe therapists or leaders as being somewhat like a foster parent to those being helped. From this perspective the leaders are not just technicians who know and can teach specific relationship skills.

In addition to knowing the techniques of relationship skills, leaders provide corrective emotional experiences for participants. This may be done by a married couple who become real-life examples of marriage and through this enable participants to change the images of marriage that they have received from other sources. This corrective experience may be directly between leaders and participants through the ways that leaders respond to participants' questions, comments, and discussions. This also may happen when the leader arranges group activities to encourage spouses to talk with each other and then gain feedback from the leaders or the group about the positive aspects and growth areas observed in the couple interactions. In all of these leadership issues, it is important for the leaders to offer several ways of coping with issues and to encourage every couple to make choices about what is best for them in their own situations.

Married Couples as Leaders

Mace (1975b) insists that although an individual or unrelated male-female leadership team can lead an effective experience, the best facilitators for ME weekend programs or marital growth groups are married couples who play a fully participative role and serve as models of healthy couple interaction and even to some extent as surrogate parents. The ACME model requires that leadership be provided by a married couple. In that model, leader teams often include at least one professional, but Mace and Mace (1976) suggest that lay couples may be just as effective.

Leader couples need to model enrichment skills in their own marriages and to have the ability to inspire couples in realistic ways. It is obvious that leaders must be trained and experienced in the type of event they lead. Leaders should have experience in diagnosing and treating individual, couple, and family dysfunctions, or at least should know their own limits so that they have the ability to refer participants to professional consultants when it is necessary and appropriate. Skills in answering questions, being open, limiting and containing couple anxieties, and nurturing positive growth in couples are essential for leaders.

There is much in the way of subjective, personal testimony from leaders and participants that affirms the value of having married couples as leaders. Mace and Mace (1976) also suggest that clinically trained leaders should be available in at least a supervisor capacity for all ME programs. However, research that either supports or denies this position has yet to be performed (Guerney & Maxson, 1990). Otto (1976) surveyed 30 professionals involved in ME programming and found that 90% reported that they used either husband-wife or other male-female leadership teams. However, many of the more recently developed programs use one leader, perhaps with additional assistants or coaches according to the number of couples.

The importance of the gender and marital status of ME leaders involves several assumptions. Having both gender perspectives represented in the leaders is advantageous to emphasize egalitarian co-equal balance in marriage, to help avoid gender biases, and to model the value of both female and male perspectives. Having leaders who are experiencing satisfaction and wellness in their own lives enables them to speak from their own experience in practicing the relationship skills that they are teaching and demonstrating.

The counterargument to gender and marital-status concerns is that a well-trained leader should be able to teach and model skills and coach others in applying them independently of the leader's own personal life. The connections of a leader's competence to his or her gender, marital, and professional status are complicated and not yet well understood. Where payment of leaders is an issue, if one well-trained leader can accomplish as much as two, then costs can be reduced by having individuals as leaders.

It seems preferable to have competence along with representation of gender and marriage in leaders of ME events. Use of married couples as leaders automatically brings gender balance and represents marriage. A nonprofessionally trained couple may mean only that neither spouse is licensed or certified in a helping profession as typically defined. However, one or both spouses may have formal training in related areas, such as human services, education, or personnel management, or in-service training as part of volunteer work in lay counseling, telephone hotline services, and other areas.

Leaders as Participants

Leadership styles vary from nonparticipant leader-director to full participant-leader (Mace, 1975a). At least three elements define participation: presentation of information, demonstration of skills, and self-disclosure of personal information. The leader's presentation effectiveness is essential in all programs, even those that have much videotape, audiotape, or computer-presented materials (e.g., TIME [Dinkmeyer & Carlson, 1986a,b]). Leaders may demonstrate skills with a real-life or role-play partner or in directed role-play situations. In self-disclosure, the leader describes his or her own experiences and inner feelings or couple leaders talk together as husband and wife about personal matters while the participants observe that process.

Some programs, such as Relationship Enhancement and PAIRS, do not encourage the group leader to be a participant who self-discloses personal moods, feelings, or reactions that arise as the group is led. On the other hand, leaders of the ACME model are full participants. Both ACME and Marriage Encounter expect leader couples to model self-disclosure of thoughts, feelings, and intentions, as well as risk taking, vulnerability, and positive affirmation. Regardless of the style, most writers seem to agree that it is important for the leaders to model the skills they seek to teach and the growth-oriented relationship they value.

Nonprofessionals and Paraprofessionals as Leaders

Most ME programs permit and encourage the use of appropriate nonprofessionals or paraprofessionals as leaders or facilitators (e.g., Guerney, 1977; Hopkins et al., 1978; L'Abate, 1977). Truax and Carkhuff (1967) emphasized the therapeutic value of personality variables of the therapists, as opposed to formalized techniques. Empathy, warmth, and genuineness are identified as exerting a personal influence that contributes to successful outcomes (Goldstein, 1973). Truax and Carkhuff (1967) also demonstrate that training in empathy, warmth, and genuineness is possible. Goldstein (1973) refers to about 20 research reports that suggest or demonstrate the therapeutic potency of nurses, patients' parents, college undergraduates, psychological technicians, convicts, housewives, auxiliary counselors, human service aides, and foster grandparents. Collins (1991) and Guerney (1977, 1987) strongly suggest that nonprofessionals trained in empathy and appropriately supervised can be effective agents of change.

All of this suggests that the use of appropriately trained and supervised nonprofessionals to facilitate growth with nonclinical, couple enrichment groups, and even with clinical couples or groups of couples (L'Abate, 1977), is appropriate. Recent developments in lay counseling (Tan, 1991) continue to support the many ways in which nonprofessionals can be effective in extending mental health and enrichment services.

The better use of nonprofessionals can lead to the dissemination of important growth-oriented services, at a reduced cost, to a larger portion of the population than would be reached if leadership were restricted to professionally trained persons. The use of nonprofessionals also conserves professional resources, allowing professionals to serve as program developers, supervisors, and leadership trainers (Guerney, 1977; Tan, 1991).

LEADER TRAINING

Otto (1975, 1976) found that of the 30 professionals conducting enrichment programs that he surveyed, over 80% were training other persons to lead programs as well. Most national ME organizations have training guidelines and clearly defined standards for leaders. The need for highly qualified, trained leadership becomes evident when it is realized that the most important variable in the success of enrichment programs is identified as the quality of the leader's skills and relationships (Lieberman et al., 1973; Mace & Mace, 1976; see also chapters 7 and 8, this volume).

ACME (Hopkins et al., 1978; Mace & Mace, 1984) developed standards for the selection, training, and certification of leaders of ME programs, which have been maintained. Many of the national ME organizations have adopted these or similar standards. Standards for selecting potential leader couples include the following qualities:

1. Actively committed to marital growth for themselves and for others;
2. Able to work together cooperatively as a team;

3. Communicate in a warm and caring manner to other couples and are sensitive to others in the group;
4. Ready and able to share themselves openly and to be vulnerable;
5. Aware of group processes and couple processes occurring around them;
6. Have some basic knowledge of human development, marital interaction, and group process dynamics.

ACME's training and certification standards for leaders (Mace & Mace, 1984) include the following:

1. Participation in at least one ME event;
2. Reflection on experiences regarding enrichment leadership and component parts of the program;
3. Exposure to and discussion of a variety of styles, resources, and support systems for ME;
4. Practice under supervision in designing a ME experience;
5. Practice under supervision in leading a ME event;
6. Marital exploration, such as an intense marital dialogue, in front of other trainee couples;
7. Reflection on, and evaluation and development of, an ongoing growth plan for themselves;
8. Provisional leader certification by ACME;
9. Participation in an advanced training workshop;
10. Leadership of five ME events with evaluation and feedback from participants;
11. Full certification for a three-year period;
12. Review every three years, with evidence of continuing marital growth and satisfactory couple group leadership, for continuing certification.

Other leadership training programs differ somewhat from the ACME model. For example, the training programs of Guerney and L'Abate do not share ACME's emphasis on the leadership couple's active participation and sharing of themselves and their personal experiences within the program. In the Guerney and L'Abate programs, leaders serve as facilitators, not as co-participants, whereas, in the ACME model, the facilitator and co-participant functions are emphasized equally. In addition to this difference, (Guerney 1977, 1987) uses a more behaviorally oriented training approach, which he suggests is applicable to a variety of programs. L'Abate advocates the use of detailed written instructions incorporated into training manuals, designed for varied content areas (L'Abate 1977, 1981, 1985a).

Training and certification of ME leaders is becoming more specific and standardized as experience and research identify components and leader qualities that contribute to participants' goals and benefits. A combination of skill development, didactic learning, and actual supervised experiences as a leader are common elements of all training programs. Attention to the careful selection and training of competent leaders continues to be a goal of programs (Guerney & Maxson, 1990).

Programs also differ in the extent to which leaders are permitted or encouraged to change the format for each client group or event. Programs seek to achieve a flexible balance between maintaining standards of program content and structure that typically are assumed for ME events and the local leaders' resources, creativity, and emphases. Where programs utilize both general presentations of specified information and individualized coaching of couples, such as PREP (Markman, Floyd, Stanley, & Jamieson, 1984; Markman et al., 1994), training to criterion involves much effort and expense. Other programs (e.g., Creative ME Program [Hof & Miller, 1981] and PAIRS [Gordon, 1988]), encourage leaders to adapt resources to their own program and modify them according to the emerging needs of a particular group of couples.

All programs need to be guided by a clear theoretical rationale and a knowledge of research on and experience with each program element in which clients are requested to participate. These values are especially important for leaders who develop their own variations of enrichment events. It is also important that clinically trained professionals realize that their training as a marital or family therapist is not necessarily sufficient to qualify them as ME program leaders. It is equally important for enthusiastic nonprofessionals to realize that having a growth-oriented, mutually satisfying marital relationship, and participation in a few ME programs does not qualify them to be effective program leaders. Supervised training and experience is essential for leaders to know both the range of possibilities and the limits in ME programs and experiences.

PROGRAM ELEMENTS AND CONTENT

The content focus of most enrichment programs today is a combination of information about relationship functioning and commitment, demonstrations of relationship skills, opportunity for practice of these skills, and encouragement to couples to renew their commitment to change toward positive goals. Chapter 2 describes details of these content areas. Both didactic and experiential elements are to be found in most programs.

Programs typically emphasize the application of general communication skills to specific concerns that a couple has, although some programs may be designed to focus primarily on a specific topic. Topics usually include general communication skills, increasing affection and sexual affirmation, and other topics that a group may request.

Content should be appropriate to the growth levels of participants in ways that stimulate couples to consider issues and to share clear expressions of marriage values, possibilities, and options. Resources, materials, and handouts enable couples to remember content. Clear instructions provide a sense of security and confidence to participating couples, yet give enough freedom for couples to adapt content to their own growing edges.

ACME affirms that all of the programs that it recognizes, whatever the content and format, should meet the following guidelines:

1. The program should be led by one or more qualified married couples whose leadership reflects an ability to interact and participate effectively.
2. The program should be experiential and dynamic, as opposed to a didactic and purely intellectual.
3. The program should provide an opportunity for couple dialogue and interaction with feedback and encouragement from others in the group as well as in private.
4. Structured exercises should be used to facilitate dialogue or as a basis for response to and discussion of specific issues or processes.
5. There should be a ratio of one leadership couple for each four to eight participant couples.
6. Participant couples should have some voice in setting the agenda.
7. Program time should be at least 15 hours, either in a weekend setting or in a series of sequential weekly meetings (deGuzman, 1996; Hopkins et al., 1978; Mace & Mace, 1984).

Guidelines such as these provide a base for ongoing evaluation of specific programs as well as discussion and research regarding the effectiveness of various program formats and designs.

SCHEDULE AND FORMAT

ME can take place in a variety of formal or informal settings. The two most common time-schedule formats are

1. The intensive retreat, conference, or marathon, which can last from a weekend to five days. The usual format is a weekend, from Friday evening through Sunday lunch. Other formats may be Friday evening through Saturday evening, all day Saturday, or evenings across four or five weeks.

2. A series of weekly meetings in the form of either a marital growth group or a couple communication program (Hopkins et al., 1978; Mace & Mace 1974, 1976, 1984).

Overnight formats allow more concentrated time for couples with fewer potential interruptions, yet usually are more difficult for couples to arrange to attend. Those who are willing to give the additional effort and expense for a weekend event usually feel that it is well worth it. *One-day formats* may enable additional couples to participate in enrichment although there is less time available. *A series of sessions* spaced at weekly (or other) intervals gives participating couples much more opportunity to practice what they learn in the sessions and to obtain support and feedback about these real-life applications. Because sessions are mixed with the rest of weekly living, some couples may miss sessions or not have time to concentrate when they do attend.

ACME differentiates ME events into several types (deGuzman, 1996). These can be clustered according to the number of participants:

1. Events for small groups, usually six to eight couples:
   a. ME Retreat—$1\frac{1}{2}$ to $2\frac{1}{2}$ days in a retreat setting, emphasizing information, skill development, and couple experiential activities;
   b. ME Series—weekday evenings in a local community over a period of four to six weeks with six to eight couples on a specific topic;
   c. Ongoing ME Groups—support groups of three to six couples that meet regularly for marital growth over a period of a year or more;
   d. ACME Chapter meetings, open to ACME members and potential members.
2. Events for larger groups, focused on couples:
   a. ME Workshop (miniretreat)—1 to $1\frac{1}{2}$ days in a local setting, emphasizing couple skill development and growth;
   b. ME Programs and Seminars—one educational and experiential session of one to three hours in a local community, open to the public.
3. Events for larger groups, focused both on leaders and on couples:
   a. ME Conference—a one- to three-day gathering, open to the public, with speakers, workshops, and continuing education activities;
   b. ME Festival or Rally—a one-day event open to the public with speakers, workshops, and celebratory activities.

Many couples experience several types of programs, and there are advantages and disadvantages of each type.

Formats vary as to the percentage of time scheduled for large-group presentations of information about relationships and activities, small-group practice and feedback, private-individual couple time for practice and exploration of issues, and free time for relaxation and friendship. The schedule format needs to provide for group time for leader presentations and fellowship, small groups in which two to four couples interact on practice skills, individual couple time, for couples to practice skills and discuss issues privately, and free time for relaxation.

Often the large-group presentations include some theoretical information about marriage elements, such as communication, conflict resolution, and problem solving. Often, suggestions include ways that participants can express affirmation and support as couples. Some programs may include group fellowship singing, worship, and fun activities. In smaller groups participating couples have an opportunity to practice specific skills so that each couple can both receive feedback about their skills and provide feedback to other couples.

Clear yet flexible scheduling is essential with provision for adjustments according to needs of couples and groups.

Intensive Weekend Programs

The intensive weekend experience has the advantage of providing participants with the opportunity to be together as a couple, away from normal routines, other demands, and pressures, in an atmosphere of seclusion and leisure. Couples are able to take a continuous and intensive look at their marriage relationship, working with other couples on enhancing their relationships (Mace & Mace, 1974). Programs with the intensive weekend format vary in their degree of structure and focus on the couple. The continuum ranges from highly structured and couple centered, to relatively nonstructured and couple group centered.

At one end of this continuum is the Marriage Encounter model (Bosco, 1973), in which group interaction is limited to the sharing of meals and religious services. There is no sharing of marital experiences between couples or in the total group, except by the leadership couple. The leadership couple, working with a trained religious leader, makes several presentations to the total group, after which each couple, in the privacy of their own room, writes down their personal reflections on a variety of personal, interpersonal, and spiritual issues (e.g., I, We, We-God, We-God-World [Bosco, 1973; Whitehead & Whitehead, 1981]).

Following the writing, each partner reads what the other has written, and each encourages the other to discuss verbally and further describe the feelings initially noted in writing, in an attempt to experience each other more fully at an affective level. This specific dialogue process is practiced repeatedly throughout the weekend. The opportunity is provided for participants to join ongoing support groups after the initial experience. Couples are encouraged to continue the process of daily dialogue after they return home. This model also has been adapted for engaged couples.

Highly structured, couple-centered programs such as Marriage Encounter involve less anxiety over public disclosure than programs with more focus on group interaction. However, the couple-centered programs do not provide the possibility for potentially valuable observer feedback and support in the presence of other couples, which frequently occurs following the modeling by the leadership couple or other participant couples of ways to cope with issues in the other programs (L'Abate, 1977; Luft, 1969; Yalom, 1970).

Near the middle of the structured versus nonstructured continuum are programs such as ACME's (Mace & Mace, 1976), CCP (Miller et al., 1991), and PAIRS (Gordon, 1988). Various issues and aspects of the marital relationship are addressed through a series of experiential and affective exercises, theoretical input, total group interaction, and skill practice and couple dialogue within a small-group setting of five to six couples. This type of structure, which involves interaction between and within dyads, provides the possibility for the giving and receiving of potentially valuable observer feedback and support.

The intention of these moderately structured programs is to create a supportive and trusting environment, with little or no confrontation, so that individuals and couples can feel free to risk self-disclosure and become vulnerable to each other in the presence of other persons. This frequently occurs, following the modeling of the leadership couple or other participant couples. Even within this trusting environment, however, some people are too anxious to reveal their true thoughts and feelings. Instead, they may attempt to present themselves or their relationships in an overly positive way, and thus deeper intimate self-disclosure may never take place (L'Abate, 1977).

At the more unstructured end of the continuum are programs that were originated by David and Vera Mace (1976, 1978b). These programs have much in common with the other two models, but their organization and structure are minimal (Mace & Mace, 1976, 1984). A group of couples, usually five to eight couples per leadership team, meets for a prescribed period of time and establishes its own goals and agenda. The group stays together except for an occasional private couple dialogue.

Although a few structured exercises may be used, much of the time is devoted to couple dialogue, that is, husband and wife talking and sharing together in the presence of other couples. This model provides the possibility for the giving and receiving of observer feedback, support, and encouragement. Each couple can control whether and how much feedback they want from others present. The lack of a structured agenda may lead to the avoidance or neglect of certain key issues in marital interaction. However, that need not be a detriment, because this usually is viewed as only an initial experience, and one that will be followed by other team-oriented experiences.

Multiweek Programs

Multiweek ME experiences have the advantage of allowing participant couples the opportunity of spaced learning and continuing practice and reinforcement for a number of weeks. These programs also provide the opportunity for couples to do homework and practice new skills between meetings within the context of an ongoing support group (Mace & Mace, 1974). Disadvantages of the multiweek format are the possibility of a lack of intensity, broken continuity, or the interruption and erosion of the process by the normal routines and responsibilities of daily life.

Some multiweek programs give practice assignments for the couples to do at home between meetings. This allows them to practice and reinforce what they have learned in the sessions. The assignments usually involve reading and skill practice, and focus on identifying and expressing positive feelings and experiences, effectively serving as positive reinforcement for the behaviors of each partner (Schauble & Hill, 1976; Markman et al., 1994).

Research on this subject suggests that the use of homework with couples in therapy has positive effects upon their marital relationship (L'Abate, 1977; Paul & Paul, 1975; Shelton & Ackerman, 1974). The research of L'Abate (1977) concurrently suggests that an enrichment program combined with couple work at home between sessions results in a higher percentage of positive change than does participation in the enrichment program alone (see chapter 8, this volume).

As with the intensive experiences, a variety of multiweek models and programs exists. The program content of marital growth groups is similar to the content of intensive weekend programs with the difference being in the weekly time format. As with the weekend experiences, the marital growth groups may vary in the degree of structure and focus on the couple. These programs are conducted on a weekly basis to provide specified advantages to the participants. The weekly ME group may be time-limited or open-ended marital groups that do not use leadership couples who meet the certification criteria of ACME; these are called support groups by ACME (deGuzman, 1996). ACME uses the term marital growth group for groups that are more formally organized and are led by ACME-certified couples (Hopkins et al., 1978).

Many of the communication skills training programs meet once a week, for one to four hours for five to eight weeks (e.g., Relationship Enhancement programs [Guerney, 1977], CCP [Miller et al., 1976, 1991], PAIRS [Gordon, 1988]).

These programs generally are highly structured and behaviorally or affective-behaviorally oriented. They are based on the hypothesis that marital relationships can he enhanced through the use of short-term highly structured, behaviorally oriented group experiences and program. This approach continues to receive research support (Guerney & Maxson, 1990; Rappaport, 1976).

Among widely used communications training programs are the Relationship Enhancement program (Guerney, 1977), CCP (Miller et al., 1976, 1991), the Imago Relationship program (Hendrix, 1988), and PAIRS (Gordon, 1988). Among early multiweek models were the Marriage Diagnostic Laboratory (MARDILAB [Stein, 1975]), the Pairing Enrichment Program (Travis and Travis, 1975), and the reciprocity counseling-behavioral approach (Dixon and Sciara, 1977).

L'Abate (1977), L'Abate & Young (1987), L'Abate & Weinstein (1987), Guerney (1977), and Miller et al. (1991) note that their enrichment models can be used with one couple at a time or in the more common format involving a group of couples. L'Abate's view is that "enrichment programs are a structured, manual-directed, already written and presented approach that is based on a linear model of information processing following incremental, additive, progressive and step-wise presentation of information to be used by couples and families" (L'Abate, 1977, p. 214).

L'Abate describes designs of programs for couples and families in areas such as confronting change, problem-solving skills for dating couples, sexuality and sensuality, man-woman relations, assertiveness, equality, reciprocity training, negotiation, conflict resolution, becoming parents, effective parenting, single-parent families, widowhood, and death and dying (L'Abate, 1975, 1990; L'Abate & Weinstein, 1987; L'Abate & Young, 1987). He also has developed a system of classification of enrichment programs based on the following approaches: affective versus cognitive, practical versus theoretical, simple versus complex, general versus specific, and structured versus developmental. This variety of programs and the system of classification make it possible to fit a specific couple or family to a specific program (DeMaria, 1993).

FOLLOW-UP

It is clear that programs need to provide postevent follow-up booster contacts and meetings for continued support of couples who initiate changes in the ME event. Often at the closing of an enrichment event, couples who have become better acquainted with other couples talk about plans for some type of follow-up meeting at a later time. ACME encourages couples to participate in long-term support groups (deGuzman, 1996). Retrouvaille (B. Zwann & P. Zwann, personal communication, April 15, 1997) has four phases to its program for couples facing serious problems and divorce: preweekend interview; the weekend event itself; the post-weekend series of weekly meetings across a three-month period; and Continuing Our Retrouvaille Experience (CORE), which is a continuing support group that is led by the participating couples.

The weekend ME experience is designed to free a couple from their usual networks of patterns and pressures in which their current relationship interactions are set. This advantage of the event is also a disadvantage to the couple on their return to the realities of daily living, because those who comprise the couple's larger system (children, work associates, relatives, friends) have not participated in learning similar skills, perspectives, and changes. If there is no ongoing follow-up and support group provided after the initial experience, the old reinforcement contingencies and pressures from the realities of everyday life can easily overwhelm the couple's good intentions and efforts toward improving their relationship. The results can be quite painful, leaving the couple with a feelings of isolation and inadequacy to maintain the newer skills. In such a situation, positive gains from the weekend experience can quickly fade and integration of learning and skills frequently may not occur.

SETTINGS FOR PROGRAMS

Typical settings for marriage enrichment weekend events are usually a retreat center, camp, hotel, or college campus setting. Evening or one-day event settings may be in facilities of a local church, synagogue, or private home. The qualities of the event setting are very important because they provide a supportive context for the couples and add to the positive romantic atmosphere that reduces distractions from the enrichment experiences.

Essential qualities of any setting include

- A location without distractions, conducive to openness, relaxation, and renewal;
- Child care as needed to relieve couples from concern about their children;
- Good food (prepared, catered, pot luck, etc.);
- If overnight, private sleeping rooms for couples;
- Reasonable cost to couples;
- Convenient time for travel.

Any of the ME formats may be conducted at a retreat, hotel, or religious (church or synagogue) location. A relaxing retreat location adds new experiences to the positive atmosphere of the event, although the cost of overnight accommodations is an added expense.

A local facility setting avoids overnight expenses but may break the concentration of couples on the event because they return home overnight. A hotel location may have better overnight accommodations for couples yet may be more expensive than a retreat location. Some hotel locations also may have features usually found at retreat settings, such as beach, mountains, walking trails, and recreational equipment.

This brief overview of the dimensions of ME programs demonstrates the varied designs, formats, techniques, and resources that are used. Programs are continually being revised, and more new programs appear every year. We have seen how programs vary with regard to time schedule; format; structure; use of total group interaction, dyadic interaction, and interaction in small groups of several couples; and many other dimensions. The next chapter describes some of the currently available programs.

Chapter 5

Programs

Contemporary ME programs reflect the nexus of enrichment, psychoeducation, and treatment for couples, incorporating aspects of each approach. Emphasizing the interplay between prevention and remediation, David Mace, a founder of the ME movement, repeatedly called for greater attention by the professional community to ME programs. Mace believed that ME offers several advantages: skill building, greater public access, and lessened stigma; group process for modeling and support; and suitability for research.

This chapter highlights a sample of the ME programs that have a national or international presence. Because our primary goal is to identify principles, techniques, issues, research, and strategies, each program is described only briefly. Readers who want more extensive descriptions of major programs by their originators and/or current major leaders may consult Berger and Hannah (1998). The Coalition for Marriage, Family, and Couples Education (CMFCE) Smart Marriages World Wide Web site (see Contact Information for Specific Programs, this volume) provides current information to aid in contacting specific programs.

ME is not an isolated or a new phenomenon. It is part of a tradition of strengthening the family through family facilitation programs, which began with the community mental health movement and the first family cluster intervention models. Social work, in particular, with its early roots in community and family advocacy, has supported development of these family-life education programs. Adding to the social-skills group model, ME programs have evolved to the point of drawing on treatment models for curriculum and structure. Imago Therapy, for example, offers both a treatment intervention model and a group skill-based enrichment program. This is one example in which the differences between enrichment and treatment are blurring. The evolution of ME also is being fostered by managed behavioral health care companies. Changes in the managed behavioral health care delivery system are moving toward the incorporation of skill-training models of intervention as treatment of choice for couples presenting with relationship distress.

Marriage Encounter and the Association of Couples for Marriage Enrichment (ACME) paved the way for today's ME programs. The Couple Communication Program (CCP) and Relationship Enhancement laid the behavioral foundation with specific techniques to enhance interpersonal relationships. Trademarking of programs is growing rapidly. However, there is no way to document all of the unique models and formats that have been developed by local grassroots organizations, churches, synagogues, agencies, and mental health professionals throughout the country. Their contributions are to be applauded and encouraged because they are important in the effort to expand and maximize the availability of enrichment opportunities to all couples across all socioeconomic, ethnic, and other dimensions.

There is a variety of programs that work because they include in various combinations the principles described in chapter 4. Some programs have been evaluated empirically for effectiveness; others have not. All of the programs, however, have individuals and couples who give testimonial to the effect of participating in a ME program. Giblin's (1986) meta-analysis suggested that ME programs do help couples develop the ability to strengthen their relationships and that, in particular, distressed couples make the most gains in improved satisfaction. The distinctiveness of each program model and design contributes in many ways to strengthening marital theory and intervention. Further research and theory development will only fortify the energy that was sparked so many years ago by the pioneers of ME.

MAJOR PROGRAMS

These enrichment programs, listed in alphabetical order, represent the variety now available.

ACME

ACME was established in 1973 and is now an international organization. It was founded by David and Vera Mace, leaders in both the establishment of marriage counseling centers and ME. ACME was established to work for the enrichment of member couples' marriages, to provide mutual support, to initiate and support community services that foster quality marriage and family life, and to improve the public image of marriage as an expansive rather than a restrictive state (Mace & Mace, 1975).

ACME's training standards for certifying married couples who lead enrichment programs are the most extensive and comprehensive of any program. There are over 450 trained couples who lead a variety of programs in weekend, evening, and weekly ongoing formats. Many of ACME's activities are conducted with small groups of couples. More than 60,000 couples of varied income levels have participated in ACME's enrichment programs. Trained leader couples lead a variety of experiences to cover all stages of marriage. ACME also offers a Book and Resource Catalog and has sponsored International Marriage Enrichment Conferences.

CCP

CCP began with the research and development team of Drs. Sherod Miller, Elam Nunnally, and Daniel Wackman. Sherod Miller, Ph.D., heads the instructor training and develops and writes programs. CCP is taught in both individual and group formats of six to eight hours. Originally developed at the University of Minnesota Family Study Center in the early 1970s, CCP was redesigned and updated in 1991. More than 500,000 couples have taken the program since it began and over 3,000 people have taken the instructor training. Certification requires participating in a training workshop, studying the materials, teaching 20 couples who evaluate the instruction, passing a written test, and signing a set of ethical expectations.

The goal of CCP is to help people improve communication in a relationship (not necessarily a marital relationship), from a stance of equality, intimacy, and openness, so that meaning and growth are maintained. Two kinds of skills are developed: self- and other-awareness skills, so that partners call understand their feelings, thoughts, intentions, rules, norms, and patterns of interacting; and communication skills, to help participants modify their rules, norms, and patterns of interacting, so as to keep the system flexible and viable. The program is structured with specific goals and employs experiential learning through exercises, readings, lectures, small-group discussion, and repeated skill practice in groups and through homework between sessions. The format frequently involves five to seven couples meeting for three hours one night per week for four consecutive weeks with a trained instructor.

With some 65 independent, quantitative outcome studies, CCP is one of the most widely researched programs in the field. The goals of the program are to help couples develop communication and conflict-resolution skills as well as develop a more satisfying relationship and prevent marital distress. CCP has demonstrated positive effects on communication and marital satisfaction.

Creative Marriage Enrichment Program (CMEP)

CMEP is described in detail by Hof and Miller (1981). Over 200 couples and individuals have been trained as facilitators, and over 10,000 couples have experienced CMEP in the United States and Canada. It has been used with clinical and nonclinical populations, and within religious and nonreligious communities. It has been used in a variety of formats, from weekend-long retreats, to multiple (8–15) week two- to four-hour sessions, to a combination of the two.

David Mace described CMEP as one of the best programs of its kind. Created in 1972, the program reached its core concept form in 1977 and has undergone numerous content changes and revisions since then. Training in CMEP has been offered by Hof and Miller, and the program details were made available in their 1981 book. It is impossible to know how many people have adapted or used the CMEP in their communities or practices.

The CMEP attempts to provide an atmosphere of mutual empathy, trust, understanding, and peer support. It is designed to give couples an opportunity to learn new skills in areas such as communication, conflict resolution, and intimacy while fortifying their already-existing relationship-enhancing skills. Theoretically grounded in Schultz's (1978) fundamental interpersonal relationship organizations (FIRO) theory, the program focuses on issues of inclusion (in or out), control (top or bottom), and affection (near or far). There is an emphasis on expressing feeling, wants, and needs; identifying, expressing, and affirming individual and marital strengths; understanding and negotiating gender roles in marriage; creatively using conflict; and exploring various facets of intimacy. The program is based on the belief that marital relationships are dynamic, not static, and that change in such relationship is not only possible, but inevitable.

Celebrating Marriage

Celebrating Marriage was created by David Bradley, Richard and Joan Hunt, and Jack King. Used primarily among United Methodists, this program was revised and updated in 1996. The program was first offered in 1982 and offers experiential workshops in a weekend and evening format. Using ACME standards, both married couples and professionals have been trained as leaders. Approximately 100 leaders have provided the program to more than 5,000 couples. The program emphasizes communication and conflict-resolution skills, goals and values clarification, and ways to express affirmation and support.

Getting the Love You Want (GLYW)

The Institute for Imago Relationship Therapy was cofounded in 1984 by Harville Hendrix and Helen Hunt. Through its network of workshop leaders, the Institute offers "Getting the Love You Want: A Workshop for Couples" and "Keeping the Love You Find: A Workshop for Singles" in a weekend or weekly format. There are approximately 1,100 certified Imago therapists, 130 certified workshop leaders, and 20 clinical instructors who train therapists. Imago Relationship

Therapy was detailed in the best-selling *Getting the Love You Want* by Hendrix (1988).

The GLYW workshop is designed to help couples resolve deep issues from childhood and rediscover joy. An adaptation, Keeping the Love You Find, is designed to help single persons to prepare relationship skills and identify childhood issues. The primary workshop format for the couples' workshops is a 20-hour intensive weekend (Saturday and Sunday, all day). In addition, Imago therapists offer introductory and advanced workshops in one-day workshops, a ten-week series of one evening per week, and advanced workshops.

The intensive 20-hour GLYW workshop is designed to help couples resolve issues from childhood and rediscover the joy and spiritual potential of being together and using their relationship for personal growth and change. The workshops are designed to empower couples to create a conscious relationship by helping them to learn principles and procedures of couple relationships with a focus on the couples dialogue. The basic premise of the Imago model is that the unconscious purposes of a committed relationship are personal healing and self-completion. To that end, the aim is to help couples to identify and integrate their unconscious developmental issues and use them in their relationship for mutual healing and collaborative self-development. The exercises include identification of exits that partners may take from their relationship, affirmation and holding exercises, identification of unresolved childhood hurts and wounds, listening and expressing skills, and how each partner can affirm the other and move to a conscious, intentional, and committed couple relationship.

Keeping Love Alive

Since the early 1980s, Michele Weiner-Davis has worked to develop and apply the theory of Solution-Oriented Brief Therapy. She is the author of *Divorce Busting: A Step-By-Step Approach to Making Your Marriage Loving Again* (Weiner-Davis, 1992). She has created a home study program for the public called Keeping Love Alive, a program of six audio tapes and a guidebook.

Making Marriage Work (MMW)—An Example
of Jewish Marriage Enrichment

MMW was designed in 1978 by Sylvia Weishaus, Ph.D., and Rabbi Aaron M. Wise to educate engaged and recently married couples in the Los Angeles community to help them to begin their marriages with more realistic expectations and relationship skills. MMW is offered under the auspices of the University of Judaism in Los Angles, with classes on its Los Angeles campus, as well as in Conservative and Reform synagogues in Southern California, and in Jewish Family Services Facilities in Orange County, California, Southfield Michigan, and the Jewish Theological Seminary in New York City. Classes meet for 10 weeks, and instructors are mental health professionals. Six sessions are led by the instructor, three by a rabbi, and one by a financial planner.

MMW also offers an Interfaith session, Success in Your Second Marriage, and Married Life: Challenges of Growth for couples married 2 to 15 years. A recent evaluation of MMW by Weishaus, Marston, and Shieh (1994) found a divorce rate of 8.9% and a mean marital satisfaction of over 8 on a 10-point scale for participants of MMW.

Marriage Encounter

Marriage Encounter began in the early 1960s under the leadership of Father Gabrael Calvo who gathered together a group of couples in Barcelona, Spain. It has been an important force in the ME movement. Marriage Encounter has reached more couples than all other ME programs combined. It is estimated that well over one million couples world wide have participated in some version of ME.

Marriage Encounter is largely a weekend consciousness-raising experience. Although conducted in a group setting, the exercises are carried out individually by the couples who are attending. The emphasis is on letter writing and sharing. The weekend closes in a renewal of vows, which is often quite emotional for many couples.

Marriage Encounter is offered through three separate organizations: National Marriage Encounter, International Marriage Encounter, and Worldwide Marriage Encounter. International Marriage Encounter publishes marriage and family enrichment materials including *Marriage* magazine. Marriage Encounter has extended beyond its original Catholic base and has been adopted by 12 other denominations.

Practical Application of Intimate Relationship Skills (PAIRS)

PAIRS was developed by Lori Gordon, Ph.D., and was first taught in 1977. The program is a 16-week, 120-hour, intensive, experiential program designed to provide skills to sustain love. Approximately 500 mental health professionals have been certified as PAIRS leaders since 1984, and more than 8,000 people have participated in the PAIRS course. There are more than 50 active leaders teaching the course throughout the United States, Canada, France, England, Russia, Israel, Australia, Costa Rica, Italy, Taiwan, and South Africa. PAIRS leaders are mental health professionals from a variety of disciplines who participate in a three-week training program to become certified to teach the PAIRS course.

PAIRS is best categorized as a humanistic and experiential model that emphasizes that the importance of acknowledging and encouraging the uniqueness of the individual, establishing and maintaining positive self-attitudes, and promoting bonding as a biologically based need for physical and emotional connection (Gordon, 1990). *Passage to Intimacy* (Gordon, 1993) describes key concepts of the PAIRS course. Participants who take PAIRS come with a wide range of relationship problems and levels of satisfaction and distress. Recent data suggest that PAIRS is serving a very distressed, devitalized population of couples. Analysis of PAIRS (DeMaria, 1993) suggests that it addresses the full range of theoretical models for marital intervention. Each week is structured to provide theory, experiential exercises, and opportunities for group and individual processing and sharing.

Differences in learning styles among participants are addressed by the variety of methods used in the PAIRS. A combination of weekly classes with intensive weekends increases opportunities for attitude and behavior change. PAIRS uses a variety of techniques to enhance personal awareness, to effect attitude changes, and to develop communication and conflict-resolution skills, including readings, journal writing, and practice sessions. In addition, there are four intensive weekends that are considered key to the success of the PAIRS experience. The first weekend focuses on conflict management with peer support and professional guidance. The second weekend addresses bonding as a biologically based need and provides opportunities for emotional expression and reeducation, emphasizing emotional literacy. This focus on bonding is an aspect of the PAIRS course that helps to distinguish the PAIRS program from most enrichment programs as well as some models of couples' therapy. The third weekend, also a unique aspect of PAIRS, teaches couples about sexuality and sensuality and provides opportunities to discuss sexual needs, desires, and conflicts. The fourth and final weekend addresses the need for conscious agreement in relationships and uses contracts as an instrument.

Passionate Marriage Couples Enrichment

An adaptation of the Sexual Crucible approach, Passionate Marriage Couples Enrichment is a three-day psychoeducational experience developed by Drs. David Schnarch and Ruth Morehouse. There are also nine-day retreats. These workshops emphasize understanding adult sexual potential, integrating sex and spirituality, and enhancing intimacy during sex, and developing strength to love and want your partner.

Prevention and Relationship Enhancement Program (PREP)

PREP is a research-based program that teaches couples (premarital or marital) how to communicate effectively, to work as a team to solve problems, to manage conflicts without damaging closeness, and to preserve and enhance commitment and friendship. Drs. Howard Markman, Scott Stanley, Susan Blumberg, and many colleagues and assistants have studied factors that predict marital breakdown. They have written *Fighting for Your Marriage* and produced accompanying video and audio tapes.

PREP is based on the cognitive/behavioral tradition of marital therapy. The focus is on attitudes, commitment, expectations, communication, and conflict-resolution styles. The goals emphasize reducing risk in relationship and raising protection and enhancing the positive bonding that comes from fun, friendship, and sensuality. *Fighting for Your Marriage* provides ground rules for fighting and loving, using the speaker-listener technique to manage conflict, problem solving, and working through hidden issues to promote intimacy.

PREP has developed as a result of prediction research, outcome research, and survey research (Stanley, 1993). Drs. Howard Markman and Scott Stanley have been conducting their research for over 20 years and PREP is unique in its research-based design. Much of the specific research on PREP has been conducted at the University of Denver for the past 15 years. In a large-scale study in Denver, 5% of PREP couples had dissolved their relationship at 3-year follow-up in contrast to 24% of control couples. Up to eight years after completing the program, PREP couples were still communicating significantly better than couples who have not received the training.

PREP has been adapted for Christian groups as well (Stanley, 1998). More than 1,700 professionals and paraprofessionals have been trained to lead the PREP program. Included in this number are over 650 trained Christian PREP leaders. PREP instructor training requires a three-day commitment and is offered at PREP, Inc., in Denver by Drs. Markman, Stanley, and Blumberg, and also at New York University by Peter Fraenkel, Ph.D.

PREPARE/ENRICH—Growing Together Workshop

Growing Together is a group workshop model that is designed to assist couples in talking about their relationships, using their results from the PREPARE inventory.

PREPARE was created by Dr. David Olson in 1977 after considerable research. ENRICH was completed in 1981 by Drs. David Olson, David Fournier, and Joan Druckman. Designed to help couples dialogue with each other about their relationship, four inventories have been developed: PREPARE, PREPARE-MC, EN-RICH, and MATE. PREPARE has been revised three times, in 1982, 1986, and 1996 (Olson et al., 1996). ENRICH was revised and updated in 1986. Version 2000 of the PREPARE/ENRICH inventories was released in 1996.

PREPARE/ENRICH has been used by over 30,000 counselors and clergy of all denominations in the United States with premarital and married couples. There are also branch offices in six countries: Australia, Canada, Japan, Germany, South Africa, and Sweden. Counselors, clergy, and lay couples can offer the PREPARE/ENRICH inventories. A one-day workshop is required for all leaders. A self-study training course is available. More than 1 million couples have taken the PREPARE/ENRICH inventory throughout the world.

Based on the PREPARE/ENRICH inventories, a typology of couples has been developed. Four premarital types have been identified: Vitalized, Harmonious, Traditional, and Conflicted. A fifth type, Devitalized, was identified among married couples. These typlogies provide a descriptively useful method for assessing and following couples.

Norms were established on 350,000 couples for PREPARE, 150,000 couples for PREPARE-MC, and 150,000 couples for ENRICH. There are 165 items on the inventory and, when scored, a 15-page computer report, assessing the couple's strengths and growth areas in 14 different categories, is produced for the counselor. The couple receives a 24-page *Building a Strong Marriage Workbook*. The counselor meets with the couple for several sessions to address six areas: building strengths and working on growth areas, couple communication, conflict resolution, family-of-origin issues, financial planning and budget, and goal setting. Version 2000 adds four personality measures.

Relationship Enhancement

First developed as a form of brief couples therapy, the emphasis of Relationship Enhancement is on teaching empathic communication and problem-solving skills using weekend and multiweek formats. More than 400 professionals have been trained in Relationship Enhancement, and over 6,000 couples have participated in the programs. Nording (1997) has adapted this program for the Washington, D.C., Catholic Archdiocese. His program is called "To Love and To Cherish." By 1997, there were over 200 trained lay-couple leaders in 25 parishes.

Relationship Enhancement skills were developed by Dr. Bernard Guerney, Jr., and have been refined by him and his colleagues over the past 30 years. Along with CCP, Relationship Enhancement has been one of the most widely researched programs. It is based on Rogerian concepts and has carefully detailed the empathic process. The research literature suggests that this is the most effective program available. Giblin's (1986) meta-analysis of ME programs found that Relationship Enhancement had the most significant effects (i.e., highest effect sizes) in the study. In another study involving over 4,000 couples at Purdue University, Relationship Enhancement was responsible for the most powerful improvement of any of the 12 major approaches to improving couple and family relationships that were investigated.

The Relationship Enhancement Program (Guerney, 1977, 1987) and the Conjugal Relationship Enhancement Program (Rappaport, 1976) are highly structured, short-term educational models for improving communication, enhancing personal and marital relationships, and preventing problems that could arise within them. All of the Relationship Enhancement programs employ and emphasize Rogerian, client-centered therapeutic principles, including direct expression of feelings and empathic listening concepts. Specific skills are taught through didactic and experiential modeling methods and are practiced within each session and at home between sessions. Skills taught include the following: recognizing feelings, desires, and motivations in oneself and in others; learning to express oneself honestly and congruently; learning how to respond to others with understanding and acceptance; and learning how to help others to behave in a similar fashion. Program formats range from weekend marathon groups to a series of one-hour weekly meetings. The program is designed for use with individuals, couples, families, as well as other client and professional groupings.

Rappaport and Harrell (1975) use an educational, behavioral exchange model to implement their Conjugal Relationship Enhancement Program (Guerney, 1977; Rappaport, 1976), and they see the program as being effective after a married couple has learned specific effective communication skills. The goal of their program is to enable motivated and willing couples to resolve marital conflict more effectively. This is accomplished through the teaching of specific reciprocal exchange and bargaining skills, which are based on the assumption that each partner has resources of value to the other. From the beginning of the program, participants are encouraged to utilize their own resources and to negotiate their own contracts. The leader-educator-therapist thus is not the architect of change, but is a facilitator of change.

This model differs from most ME programs in that it starts with a problem focus and the identification of undesirable behaviors, and then moves to the positive restatement of them. Generally speaking, ME programs start with an emphasis on the identification and expression of positive behaviors and feelings. However, the educational nature of this model (i.e., skills are taught), the immediate use of the couples' resources, and the underlying assumption that they are capable of accomplishing the task, all of which are foundations of the growth model, link this program to other ME programs.

Retrouvaille

Retrouvaille began in 1977 with roots in Marriage Encounter. Retrouvaille is an independent ministry for troubled marriages, which began as a French language program in Quebec, Canada, in 1977. In 1978, the program was translated into English and later was expanded to include the postweekend sessions. Today Retrouvaille, in either English or Spanish, is offered in over 158 communities in the United States, Australia, Canada, Mexico, New Zealand, Trinidad, the Philippines, Singapore, Central America, Germany, Ireland, and Africa. Approximately 50,000 couples have attended Retrouvaille worldwide. In 1996, over 7,000 couples attended Retrouvaille.

There are four phases of the program: the interview, the weekend, the postweekend (three months long), and Continuing Our Retrouvaille Experience (CORE). Although Catholic-based, there is a Christian multidenominational outline.

Training in Marriage Enrichment (TIME) and Other Adlerian Programs

The TIME program, developed by Dinkmeyer and Carlson (1986a,b), teaches couples skills for enhancing marital satisfaction. Based on Adlerian concepts, TIME is conducted over a 10-week period or over a weekend. Malcolm (1992) describes the Personal Growth in Marriage program based on Adlerian principles. The four main objectives of this program include building partner self-esteem, taking responsibility for one's own behavior, developing relationship skills, and providing relationship education.

Sherman and Dinkmeyer (1987) see Adlerian theory as integrating other systems theories of family therapy with its emphases on creativity in relationships, subjective perception, wellness, social interest, purposiveness of behavior, the holistic nature of person and social system, roles and places in the interactive system, patterns of communication, and the capacity for change. They distinguish Adlerian family therapy from family counseling. Many case examples demonstrate educational and enrichment models for use as an adjunct to therapy.

SEMINARS AVAILABLE AS VIDEO AND AUDIO PROGRAMS

Psychologists, psychiatrists, family therapists, and pop authors commonly develop seminars to present to the public based on their self-help relationship books. Many programs have been developed and are available as video and audio tape series with workbooks. These include, but are not limited to, John Gray's (1992) *Men Are from Mars, Women Are from Venus*, Gary Smalley's (1993) *Keys to Successful Relationships*, Michele Weiner-Davis's (1992) *Keeping Love Alive*, Pat Love's (1994) *Hot Monogamy*, and David Schnarch's (1997) *Passionate Marriage*.

John Gray has recently expanded his outreach significantly to the public through the Mars and Venus Institute and Counseling Centers. Michele Weiner-Davis, Pat Love, and David Schnarch provide training for mental health professionals as well.

The Mars and Venus Institute was established in July 1996 to offer ME workshops based on the principles in John Gray's best-selling work, *Men Are from Mars, Women Are from Venus*, which has sold over 10 million copies since it was first released. In addition to Gray's workshops and lectures over the past 15 years, the Mars and Venus workshop is an eight-hour program that has been taught to over 1,000 couples by 150 trained facilitators. In 1996, Mars and Venus Counseling Centers, Inc., was established, and counselors in these programs also lead Mars and Venus enrichment workshops.

Gray's model identifies differences between men and women and offers ways of addressing these differences. In addition to identifying different communication styles, many of Gray's techniques come from his book *What You Feel You Can Heal: A Guide for Enriching Relationships* (Gray, 1984).

OTHER PROGRAMS

David Mace would be pleased to see the scope of influence that ME techniques are beginning to have in a variety of settings. Many different kinds of programs are applying concepts and techniques to improve couple relationships. Religious denominations require a wide range of premarital preparation. The religious community is expanding its efforts to make ME more readily available through programs such as Marriage Mentoring and the Community Marriage Policy, which are discussed in chapters 12 and 13. The variety of ME programs and services now being offered to military families, to employees in corporations through Employee Assistance Programs, to senior high school students through special curricula designed for teachers, to patients in cardiac rehabilitation, and in other settings are described in chapter 13.

SUMMARY

ME programs are concerned with enhancing a couple's communication, emotional life, and sexual relationship. As ME programs have evolved, they have become an important resource for marital intervention and have contributed to marital theory and practice. Traditional ME methods combined with systems theory, cognitive and behavioral theory, and other models of marital intervention now form the theoretical bases and variety of programs. Models of couples therapy, such as Imago, now offer enrichment programs based on a particular theoretical model.

This chapter provides an overview of programs that offer ME. Although there are many programs offering services internationally and nationally, there are many other programs developed locally by churches, synagogues, community centers, human service agencies (public and private), mental health practitioners, family-life educators, teachers, health care professionals, among others. What they all share is a desire to impart knowledge, experience, and skills that will help couples gain greater satisfaction with their relationships. The hopes and dreams of those who paved the way for a growth-oriented marital philosophy throughout our society are beginning to be realized through the many contributions of increasing numbers of practitioners to the ongoing development and dissemination of ME.

The increasing variety of ME programs illustrates the many ways that basic tools and techniques can be combined. Common essential elements are likely to become recommended, if not required. Analogies to medications or automobiles may be helpful. Generic drugs provide the basic medication combination that is effective in treating a specific medical condition. Brand names, then, in some way seek to enhance this combination. All automobiles have a steering mechanism, engine, safety devices, passenger seating, and other elements that distinguish them as passenger vehicles, yet millions of dollars are regularly spent to make one make and model stand out to be purchased. In the next chapter some ME tools that make certain programs stand out are described, with suggestions for their use and further development.

Chapter 6

Resources for Couples and Leaders

In feedback to their marriage enrichment (ME) leader, Maria and Leo gave these comments:

Leo: The lecture presentations were okay and usually interesting, but the most helpful to us was when you watched us trying to reflect each other's messages, put a hold on the conversation, and coached us to improve in specific ways.

Maria: Just the experience of being very uncertain about what to change, yet seeing other couples actually being willing to be vulnerable and open to change, gave us confidence that we can risk trying something new.

Leo: The one-page handouts with specific illustrations were much better than a book. These gave me handles to practice using the skill on topics that matter most to us.

Maria: The general group atmosphere of support and affirmation meant so much to me. You encouraged us and challenged us to grow without embarrassing or condemning us. We hope we can continue with some of these couples in an ongoing support group such as you described.

Maria and Leo imply several tools that they found in their ME program. In this chapter we give some examples of structured exercises and techniques to illustrate the wide range of resources, tools, and techniques now available to professionals and couples in any therapeutic growth setting.

ACTIVITIES AND RESOURCES FOR COUPLES AND LEADERS

David Mace attributed his conviction that marriage is the major relationship in the family to his experiences as a counselor and pastor in London in the late 1930s.

He described how, after visiting in many homes, he went to the city library and in one afternoon he read all the books on marriage he could find, which, he said, was not too difficult because only three were available. Since that time, practitioners and researchers have produced many useful books, journals, magazines, newsletters, and videos on every facet of marriage. Many hundreds of self-help and professional resources concerning marriage are now widely available.

One goal of ME is to enable couples to experience, learn, and apply the findings and skills available through these media. To this end, ME leaders have created many techniques for helping couples to expand their range of positive responses. Some exercises originally designed for group settings also can be used with individual couples in therapy. For many years Satir (1967, 1972) used role playing and dramatizations on many types of audiences to illustrate marriage and family relationships and processes from a systems theory perspective. The experiential emphasis of her skillful illustrations made them available and useful in both therapy and enrichment settings.

Gottman et al. (1976) provided an early version of printed aids that couples can use. Most are still very useful for individual couples and couples groups. Many have been updated (Markman et al., 1994). Some, such as the intent-encoding–message-decoding–impact approach to communication, have appeared in various forms in many enrichment programs. Especially helpful is the "up deck" of things one partner can do to help the other partner feel more appreciated and valued. The list of 85 activities can be cut into small squares to form a deck that partners can use like a game. A similar approach is the "fun deck" of enjoyable activities that couples can do together.

Gottman et al. (1976) also offer brief assessment and troubleshooting guides for couples. They describe the "floor exercise" as a way to assist partners to take turns as speaker and listener. The "floor" is a small square or rectangle that represents the speaker role. The person with the "floor" is the speaker while the other listens and then gives summary feedback to the speaker. When the speaker is heard, the "floor" is passed to the other partner and the roles are exchanged. In one version of this exercise (S. M. Stanley, personal communication, June 24, 1994), the "floor" has several printed reminders of key communication skills that each partner is to use.

Miller et al. (1991), on the basis of 20 years of experience, provide several easy-to-use communication aids. The "awareness wheel" has five components (sensory data, thoughts, feelings, wants, actions) that remind the person of the major elements involved in communication. Many examples of each component are included. The "listening cycle" (attend, acknowledge, invite, summarize, ask) reminds the person of important components of accurate listening. Both are also available in a large floor-mat size that allows partners to move from one location to another on the mat that corresponds to the skill that they are currently using in the dialogue. Small handheld reminder cards also make summaries of skills easily available. They note that the physical movement gives kinesthetic feedback and further aids persons to use and incorporate the skills into everyday conversations. Presession and postsession questionnaires enable participants to make self-checks of progress. These techniques and materials can be used in enrichment communication workshops and with individual couples.

Hendrix (1988) integrates in a specific order a series of exercises into the Getting the Love You Want enrichment program. Creating a specific relationship vision, much like the vision and core values of a company, enables partners to identify their strengths and clarify common goals and differences. Hendrix describes how to use exercises to become aware of childhood wounds, frustrations, and unfinished childhood development that each partner may expect to get from the other. The "closing exits" exercise moves spouses to greater commitment to work at strengthening their relationship. Hendrix and Hunt (1994) offer a day-to-day guide consisting of 365 meditations and exercises that a couple can use throughout the year. They also describe their own marriage growth and emphasize meditation as a form of personal empowerment that then can be shared in marriage.

Many ways of enabling couples to remember the good times in their relationship have been developed. A "walk down memory lane" is used in the Celebrating Marriage (General Board of Discipleship, 1982) enrichment program of the United Methodist Church. In this activity, couples are invited to relax and recall significant events in their relationship history, such as their first date, honeymoon, or other positive events. Bassoff (1985) developed the "memory board" as an enrichment activity for married couples to help them recall the positive experiences of their marriage. This consists of partners writing out brief descriptions of events and activities that they have enjoyed or would enjoy.

L'Abate and Young (1987) present examples of applications of enrichment techniques to different types of couples, parent-child relationships, and family situations. Contributors show how these techniques can be applied to couples coping with stress, depression, chaotic interactions, alcoholism, conflict, and emotional triangles. L'Abate and Weinstein (1987) also describe these structured enrichment techniques to enable persons to be more successful marital partners and parents by increasing their positive interactions. Structured enrichment is effective with many types of couple situations in increasing sexual fulfillment, improving helpful attitudes, clarifying values, and relational skill building. They provide many exercises and suggest how these can be applied to specific situations.

In the context of an educational approach to family relationships and interpersonal effectiveness, Crow and Crow (1988) offer activities for evaluating the functional level of couples and families and educating them toward a more positive interpersonal style. Activities involve marriage assessment and enrichment, parent-child relationships, and parental style and effectiveness.

As described by Dinkmeyer and Carlson (1986a,b), the Training in Marriage Enrichment (TIME), based in Adlerian theory, is a highly structured, systematic, 10-session program to enable couples to build a loving, supportive relationship. Each session outline has practice exercises, to be done between sessions, and homework applications.

The emphasis on positive change is a major part of most therapeutic programs. Stuart's (1980) plan of action for initiating "caring days" encourages the couple to identify desired behaviors and do them consistently. In another variation, Hendrix (August 2, 1995, personal communication) asks each partner to describe three actions (or gifts) that he or she is willing to give to the other, and then allow the other partner to select one of the gifts. A parallel exercise for stretching or expanding positives is for one partner to describe three gifts (affirmations, changes, supports) he or she would like to have from the partner and the partner then selects which one to provide.

Exercises and exploration activities are included in guides for premarital and married couples (Hunt & Hunt, 1981, 1994). Hunt and Hunt (1976) provide a guide to encourage couples to explore the ways that marriage and career goals and activities both complement and conflict with each other.

Most of these activities can be used in enrichment workshops, educational settings, and other group settings with couples as well as with individual couples in therapy. Some exercises, such as those that involve deeper contact with family-of-origin issues or self-disclosure of repressed material, are considered so powerful that they should be used only with the guidance of a trained leader or therapist (Hendrix, 1988).

This brief summary illustrates the many tools and techniques that have emerged from ME programs to be available in other educational settings and for use in therapy. Because these activities and exercises usually are described clearly with skill-building helps, they probably have helped to increase the structure and precision of couple therapy as well as enrichment and mentor training.

THERAPY INTERVENTIONS AND REFERRALS

Nelson and Trepper (1993) bring together over 100 specific interventions that have been used by family therapists. Many of these are also useful in ME settings. Each contributor describes a particular intervention method and specific indications and contraindications for its application, and provides a case illustration of its use.

Among methods included are the communication stone, functional dysfunctions, ways to facilitate marital dialogue, problems with problem solving, charting the transactional map, problem definition for multiproblem families, dual-career couples, a cross-cultural double date, healing of memories, a ritual for starting over and recommitting after an affair, Bowen's differentiation-of-self scale in marital conflict, combining individual and conjoint sessions in couples therapy, and using the tape recorder as a behavior modification device for couples.

Gillis and Gass (1993) document the use of adventure experiences in marriage and family therapy and enrichment, giving illustrations of actual techniques in enrichment and therapy. Adventure involves using new experiences to create functional change for couples. The steps include assessment, structuring, intervention, debriefing, and follow-up.

The emphasis today is on how ME and marital therapy can work together to benefit the participant couple. Referrals and resources need to be selected according to the needs of the couple, regardless of the setting. To this end, Flather (1996) provides a comprehensive reference of hundreds of resources on 46 topics related to marriage and family issues. Compiled from over 200 publishers, professional organizations, and individuals, these materials include problem-specific treatment manuals, studies of professional development, journal sources, and reference works. This source illustrates the wide range of information now available on support groups, hot lines, self-help materials, meditations, and aids for working with couples, children, and families.

MARRIAGE INVENTORIES AND RATING SCALES

Relationship skill exercises often include rating scales and other methods for assessing how much progress the participants make in learning a skill. Informal measures of values, attitudes, perceptions, information, and other aspects of marriage can be useful to couples to increase their awareness of strengths and growth areas and to elicit discussion, decisions to improve, and plans for change. The focus of this section is on measures that can be useful in enrichment and other applied settings. Chapters 7, 8, and 9 focus on research and technical considerations of measurement.

In the decades since Terman's classic research on marital happiness (Terman, Buttenweiser et al., 1938), many measures of marital relationships and patterns have been devised (Touliatos et al., 1990). In some ways these instruments are variations of asking the general happiness/satisfaction question that initially appeared in the Locke (1951) and Locke and Wallace (1959) measures, and continued in the Spanier (1976) Dyadic Adjustment Scale. This general perception of overall marriage quality is still useful (Goodwin, 1992).

Mace and Mace (1978a) devised a simple assessment of how partners see their marriage. This consisted of having each partner write down 10 specific qualities or characteristics that they want or have in their marriage and then, on a scale of 1 to 10, give an estimate of how well they are doing in each area in their relationship now. This assists partners to clarify values and perceptions as a basis for making desired changes and affirming progress. This approach encourages a couple to specify areas of progress and concern in order to address them constructively.

The Locke-Wallace Marital Adjustment Scale (Locke & Wallace, 1959) has been revised and updated by Spanier (1976). The 1989 Spanier Dyadic Adjustment Scale (DAS) arranges the 32 questions into four scales: dyadic consensus, dyadic satisfaction, dyadic cohesion, and affectionate expression. The DAS is widely used in couple research as a benchmark measure of couple functioning.

Early marriage research tended to focus on demographic factors in marital success, which tended to minimize the current interactions of partners. As psychological factors were increasingly acknowledged, instruments originally designed for individuals were extended to couples. Two examples of this approach are the Taylor-Johnson Temperament Analysis (TJTA [Taylor & Morrison, 1996]) and the 16 Personality Factor (16PF [Cattell et al., 1970; Russell & Karol, 1994]) inventories.

To use the revealed-differences ("crisscross") technique, the TJTA presentation format has each partner answer 180 questions about one's own psychological functioning and then answer the same questions as they apply to the partner. In this way, four views are available—male self, female self, male view of female, and female view of male—giving six combinations. The TJTA profile organizes these answers in nine scales: nervous vs. composed, depressive vs. light-hearted, active-social vs. quiet, expressive-responsive vs. inhibited, sympathetic vs. indifferent, subjective vs. objective, dominant vs. submissive, hostile vs. tolerant, self-disciplined vs. impulsive. Eight supplemental scales are overall adjustment, self-esteem, alienating, industrious-persevering, emotional stability, interpersonal effectiveness, persuasive/influential, outgoing/gregarious. The TJTA computerized scoring format provides a choice of a brief report or an interpretative report.

The 16PF approach arranges each partner's individual answers to the standard 16PF questions into 16 factors and 5 second-order combinations of themes. The 16 bipolar basic scales are reserved vs. outgoing, concrete vs. abstract, reactive vs. stable, deferential vs. dominant, serious vs. lively, expedient vs. conscientious, shy vs. bold, utilitarian vs. sensitive, trusting vs. vigilant, practical vs. imaginative, forthright vs. private, self-assured vs. apprehensive, conservative vs. experimental, group-oriented vs. self-reliant, disordered vs. perfectionist, and low drive vs. high drive. Five second-order factor scales are introverted vs. extroverted, low anxiety vs. high anxiety, empathetic vs. tough-minded, accommodating vs. independent, and unrestrained vs. self-control. The 16PF marriage counseling report contains analyses of each partner and of their possible interactions. The profile presentation format compares the two profiles and offers many suggestions to the couple and the therapist about the couple's strengths and growth areas.

Theoretical development of the continuing systemic interactions between each partner's actions and personalities in the marriage relationship has led to the development of several instruments that focus specifically on couple issues. Spanier's (1976) research on the Locke-Wallace scales led to the four factors that the DAS measures.

Olson and his colleagues have made the PREPARE, PREPARE-MC (for couples with children), and ENRICH inventories widely available (Olson et al., 1996). More recently the MATE inventory has been developed for older couples. Eleven scales provide the following measures: marriage expectations, personality issues, communication, conflict resolution, financial management, leisure activities, sexual relationship, children and parenting, family and friends, role relationships, and spiritual beliefs. Scores are adjusted for idealistic distortion.

Version 2000 with 165 questions includes measures of closeness and flexibility in both family of origin and the couple, allowing each partner to describe his or her family of origin and the way he or she sees the current couple relationship. These scales allow placement of each of these four views along the closeness and flexibility dimensions of Olson's circumplex model. The closeness points have been revised from enmeshed-connected-separated-disengaged to five points on the dimension of closeness (togetherness or cohesion)—overly connected–very connected–connected–somewhat connected–disconnected. The dimension of flexibility (change or adaptability) has been revised from rigid-structured-flexible-chaotic to inflexible–somewhat flexible–flexible–very flexible–overly flexible.

The PREPARE and ENRICH inventories compare the responses of the man and woman according to whether they both agree with values and procedures that facilitate success in marriage (positive couple agreement [PCA]) or both disagree on these (special focus [SPF]). The PCA correlates very highly ($r = .82$) with the overall DAS score (Waterman, 1990).

In addition to the original 11 relationship scales, the revised Version 2000 of PREPARE/ENRICH inventories also include attention to relationships between life events and the couple's functioning. The counselor's report includes a profile of the couple's positive couple agreement on each scale and how well it matches one of four types of couples (vitalized, harmonious, traditional, conflicted). In Version 2000, there are 28 questions about demographic, background, and individual characteristics of each partner and four personality assessment scales (assertiveness, self-confidence, avoidance, and partner dominance).

Hunt and Hunt (1994) also used the revealed-differences approach to have self and partner views on their MIRROR instrument, which organized marriage issues into two dimensions: content (topics) and process (psychological functioning). On the basis of analyses of this instrument, they are researching an interactive computer inventory (LovePower [Hunt & Hunt, 1994]) that uses a personal computer to present the LovePower items, provide immediate scoring, and display feedback results on scales and items, with an extensive printout of results. Designed for couples to use to explore their relationship, each partner answers items as they see self and as they see the partner. The LovePower scales are love/nourishment, future, resources, positives, negatives, communication, and outreach.

The LovePower procedure allows for positive-agreement and negative-agreement comparisons of answers by the woman and the man. These correlate highly with the equivalent PCA and SPF scores on ENRICH (Hunt & Chia, 1996). The convergence of these ENRICH, DAS, and LovePower scales suggests that agreement of partner perceptions about their relationship is a significant element in their understanding and in growth in their relationship.

USING MOVIE, VIDEO, AND TELEVISION RESOURCES

It is possible to utilize commercial drama in any medium to enable couples and families to consider their own interactions. Most stage, screen, and television dramas focus on the interactions between couples, often between the leading-man and the leading-woman characters. Commercial drama must balance between economic viability, artistic quality, and realistic human qualities. Even when the dramatic plot is modified to increase potential market and sales, it is still possible to consider drama as case studies of interactions between a woman and a man in a couple situation. The widespread availability of screen dramas on videotape makes them potentially available to leaders and couples. Subject to rental and user limitations in group presentation situations, couples can view many movie and television productions as homework assignments.

An interactive approach to case studies (Hunt & Rydman, 1979) can be useful for considering any type of drama. This approach has three major levels: Level 1 considers the story from the perspective of an interested observer outside the situation. Level 2 invites the observer to become aware of his or her personal responses to the situation. Level 3 considers the ways in which the first two levels affect the observer in her or his own life as a partner in a couple.

Level 1: What Is Happening between the Characters in the Drama?

As viewers outside the drama, a couple can focus on a specific couple in the story and describe each person as a partner in that couple, the influence of each partner's family of origin on that partner, any other individuals relevant to the couple, and interactions between the partners and between the couple and others in the drama. Observers also can describe key scenes with dialogue segments that are examples of how the partners function as a couple or with others. The couple then can explore explicit and implicit value assumptions of specific characters along with symbols and other elements that have significance for them.

From this basic information the observing couple can consider changes that might be made in the story, script, and other elements to cause the story to go in a better direction. In this process the couple might assume that they are scriptwriters whose assignment is to show how the characters can improve their values, apply good communication skills, increase commitment, resolve problems, and change in other realistic ways that will improve their wellness as a couple. In situations where the couple ends the relationship, what might each character as a partner have done to keep the relationship going well? If a third-party character seems to have enticed one of the partners away from the marriage or other committed relationship, what was already happening in the marriage that made it vulnerable to this enticement?

Observers can identify values that are implicit in any dialogue or play, the intent that each character expresses in specific dialogue and actions, and the affect of that character's words and actions on other characters. As writers, the observing couple can try to script these changes and explore alternative outcomes, without considering whether there is enough casual sex, violence, or other emphases that some assume is necessary to sell the production.

Level 2: What Are the Effects of the Drama on the Viewing Couple?

Good drama elicits many feelings and other personal reactions from viewers. Couples move to this level as they identify feelings and thoughts they have in response to the drama. A couple can identify similarities to and differences from characters in the drama and themselves. Describing specifics of the characters, scenes, and other elements of the drama that made the most positive or negative impacts on the viewer offers opportunities for the couple to become more aware of how their own memories and assumptions contribute to their responses to each other.

Level 3: How Will the Viewing Couple Change?

At this third level the viewing couple moves its focus away from the drama to its own daily interactions. They now consider how they relate to each other in the light of what they have seen in the drama. By considering ways in which they are similar to or different from the couple portrayed, the couple can identify specific ways they would like to change. Questions they can explore focus on what have they learned from the drama that can be applied in their own lives. They can specify ways that they will modify their own insights and ideas about goals, habits, interactions, and other aspects of their relationship. Where negative outcomes have been portrayed in the drama, the viewing couple can move beyond a vague hope that they will never be like the couple portrayed in the drama to identifying how they will implement positive changes in their own patterns of marital interactions, thus avoiding negative outcomes.

These three levels of interactions can be applied to any situation. Most couples already do this as they talk about a marital or family situation that they know about among their families, friends, or through media reports. The advantage of movies about couples and families is that all observers have access to the same information, even though they know that the movie writers, directors, and producers have shaped it to maximize artistic and commercial goals. In all of these sources the distinctions between insider and outsider reports (chapter 7) still are important. Clarifying the three levels and exploring each level more completely offers an opportunity for couples and leaders to apply communication skills, clarify values, and commit to desirable goals in relation to their own situations.

USING VIDEO FEEDBACK FOR COUPLE SKILL TRAINING

Early studies of the effects of videotape playback on couples present mixed results about the value of videotape feedback (Fichten & Wright, 1983; Mendez, 1992; Padgett, 1983). One possible answer is self-modeling (Dowrick & Biggs, 1983, p. 105) using videotapes that show only desired target behaviors (Mendez, 1992). It seems that persons who see their videotaped performance as inferior to their idealized standard experience negative affect, which counters any beneficial effects. Persons who see videotapes of themselves that consist of only positive behaviors tend to respond positively because the observed behaviors match their idealized self more closely.

There are several methods for creating positive self-modeling videotapes. Couples may videotape their role-plays of positive exchanges, or videotapes of existing behavior may be edited to leave only positive exchanges. Positive results are most likely to occur when videotape self-observation is combined with clear instructions, verbal feedback, and guided discussion (Mendez, 1992).

Cleaver (1987) compared the effectiveness of teaching communication skills to married couples with and without the use of a structured videotape. The videotape explained communication principles, had models who demonstrated the skills, and offered practice exercises. Both groups improved, and the group receiving the additional videotape demonstrations had more lasting improvement two months after the workshop.

Whether videotape feedback assists a couple in positive ways seems to depend upon the partners being able to assimilate their observations and then practice them with guidance from a supportive facilitator or coach. Some enrichment leaders illustrate this feedback process in their programs, and some programs provide for this by having small practice groups of two or three couples in which each couple can practice skills and receive feedback from the others, usually without using videotapes.

The key element in using videotapes seems to be the quality of the feedback and the supportive encouragement provided to the couple (Markman et al., 1993; Floyd et al., 1995). The progression from receiving new information to applying it in daily living involves each partner in becoming aware of possible changes and practicing them without becoming so discouraged that one or both partners give up. Using videotape feedback requires the facilitator/coach to give encouragement and provide examples of improved responses in a specific situation.

INTERNET AND INTERACTIVE COMPUTER RESOURCES

Gould (1993) has developed his Therapeutic Learning Systems, which provide self-paced psychoeducational programs that an individual can utilize in the context of a professionally led group and individual experience. The branching structure of this system makes a psychoeducational developmental model available via interactive computer with flexibility in meeting specific concerns and issues of an individual. It would be possible for both partners to utilize this type of system and compare their findings in the supportive atmosphere of a professional leader.

Hunt has developed interactive computer programs that allow each partner in a couple to enter answers to relationship and other questions and then obtain immediate feedback and printed results. Still in development, these procedures have been applied to the Growing Love in Christian Marriage (Hunt & Hunt, 1981) and the LovePower approaches to marriage (Hunt & Hunt, 1994).

As of mid-1998, computer-administered inventories and feedback for couples are still in experimental stages. However, with the widespread availability of faster computers and the rapid development of the Internet and of World Wide Web home pages, these media are likely to provide important resources for ME and mentoring. The emerging availability of high-quality video training makes these media even more promising for enrichment and mentoring applications. The Coalition for Marriage, Family, and Couple Education Web site contains current information about some of these resources.

These descriptions of representative resources sample the increasingly diverse resources that are now available through standard programs. More resources are being created by the expanding numbers of marriage and family professionals who seek to offer researched-based enrichment and mentoring resources for couples and families. Especially promising are the computer and video media that newly developing technologies are making possible. The abundance of resources gives many more opportunities to deliver validated training and skill development to couples who then can share them with other couples through mentoring and outreach. Because those with greatest need often are least likely to access research-based and validated resources, the continuing challenge is finding ways for couples and professionals to reach those couples and families.

PART THREE

RESEARCH ON MARRIAGE ENRICHMENT

We turn our attention to the research literature on marriage enrichment (ME). Research on marital enrichment programs has made much progress, yet there is still much to do. When viewed within the context of the large number of couples who have been participants in these programs, the amount of research seems very small. In this section we examine some reasons for the limited research in this field, briefly discuss the methodological problems of marital enrichment research, critically evaluate the published studies, and suggest directions for future research.

Chapter 7, Dimensions of Research, examines the evidence from many sources that ME provides positive benefits to couples. Some methodological considerations in research design and appropriate measures of change are considered with some representative findings.

Chapter 8, Measuring Program Effectiveness, considers ways to measure program quality in relation to changes in couples and to move toward ways to evaluate and improve measures of enrichment events and programs.

Chapter 9, Essential Elements for Enrichment Changes in Couples, considers interactions between theory, research, and applications, and then explores major dimensions of couple commitment, program structure, leader qualities, use of homework, and interaction with therapy in relation to ME as major elements that produce positive changes in ME participants.

Chapter 7

Dimensions of Research

The overall findings of research on marriage enrichment (ME) show that, in general, enrichment programs do benefit most couples. However, research on marital enrichment continues to face several difficulties. This is partly because of the difficulty of evaluating the effectiveness of ME programs, the expense of empirical research follow-up, the imprecision of measuring subjective impacts and results, and other factors. Outcome research on ME shares the numerous scientific, ethical, and practical problems encountered in the measurement of outcome of other psychological change processes. For example, researchers must ensure that the treatments are specified precisely, clarify how changes relate to the characteristics of the particular therapists involved, and control adequately factors such as passage of time and placebo effects.

SUCCESS OF MARRIAGE ENRICHMENT

The overall answer from research is that ME has positive benefits for participating couples. Empirical research on ME seems to have reached a peak between 1977 and 1982. According to Guerney and Maxson (1990), there were 29 studies of programs from 1962 to 1976 (about 2 per year), 56 studies in the years 1977–1982 (about 11 per year), and 18 studies per year from 1983 to 1990 (about 2.5 per year). Several literature searches of the period 1991 through 1993 completed as part of the series of dissertation studies of marital enrichment programs found three additional studies. In 1997, PsychLit searches on combinations of "marriage" and "enrichment" produced 85 studies, including 10 studies since 1993.

These counts are subject to variability for several reasons. It is sometimes difficult to decide whether a report is a description of a program or an empirical research study. A few separate reports apparently are variations or updates of the same basic research study. Some useful studies may be missed because they have not been published or because their title and keyword information may not be identified readily as ME or couple enrichment. Some studies may omit reference to marriage or couple enrichment yet can be included because they describe the application of psychoeducational techniques to couples.

Many of the early empirical research studies focused on whether ME programs produced positive results, whether more seriously dysfunctional couples could be helped by programs, and whether certain techniques were effective. The meta-analyses of Giblin (1986) and Hahlweg et al. (1988) and the research summaries of Bradbury and Fincham (1990), Guerney and Maxson (1990), Hof and Miller (1981), and Zimpfer (1988), indicate that ME programs do produce positive results for both premarital and married couples, that some techniques are more effective than others, and that well-designed programs can help a much wider range of couples.

Since the emergence of ME programs in the early 1960s, considerable research efforts have attempted to ascertain several dimensions of ME program effectiveness. Giblin's (1986) meta-analysis of 85 studies of program effectiveness, involving 3,886 couples, provides the most comprehensive overview of research on the effectiveness of ME; it included 23 of the 40 studies reviewed by Hof and Miller (1981). His meta-analysis identified several key factors in measuring the effectiveness of ME programs.

It is clear from Giblin's (1986) study that ME does make a difference in participants' lives and relationships. The most likely improvements are in specific skill areas, such as communications (speaking for self, active listening, using feeling statements, empathetic responses) and constructive problem-solving techniques. Smaller changes are likely in marital happiness, satisfaction, relationship quality, and intimacy, all of which are more global, longer-term aspects of relationships.

Participants may experience some disruptions or shifts in marital expectations and some awkwardness in using new skills as they try to implement new learning from the enrichment experience into their daily lives. In general, the longer and more intensive the program, the more change that can be expected. Greatest changes occur from experiential behavioral rehearsal and practice processes, whereas little change can be anticipated from lecture and discussion processes that do not involve feedback and coaching.

Many hypothesized main effects and interactions are yet to be examined through empirical research. Among these are subject variables such as age, education, vocation, quality-of-life effectiveness, religious involvement, family of origin, and previous marriage relationship experiences; program variables such as amount and type of structure, type of format (weekend and/or weekly sessions), how the program addresses levels of dysfunction and relationship development stages.

In the Giblin (1986) study the Relationship Enhancement program of Guerney (1977) had highest effect sizes (ES = .96, compared to an average ES of .44).

Zimpfer (1988) updated the Hof and Miller reviews (apparently without noting Giblin's 1986 meta-analyses), noting that in the 10 years since the Hof and Miller reviews of ME programs had expanded to include premarital and dating couples as well as couples with more severe difficulties and dysfunctions. Zimpfer proposed using relationship enrichment to refer to this wider couple audience for preventive programs.

Zimpfer (1988a, p. 47) describes 13 different outcome studies that he clusters into "three general types: (1) those that offer a variety of contents and experiences, (2) those whose focus is primarily on communication training, and (3) those based mainly on behavior exchange principles." Included in the 13 were 3 studies of the Minnesota Couple Communication Program (now Couple Communication [Miller et al., 1991]) and four studies of the Relationship Enhancement program (Guerney, 1977). In all there were eight communication training programs and five mixed-experience programs.

Several conclusions are offered by Zimpfer. There is clear evidence that relationship enrichment programs generally are effective. More studies have placebo controls and obtain follow-up measures, which increases our confidence in the empirical validations of the effectiveness of relationship enrichment programs. The audience for relationship enrichment programs can include dating and engaged couples, couples who are experiencing more serious difficulties, as well as the original intended audience of couples who want to improve or enrich their good marriages. More recently, intervention and enrichment programs for couples facing divorce or dysfunctions have been designed and implemented with apparent success (see chapter 5, this volume). As discussed in chapter 8 (this volume), using enrichment and therapy together increases benefits from each type of program service.

O'Leary and Smith (1991) reviewed research on marital interaction, including psychodynamic and social learning theories of marital satisfaction and discord as well as approaches to treatment (such as premarital relationship enhancement, ME programs, and marital therapy). They found these approaches to be helpful and suggested some directions for marriage research in the 1990s.

Research on ME also allows us to identify the specific types of changes and to determine the stability over time of changes that are associated with participation in the program. Through research, we can directly compare the effectiveness of two or more different programs and identify components of those programs that produce desired effects. Finally, research can answer questions about the suitability of various programs for people with varying degrees and types of problems, personality types and traits, and social and demographic characteristics.

CRITERIA FOR RESEARCH

For research to provide the answers we need, it must meet certain scientific criteria. It is not our purpose to provide a detailed treatment of experimental design and analyses of data. We suggest guidelines that the reader can use to evaluate the quality of research, and we highlight certain methodological issues particularly relevant to research on ME. What follows is a brief discussion of the most important criteria for evaluating research on the effectiveness of ME programs.

Generalizability

The results of research can be extended from the sample to a given population only if the sample has been drawn randomly from the population. Unfortunately, this has not been done in ME research for several reasons. As far as we can determine, all studies of enrichment have been done on couples who in some way volunteered or responded to advertisements about a program. Thus the results can be generalized only to couples who do volunteer or in some way indicate that they are willing to participate in a program.

This limitation leaves the motivation of couples to participate in enrichment in need of much additional study. Undoubtedly, issues of cost, time involvement, and availability differentially affect the involvement of couples in enrichment programs. Additional researchable motivation factors include the level of distress of a couple, the requirement of preparation for marriage, the awareness of program availability, the encouragement of others to participate, and the willingness of both partners to enter a program.

Randomization

When couples are assigned to two or more experimental conditions, for example, a group of couples participating in a ME program and a group of couples on a waiting-list (control group), assignment of the couples to one group or another should be done randomly. Without such random assignment, we cannot know whether differences between groups at the end of the program are due to differences in the experimental conditions or to differences that were present at the start between the couples in the different groups.

Control Groups

Any of a number of control groups may be used, but at the minimum, a waiting-list control or a no-treatment control group is necessary. These control groups allow researchers to separate changes that may occur as a result of the ME experience from changes that are due to the passage of time and effects of ongoing life experiences.

Beyond this basic requirement, other comparison groups can be useful. For example, an attention-placebo control group, which involves assignment of a group of couples to a treatment condition believed to be therapeutical or educationally inert, permits the assessment of the degree of change caused by nonspecific treatment factors such as expectancy for change or suggestion.

Another experimental design would entail assigning couples to two or more experimental treatments of different enrichment programs. A waiting-list or no-treatment control group still would be needed because demonstration of the superiority of one program over another does not tell us how changes that may occur with either program compare to changes that result spontaneously and with the passage of time.

The way in which change actually is measured should be influenced by several factors. The measurement process is a major concern in outcome research because no amount of elegance in experimental design or statistical analysis of data can overcome the use of poorly selected measurement tools. The following factors need to be considered when evaluating measurement techniques.

Timing of Measurement

The most commonly encountered design in marital enrichment research involves measurements a short time before (pre) and a short time after (post) the enrichment experience and at a comparable time interval for the waiting-list control group. However, there must be provision for testing at yet another time, as a follow-up to the enrichment program. Without follow-up evaluation, we have no way of knowing whether changes that are seen at post-testing persist for any length of time after participation in the enrichment experience has ended. At the least, the time between post-testing and follow-up should be one month.

Use of Multiple Outcome Measures

Assessments of feelings, attitudes, beliefs, and behaviors can be made in a variety of ways. The participants and leaders can provide their own self-reports, and such self-reports can be obtained through structured or unstructured tests, questionnaires, or interviews. Observational measures may be obtained by independent judges or raters either in an experimentally controlled situation or in the naturalistic setting.

No one measurement technique is inherently better than another. The two major types of measurements, self-report and observation, have their own strengths and weaknesses (Olson, 1977). Reliance on only one measurement technique necessarily will exclude some important information needed to evaluate outcome. As valuable as observation of couple interaction can be (Gottman, 1994; Weiss & Heyman, 1990), observational methods seldom have been used in studies of ME.

Reliability and Validity of Measurement Devices

Reliability of measurement refers to the degree to which multiple measurements with the same instrument or procedure produce similar scores. The validity of a measurement device refers to the extents to which the device measures what it purports to measure. Any study on the effectiveness of ME should employ measurement devices of known reliability and validity or should seek to demonstrate the reliability and validity of the devices as part of the study. Relying solely on homemade tests and questionnaires of unknown reliability or validity throws into question the meaning of the results.

Fincham and Bradbury (1990, pp. 375, 477) outline a five-step plan for research:

1. Obtain more knowledge of basic factors that shape the quality of marriage.
2. Identify the relationship competencies that couples need for a successful marriage.
3. Design specific interventions that enable partners to increase these competencies.
4. Incorporate these interventions into programs for couples and for individuals.
5. Assess the effectiveness of these changes.

This discussion highlights the major methodological issues that must be considered when evaluating research on the effectiveness of ME programs. We now turn to an examination of the existing research literature on ME. This examination addresses two questions: Do the available studies of ME meet the methodological criteria for good research? What questions do the existing studies answer or raise?

REVIEW OF RESEARCH STUDIES

Reviewing the research literature is made difficult by the lack of a generally accepted definition of ME and the fact that different clinicians and researchers have defined the term in a variety of ways. It is difficult to determine whether a particular study should be included or excluded from a review of research on enrichment. For example, Beck (1975) classified only five of the outcome studies of marital counseling that she reviewed as studies of ME. Yet, many of the 29 studies that Gurman and Kniskern (1977) included in their review of ME programs can be found in Beck's article, but listed by Beck as studies of marital counseling or communication training. More recently, distinctions between communication programs and enrichment programs have all but disappeared. Interventions that are designed for marital therapy may be applied in couple enrichment programs, and vice versa (e.g., L'Abate & McHenry, 1983; Nelson & Trepper, 1993).

Tolman and Molidor (1994) reviewed group work from 54 social-work studies over the past 10 years and found that (a) conjoint therapy using cognitive behavioral treatment for 10–18 hours has been the predominant mode of marital therapy, (b) group or psychoeducational treatment have been used primarily with premarital couples, and (c) every type of marital intervention was an improvement over no treatment with few treatment differentials. After evaluating different approaches to marriage counseling, Cookerly (1977) found that conjoint group marriage counseling is more beneficial and advisable than traditional conjoint treatment if there is a high likelihood of divorce.

For the present review, we include studies of couples who have participated in programs that either have been identified clearly by the investigators as marital enrichment programs or consist of procedures and techniques that are major programmatic elements of ME programs. We have included, therefore, not only studies of programs such as Marriage Encounter (Huber, 1977) and the Pairing Enrichment Program (Travis & Travis, 1976b), but also research on such closely related programs such as the Couples Communication Program (CCP [Miller et al., 1976]) and the Conjugal Relationship Enhancement (CRE) program (Guerney, 1977). The originators of the latter programs have clearly associated them with ME and have been affiliated with ME organizations such as the Council of Affiliated Marriage Enrichment Organizations (CAMEO [Hopkins et al., 1978]). Finally, a number of reports on other communication training and behavioral exchange procedures are included in the research review. Although some of these studies do not purport to be assessments of ME, the training techniques are similar or identical to the main programmatic elements of many ME programs.

The programs studied differ markedly in their definition of marital enrichment, format, goals, and scope. These programmatic differences, as well as differences in research methodology and in the type of dependent measures used, make it difficult to draw general conclusions from the studies reviewed.

With few exceptions, research on the outcome of marital enrichment experiences has involved a preassessment–postassessment format with two groups, the treatment group and a waiting-list or no-treatment control group. Because of this similarity in research design, we have decided not to present a detailed examination of each study. Rather, our intention is to summarize what is and is not known about the effectiveness of marital enrichment. The reader who is interested in the specific details of any of the studies reviewed is referred to the original reports and to Table 1.

Table 1
Outcome Research of ME Experiences

Reference	Control groups[a] WL/NT	Pl.	AT	Outcome measures[b] Class	Self-report	Independent ratings	Follow-up	Results[c]
				Mixed experiences/exercises				
Adam & Gringas (1982)	Y	N	N	MA, P, RS	Y	Y	Y	MA = +; P = +; RS = ±
Bruder (1972)	Y	N	N	MA, P, RS	Y	N	N	P = +; MA, RS = −
Burns (1972)	Y	N	N	P	Y	N	Y	±
Huber (1977) (Marriage Encounter)	Y	N	N	P	Y	N	Y	Mostly +
Kilmann, Moreault, & Robinson (1978)	Y	N	Y	MA, P	Y	N	Y	+
Kilmann, Julian, & Moreault (1978)	Y	N	Y	MA, P, RS	Y	Y	N	+
L'Abate (1977)	Y	N	N	P	Y	N	N	+
Lester & Doherty (1983) Marriage Encounter	N	N	N	MA	Y	N	Y	Mostly +
Strickland (1982)[d]	Y	N	Y	MA, RS	Y	N	Y	+
Strozier (1981) Marriage Enrichment Retreat	Y	N	N	MA, RS	Y	N	Y	MA = ±; RS = −
Swicegood (1974)(ACME)	Y	N	N	P, RS	Y	Y	Y	Mostly +
Travis & Travis (1975) Pairing Enrichment Program	Y	N	N	P	Y	N	N	Mostly −
Travis & Travis (1976b)	N	N	N	P	Y	N	N	+

					Communication training				
Weinstein (1975)	Y	N	N	Y	P	Y	N	N	+
Wilson (1980)	N	Y	N	N	MA, P, RS	Y	N	Y	+
MCCP									
Beaver (1978)	Y	N	Y	Y	RS	Y	N	N	±
Brown (1976)	Y	N	Y	Y	P	Y	N	N	+
Campbell (1974)	Y	N	N	N	RS	N	Y	N	+
Dillon (1975)	Y	N	N	N	MA, P, RS	Y	N	Y	+
Huppert (1984)	N	N	N	N	MA, RS	Y	Y	N	MA = −; RS = +
Joanning (1982)	N	N	N	N	MA, RS	Y	Y	Y	+
Larsen (1974)	N	N	N	N	P, RS	Y	Y	N	±
Miller (1971)	Y	N	N	N	P, RS	Y	Y	N	**P** = ±, RS = +
Nunnally (1971)	Y	N	N	N	RS	Y	Y	N	Mostly +
Schwager & Conrad (1974)	N	N	N	N	P	Y	N	N	+
Wampler & Sprenkle (1980)	Y	Y	Y	Y	MA, RS	Y	Y	Y	+
Thielen, Hubner, & Schmook (1976)	Y	N	N	N	MA, P, RS	Y	Y	N	Mostly +
Witkin (1977)	Y	N	Y	Y	MA, RS	Y	Y	Y	±
Relationship Enhancement Program									
Collins (1971)	Y	N	N	N	MA, RS	Y	N	N	±
D'Augelli, Deyss, Guerney, Hershenberg, & Sborofsky (1974)	Y	N	N	N	RS	N	Y	N	+

(Continued)

121

Table 1
(Continued)

Reference	Control groups[a]			Outcome measures[b]				Results[c]
	WL/NT	Pl.	AT	Class	Self-report	Independent ratings	Follow-up	
Ely, Guerney, & Stover (1973)	Y	N	N	RS	Y	Y	N	±
Jessee & Guerney (1981)	N	N	Y	MA, RS	Y	N	N	Mostly +
Nix-Early (1984)	N	N	N	P	Y	N	N	+
Rappaport (1976)	Y	N	N	MA, P, RS	Y	N	N	+
Ridley & Bain (1983)	N	Y	N	RS	Y	N	Y	±
Ridley, Jorgensen, Morgan, & Avery (1982)	N	Y	N	MA, P, RS	Y	N	N	+
Schlien (1971)	Y	N	N	P, RS	Y	Y	N	Mostly +
Wieman (1973)[d]	Y	N	Y	MA, RS	Y	Y	Y	+
Other Communication Training								
Epstein & Jackson (1978)	Y	N	Y	RS	Y	Y	N	Mostly +
Henss & Boning (1984)	N	N	N	MA, P, RS	Y	Y	N	MA = +; P = ±; RS = ±
Hines (1976)	Y	N	Y	RS	N	Y	N	+
Nadeau (1971)	Y	N	N	P, RS	Y	Y	Y	±
Neville (1971)	N	N	N	P, RS	Y	N	N	+
Orling (1976)	Y	N	N	MA, P	Y	Y	N	+
Pilder (1972)	Y	N	N	P, RS	Y	Y	N	±
Strickland (1982)[d]	Y	N	Y	MA, RS	Y	N	Y	+
Van Zoost (1973)	N	N	N	P, RS	Y	N	N	±

Venema (1976)[d]	N	N	Y	MA P, RS	Y	N	N	Mostly −
Williams (1975)	Y	N	Y	MA RS	Y	N	N	−
Behavior Exchange								
Dixon & Sciara (1977)	N	N	Y	P, RS	Y	N	N	Mostly +
Fisher (1973)	Y	N	Y	P	Y	N	N	Mostly +
Harrell & Guerney (1976)	Y	N	Y	MA P, RS	Y	Y	N	RS = ±; MA, P = −
McIntosh (1975)	Y	N	Y	MA P, RS	Y	N	N	−
Roberts (1975)	Y	Y	N	MA P	Y	N	N	+
Venema (1976)[d]	N	N	Y	MA P, RS	Y	N	N	Mostly −
Wieman (1973)[d]	Y	N	Y	MA RS	Y	Y	Y	+

Note: Y = Yes; N = No. Table 1 originally appeared in Hof and Miller (1981). The subsequent entries are from Zimpfer (1988), reprinted with permission from the Journal for Specialists in Group Work, Vol. 13(1), pp. 46–47, © American Counseling Association.

[a]WL/NT = Waiting list or no-treatment group; Pl. = placebo-control group; AT = Alternative Therapy, i.e., the experimental group is compared with another therapy or enrichment group.

[b]Outcome measures are divided into three classes or groups: MA = measures of marital adjustment, P = perceptual and personality measures, RS = relationship-skill measures. Measures also may be based on self-report or ratings by independent observers or judges.

[c]+ = statistically significant pre/post change and, when used, greater change than control group; ± = mixed results; − = negative results.

[d]Three studies, Venema (1976), Wieman (1973), and Strickland (1982), are listed twice because each study can be grouped under two different categories of enrichment.

Table 1 presents some basic information about 40 different studies of marital enrichment, plus 14 studies reviewed by Zimpfer (1988). (There are 54 listings in the table, but 2 studies are referenced under each of two different program formats.) As mentioned earlier, marital enrichment programs vary considerably in format and structure. To facilitate comparisons between studies, we have identified three general types of marital enrichment programs: those that focus primarily on communication training; those based mainly on behavioral exchange principles; and those that offer a mix of experiences and exercises. The various outcome measures have been separated into the three categories suggested by Gurman and Kniskern (1977): overall marital adjustment; perceptual and individual personality variables such as perception of spouse, self-esteem, and self-actualization; and relationship skill variables such as communication and problem-solving skills, self-disclosure, and empathy.

The most basic question to be addressed by outcome research is whether the intervention procedure is followed by specific affective, attitudinal, cognitive, or behavioral changes. As Table 1 shows, most of the outcome studies reviewed do report positive changes on some of the outcome measures. Furthermore, significant changes are not restricted to any particular type or class of variable. Are the changes that follow participation in marital enrichment programs a result of the enrichment experience, the passage of time, or nonspecific (i.e., placebo) effects? Table 1 shows that 33 of the 40 studies (82.5%) used either a waiting-list or no-treatment control group. Because the general finding for these studies is that significantly greater change occurs for the marital enrichment group than for the control group, we can view the changes that occur as being due to factors other than the simple passage of time.

Table 1 also indicates that only one study used an attention-placebo control group. Roberts (1975) formed a placebo condition by placing five couples in an unstructured group setting in which issues could be discussed, but where the various enrichment experiences and exercises were not present. This placebo condition controlled for changes that might occur as a result of group participation and discussion in the absence of the specific enrichment experiences. Roberts (1975) reported that greater changes did occur in the placebo group than in a waiting-list control group. The ME group, however, was superior to both control groups. Thus, although nonspecific treatment factors did produce positive changes, the enrichment experience itself resulted in greater changes. Dixon and Sciara (1977) attempted to demonstrate a causal relationship between treatment intervention and changes in self-ratings of the relationship through use of a multiple baseline procedure, rather than a placebo control group. Their results suggest that changes in ratings are contingent upon the introduction of specific, reciprocity-exchange procedures.

It is unfortunate that only two of the studies reviewed included some type of control for placebo effects. Such a group is particularly necessary because, as Roberts (1975) demonstrated, nonspecific treatment factors can lead to significant changes in self-reported marital adjustment and in relationships. This finding raises the obvious question of whether some of the significant changes reported in the other studies reviewed here are due to placebo effects and not to the marital enrichment experience itself.

Are the measurements made with reliable and valid instruments and are independent ratings, as well as self-report measures, used? Only 16 of the 40 studies (40%) included independent raters or judges, whereas 37 of the studies (92.5%) used self-report measures. Although self-report is more economical and convenient procedure than ratings of objective observers, there are serious dangers in relying exclusively on measures that are so easily influenced by response biases, social desirability, and demand characteristics. Another drawback to the studies that use only self-report as a measure of outcome is that the reliability and validity of the instruments often are unknown.

Do the reported outcomes represent stable or temporary changes in the participants? Eight of the forty studies (20%) included some type of follow-up assessment. Burns (1972) and Huber (1977) reported maintenance of changes in self-perception and perception of spouse, respectively, from post-test to follow-up, and Wieman (1973) found that changes in marital adjustment, expressive and responsive skill, and specific target behaviors were stable over a 10-week follow-up period. In addition, Dillon (1975) obtained significant changes in self-reported communication, self-esteem, and marital satisfaction that were maintained over 10 weeks. Nadeau (1971), Swicegood (1974), and Witkin (1977) also reported some stability in changes following marital enrichment experiences. However, in Nadeau's study, self-report changes were better maintained than behavioral changes, whereas in Witkin's study, behavioral, but not self-report, measures changed significantly with gains being maintained for a two-month follow-up period. Swicegood found that some changes in perception of the relationship, marital integration, and communication were not maintained at follow-up. Kilmann et al. (1978) also found that some changes were maintained a follow-up, but others were not. In addition, significant improvement did not emerge for some variables until follow-up testing. Although the results of follow-up are encouraging for the most part, more studies need to be done with follow-up measures before we can conclude that ME does lead to stable changes in relationships.

Are different types of marital enrichment experiences more or less effective than others? Twelve of the forty studies (30%) directly compared two types of ME programs. Wieman (1973) contrasted the CRE program, a behavioral exchange program, and a waiting-list control group. Both enrichment programs resulted in significant increases in marital adjustment, communication skill, and target behaviors, and there were no differences between the two programs. Kilmann, Moreault, and Robinson (1978) and Kilmann, Julian, and Moreault (1978) contrasted two formats of the same program and a no-treatment control group. In both studies, the sequence of treatment experiences did not affect outcome, and both treatment formats were superior to no treatment. Two additional studies that used alternative treatments found, as did Wieman (1973), no differences among the various treatments (McIntosh, 1975; Williams, 1975). These studies, however, reported no significant changes for any of the enrichment experiences.

In contrast to these results, seven studies reported superiority of one treatment format over another. Epstein and Jackson (1978) included communication training, interaction-insight, and no-treatment groups in their study. Both treatment groups reduced verbal disagreements. Only the communication training group, however, led to increases in assertive requests, decreases in verbal attacks, and increases in spouse-rated empathy. Hines (1976) also reported superiority of a communication training experience over both an insight and a control group, using a rater's estimate of the couples' mutual helpfulness as the outcome measure.

Three studies of the Minnesota Couples Communication Program (MCCP, now [Interpersonal Communications Programs (ICP)]) yielded data supporting the superiority of that particular communication enrichment program over alternative programs (Brown, 1976; Witkin, 1977) or over another format of the MCCP (Beaver, 1978). Brown (1976) contrasted the MCCP, a ME growth group, and a no-treatment group and found significant changes in sex stereotyping of self and spouse only for couples in the MCCP group. Witkin (1977) reported significantly greater changes at post-test and two-month follow-up on behavioral measures of nonverbal positives and both verbal and nonverbal negatives for his MCCP group than for a behaviorally oriented communication skill workshop group or a no-treatment control group. Beaver (1978) compared two formats of the MCCP—one with couple participation and the other with each spouse in separate groups—and a no-treatment group. Significant changes on self-report of communication and empathy occurred only for husbands in the conjoint participation condition.

Fischer (1973) found that a behaviorally oriented group made significant gains in prediction of attitudes and preferences of spouses relative to a control group and to a facilitative group based on Adlerian and functional methods. Finally, although Venema (1976) found very little change for any of these treatments, a combination of communication training and behavioral exchange led to greater change on a number of measures than did either communication training or behavioral exchange alone. In summary, studies have been made comparing the effectiveness of different marital enrichment formats. The research suggests that communication training (Brown, 1976; Epstein and Jackson, 1978; Hines, 1976) and behavioral exchange (Fischer, 1973) are superior to insight-oriented group experiences. This finding is in line with recent conclusions by Jacobson and Addis (1993). Specific contrasts of behavioral and communication-training programs have yielded mixed results (Venema, 1976; Wieman, 1973; Witkin, 1977). However, we must be cautious in making conclusions at this point because the number of relevant studies is very small.

Do programs with different formats and content produce different types of changes? The comparative studies described provide no evidence for this possibility. Comparing the results of the various studies in Table 1 does, however, suggest a possible difference in the types of changes produced by different marital enrichment experiences. Positive changes on all three general types of outcome measures—marital adjustment, perceptual and personality measures, and relationship skill measures—have been obtained in many of the studies of communication-training and behavior-exchange programs. For programs consisting of mixed experiences and exercises, there is consistent evidence for positive change only on perceptual and personality measures. Of course, only two of the studies of the mixed type of enrichment experience included both marital adjustment or relationship skill measures, and so, we cannot draw any conclusions about different types of changes occurring with different programs until more comparative studies, which include all three types of outcome measures, have been completed.

For particular interventions that result in positive change, what are the effective components of the program that produce the change? For what types of participants are the enrichment programs effective? The studies by Beaver (1978) and Roberts (1975) are the only ones we have located that sought to identify an effective component of a ME experience. Roberts (1975) examined differences in outcome as a function of therapists' experience level, using novice paraprofessional, experienced paraprofessional, and graduate-student therapists. He found that outcome was positively related to the experience level of the therapists; that is, the groups led by more experienced therapists had better outcomes. Beaver (1978) found that changes in communication and empathy occurred when partners were in the same enrichment group but not when the partners participated in separate groups. Clearly, many other variables, for example, the inclusion or exclusion of specific exercises, the time format, number of leaders per group, and social class of participants (most programs have been limited to middle-class couples) need to be related to outcomes.

Two studies have examined the response of different types of participants to ME experiences. Neville (1971) used the Myers Briggs Type Indicator to identify personality types among participants in a ME experience. He found that a significantly greater proportion of volunteer participants were intuitive-feeling types as opposed to sensing-thinking personality types. Neville concluded that these two personality types differed in their comfort and compatibility with the enrichment process, but that both groups, nevertheless, responded well to the experience.

Huber (1977) assessed the outcome of a Marriage Encounter experience using Shostrom's Caring Relationship Inventory (CRI). He reported that only the male participants showed significant positive change on CRI scales; females' scores did not change. Interestingly, Beaver (1978) found similar results. When partners participated in a communication group together, only the husbands showed significant changes on communication and empathy measures.

Thus, one of these studies (Neville, 1971) suggests that, although individuals with certain personality types may be more likely than others to volunteer for marital enrichment experiences, the outcome of the experience may not be affected by the participant's personality type. The other two studies (Beaver, 1978; Huber, 1977), on the other hand, suggest that males may be more likely than females to change following participation in at least some ME programs. In a study of 100 couples, Krug and Ahadi (1986) found that participants tend to be more like couples who have problems in their marriages, as measured by the Adult Personality Inventory (API). More research is needed before we can determine whether enrichment programs are more or less effective for different types of participants.

Hill (1991) trained 28 couples as communication program instructors and compared them to a control group of 27 couples with no formal training. Using a self-report questionnaire and a conjoint tape-recorded interview, he found that in making decisions, treatment-group participants scored higher on self-esteem, had lower disparity scores on the sex-role preference measure, and used more verbal persuasion strategies than the untrained group.

Everts (1988) describes the effectiveness and future development of a ME program used in New Zealand by John and Agnes Sturt since 1977. The questionnaire and interview data from 103 participants suggests that the program had comprehensive content, competent leadership, appropriate organization, and produced reports of lasting effects, although no built-in experimental evaluation was used. Everts then suggests changes in the program and improved training methods.

Ford, Bashford, and DeWitt (1984) compared three approaches to ME: (a) direct training of spousal communication skills by one of two male-female cotrainer teams, (b) observation of videotaped simulations of direct training, and (c) bibliotherapy with telephone contacts. They also included a waiting-list control group that also was evaluated. There were 61 couples who participated in one of the four conditions. All three approaches were better than the waiting-list group. Because changes in communication behaviors were not well predicted, these authors concluded that attitudinal changes in ME programs may be facilitated by optimal matching of different clients with the appropriate type of intervention, but that behavior changes are more a function of systematic skills training for all clients.

Russell et al. (1984) compared the MCCP and structured behavioral exchange (SBE) training programs using 32 couples and assessments of a waiting-list control group. Both treatments had immediate impact on communication content for husbands and on communication style for wives. The authors note the need for follow-up experiences to maintain treatment gains. They also suggest that MCCP may be a better fit for couples who wish to increase understanding, whereas SBE may be more appropriate for couples who want to solve problems.

One major contribution of ME has been in encouraging more planning and structure in marital therapy. L'Abate and O'Callaghan (1977) linked family enrichment to therapy and described advantages of carefully planned therapy over unstructured family therapy approaches. They show that process and outcome research, theory testing, use with nonclinical families, and comparisons of structured vs. unstructured and cognitive vs. affective strategies can be tested more precisely with a structured approach. They also point to the potential of enrichment models for training new specialists in marriage and the family.

The 10-session Training in Marriage Enrichment (TIME) program employs a sociopsychological group approach to teach skills such as accepting responsibility, understanding priorities and values, communicating effectively, listening and responding to whole messages, making choices, and resolving conflicts (Dinkmeyer & Carlson, 1985). Studies of the TIME program show that it is effective in producing positive changes in couples. Mattson et al. (1990) divided 38 couples into two groups. One group received the eight-week TIME program and the other group had no treatment. The group receiving TIME had better scores on dyadic adjustment and relationship change. In another study of 17 couples, Oliver et al. (1993) found improvement in marital satisfaction, especially for women, and a post-test increase in the level of psychological reactance of males. They conclude that psychological reactance may be a factor in determining response to ME training.

We conclude from this examination of the research that some optimism about the effectiveness of ME programs is warranted. However, we must be very cautious in our optimism. Although generally positive results have been reported, we must await the presentation of more well-designed research before we can comfortably conclude that ME produces stable, positive change in couples.

DIRECTIONS FOR FUTURE RESEARCH

Many of the suggestions offered by Gurman and Kniskern (1977) for better research on ME are still to be applied systematically. In addition, the suggestions offered by Weiss and Heyman (1990) concerning research on marriage in the 1980s also apply to ME research for the future. Among these is the need for continuing longitudinal studies, especially to identify the individual and interspouse changes that shape the direction of a marriage. An especially critical area is identifying more precisely how coercion and criticism patterns link with depression, anger, and marital distress. Using physiological measures of affect, research is needed on how enrichment can affect the highly predictive affective sequences that become escape conditioning (Gottman & Levinson, 1986) and produce marital deterioration.

Recruitment procedures that sample the population more closely, such as telephone presampling methods that identify possible participant couples, need to be used in ME research. Also needed is increased research attention to withdrawal (Gottman, 1994) as it may be expressed in the often noted reluctance of husbands (more than wives) to attend and participate in enrichment programs. Sequential analysis of changes in marital patterns can get closer to the real-life interactional effects between partners. Finally the bio-, psycho-, and socioimmunology studies of physiological linkage, marital distress, and health (Gottman, 1994; Kiecolt-Glaser et al., 1987) offer promising theoretical and practical directions concerning the systems interactions between health, marriage, and family. These research directions will help us to understand how ME and other interventions positively affect marriages and families.

Chapter 8

Measuring Program Effectiveness

Participants, sponsors, and leaders want answers about marriage enrichment (ME). Participants in ME events want some assurance that spending the time, effort, and money will produce the results they want. Sponsors of events want to know that they are supporting programs that have been proven to be effective in improving relationships. Leaders want to use effective methods that produce important changes in those who participate.

INTERACTIONS BETWEEN THEORY, RESEARCH, AND APPLICATION

Measuring marriage and family relationships involves interactions between theory, research, and applications. Typically, applied research is done in direct support of applications, such as enrichment programs and techniques, whereas basic research usually is performed to test components of theory (Olson, 1976b). Good measurements bring many benefits to participants, sponsors, leaders, and practitioners.

Predicting success in marriage has long been an interest of researchers (e.g., Burgess & Cottrell, 1939; Terman et al., 1938). Terman and colleagues' (1938) studies of marriage, as part of their research on gifted children and adults, found 10 factors that were associated with an individual's success in marriage. In order of importance, these were superior happiness of parents, childhood happiness, lack of conflict with mother, home discipline that was firm but not harsh, strong attachment to mother and father, lack of conflict with father, parental frankness about sex, appropriate discipline in childhood, and a healthy attitude about sex. Terman and Wallin (1949) explored technical issues involved in marriage inventories.

Michael Kerschner, Douglas Emerson, Timothy Hogan, and Donald Chia, School of Psychology, Fuller Seminary, contributed extensively to the preparation of this section on measuring outcomes of ME programs.

Ways to organize measurement are described by Cromwell et al. (1976). Each type of measurement, with its specific advantages and disadvantages, provides different kinds of information. Instruments can be classified according to whether the information is subjective (open-ended) or objective (precoded) item formats and whether the observer frame of reference is as insider (self-report from individual involved in the relationship) or outsider (external rater, therapist, etc.) who is not part of the marriage or other relationship (Olson, 1977). This four-part distinction among instruments clarifies data sources and offers an opportunity for convergence on primary factors in marriage growth and development.

In their survey of couple treatments, Jacobson and Addis (1993) emphasize both tools and theory. They found that all couple treatments produce improvements relative to control groups, but there are no reliable differences between different models. All approaches still leave considerable numbers of couples unimproved or still somewhat distressed. They emphasize researching specific components of a model as more important than comparisons across different models. In this way it is more likely that the same program elements will be compared across models and programs. Researching the ways in which partners' aptitudes and characteristics interact with treatment techniques, especially in prevention approaches, is a promising direction for future research.

Several enrichment programs have integrated theory, research, and application. The Prevention and Relationship Enhancement Program ([PREP] Markman, 1984, Markman et al., 1993), Relationship Enhancement (Guerney, 1977; Guerney et al., 1986), and Couples Communication Program ([CCP], Miller et al., 1975, 1988, 1991) have included carefully designed research on changes in participating couples. Others use more informal measures.

The body of research on marriage and family measurement instruments continues to advance. Giblin (1986) continued the emphasis on cataloging measurement instruments. He added dimensions of suitability of instruments for different populations; discrimination of developmental sequences (e.g., recent past vs. more distant past); behavioral, cognitive, affective, and intent dimensions; and global vs. specific qualities. Along these lines, Touliatos et al. (1990) provide a helpful summary of measurement issues, categories of measurements, and descriptions of specific instruments.

Zimpfer (1988) clustered outcome measures into three classes: marital adjustment, personality, and relationship skill. All of the studies had participant self-report measures, and four of the 13 (31%) also had independent ratings of couple functioning (compared to 40% of the studies reviewed by Hof & Miller [1981]). Five of the thirteen studies included a waiting-list or no-treatment control group, and eight (62%) included some type of follow-up assessment (compared with 20% of the studies reviewed by Hof & Miller having follow-up measures).

LONG-TERM MONITORING OF CHANGE

Program assessment can identify program elements to determine the component's effect on long-term change. The ongoing research of Markman and associates (Markman, 1981; Markman, Floyd, Stanley, & Storssali, 1988; Markman et al., 1993) demonstrates the rewards as well as the difficulties of following couples across several years. PREP (Renick, Blumberg, & Markman, 1992; Markman et al., 1994) has built booster sessions into its longitudinal follow-up procedures (Floyd et al., 1995).

PREP provides six sessions of three hours each over several weeks. Each session has both dydactic presentations followed by specific exercises that allow couples to practice the specific skills. Topics include the intent-impact model, how couples can create a safe environment for change, destructive and constructive styles of communicating, expectations, hidden issues, increasing fun times, ways to revitalize friendship and intimacy, team building, spiritual values (commitment and shared world views concerning honor, respect, intimacy, and forgiveness), sexual affection, and taking responsibility for using skills (Floyd et al., 1995).

Eighty-three couples in PREP and the control groups have participated in follow-up sessions at approximately one-year intervals. Couples who refuse to participate, usually with men who score lower on commitment and dedication, suggest that the willingness of the man to participate is critically important. At the five-year follow-up, 16% of couples in the control group had divorced or separated, whereas 8% in the PREP groups had (Floyd et al., 1995). Even so, the relatively low divorce rate in the control group suggests that they may be functioning better than the general population. It is not known to what extent these couples are typical of the unselected general population, because both groups consisted of couples who in some way expressed interest in the marital research work of Markman and his colleagues. The follow-up contacts themselves serve as booster sessions for couples and may influence control-group couples as well as PREP-group participants.

When to Offer Programs

Bader, Microys, Sinclair, Willet, & Conway (1980) showed that adding postwedding components to premarital preparation efforts improves and stabilizes couples' conflict-resolution skills. Including follow-up booster sessions after enrichment events is increasingly seen as essential for enrichment improvements to continue and stabilize (Floyd et al., 1995; Guerney & Maxson, 1990; Hendrix, 1988; Hunt & Hunt, 1996a; Mace & Mace, 1984). Efforts at designing various types of marital checkups have been attempted as preventive maintenance for couples. Some examples include Association of Couples for Marriage Enrichment (ACME) support groups (deGuzman, 1996) and the Couples Garden (Brainerd, personal communication, March 15, 1996).

What to Measure

A very important consideration in measurement of enrichment program effects is Giblin's (1986) finding that, in general, self-report measures show less effect size (average of .35 across 833 analyses) than do behavioral measures such as audio-taping or videotaping (average of .76 across 254 analyses). Giblin interprets this as participants seeing less change in themselves than do observers who rate the participants. This does not suggest that self-reports are not useful. In fact, Gottman (1994, pp. 38–41) suggests that both self-report and observational measures are useful because they provide different types of data. Recent theoretical developments in understanding the processes that support marriage wellness over long time spans offer additional ways to conceptualize and measure enrichment effects over longer time spans (Gottman, 1994). Hahlweg and Markman (1988) suggest that measurement instruments may have low ceilings for couples who are already functioning well at the beginning of an enrichment event.

The couple's agreement in self-reports of marriage values, roles, lifestyles, and assumptions seems to be closely related to marital satisfaction. In a study of 60 couples, Waterman (1990) found a very high correlation between the overall positive couple agreement score from ENRICH and the Dyadic Adjustment Scale (DAS) overall score ($r = .84$). In another study of 38 couples, Hunt and Chia (1996) found that observer ratings of 10-minute videotapes of couples correlated positively with the ENRICH positive couple agreement overall score (range $r = .51$ to .62) and with the LovePower Questionnaire positive agreement scores (range $r = .49$ to .58). LovePower self-ratings of communication skills correlated positively with the observers' ratings of communication qualities (range $r = .52$ to .65 for females, $r = .40$ to .50 for males).

The relation between self-report measures and observational measures of marital quality, adjustment, or marital functioning has been considered in detail by Gottman (1994) and by Trower and Kiely (1983) and other reviewers in Dowrick and Biggs (1983). Touliatos et al. (1990) also remind clinicians of the differences between self-report measures and observational measures in marriage and family assessment.

Programs such as PREP (Markman et al., 1994), ICP Couples Communication, (Miller et al., 1991), Getting the Love You Want (Hendrix, 1988), and PAIRS (Gordon, 1988) emphasize the importance of careful attention to details of communication. Couples can improve their communication skills with supportive feedback and guidance from a trained therapist coach.

Marital assessment inventories such as the DAS, PREPARE/ENRICH, and Taylor-Johnson Temperament Analysis, use the partners' self-reports as the basis for feedback, therapy, and change. These and other paper/pencil inventories often are criticized because they are the partners' subjective reports of their values, beliefs, and perceptions without having information about how the two partners actually interact with each other.

Observer ratings of partners are criticized because, even with appropriate and careful training, the observers do not have access to the insider information that partners have about their own functioning. Systems for rating marital interaction, such as the Marital Interaction Coding System, the Couple Interaction Scoring System, and the Specific Affect Coding System, are labor-intensive and expensive (Baucom and Adams, 1987; Gottman, 1994). However, they are very important because careful observation of marital interaction, along with each partner's physiological and self-report measures, promises to lead to much more accurate theory and effective interventions. Using a comprehensive paradigm of preevent and postevent measures with control groups would be an excellent approach to testing specific enrichment techniques across the range of couples.

Baucom and Adams (1987, pp. 174ff.) call for more study of how self-report inventories and couples' actual interactions are related. Bradbury and Fincham (1987, pp. 59–89) also support this concern.

Following this suggestion, Hunt and Chia (1996) compared self-reports of 38 couples with observers' ratings of a 10-minute videotape of the couple working on a specific topic that the couple selected for discussion. The ENRICH and the LovePower Questionnaire were computer administered. Ratings of the videotape segments were made by trained graduate students in a marriage and family program. Each couple's videotape was rated by 8 to 24 trained observers.

The self-report measures analyzed in this study were the overall Positive Couple Agreement (PCA) and the Special Focus (SPF) composite indexes from the ENRICH inventory of marital functioning. When both partners answer an item the same way and in the direction that is more conducive to healthy marital functioning, the PCA index increases. The SPF score increases for each item that the partners answer in the same (or similar) way but in a direction that is considered to be harmful to marital quality. As expected, the PCA and SPF scales correlate negatively ($r = -.76$). An earlier study of 60 couples (Waterman, 1990) found a correlation of $r = .83$ between DAS and PCA.

The LovePower Scales consist of 38 items selected in earlier studies from an original set of 75 items based on the topics in *Awaken Your Power to Love* (Hunt

& Hunt, 1994). Each item consists of a statement with a six-point Likert scale to rate how well each partner sees self and sees the other partner in specific areas of marital values and functioning. These formed seven scales with scale reliabilities ranging from .81 to .94.

High favorable agreement is considered a strength whereas agreement on needing help in an area is considered a growth need. If one or both answer in the midrange, the pattern is considered mixed. Each partner answered each question with one of six possible answers: (1) major changes needed, (2) serious concerns, (3) some concerns, (4) satisfied, (5) well satisfied, (6) near perfect.

The LovePower *Positive Agreement* was scored as the number of times that both partners rated themselves as satisfied, well satisfied, or near perfect. The LovePower *Negative Agreement* was scored as the number of times both partners reported having some concerns, serious concerns, or major changes needed. *Disagreement* was scored as the number of times one partner rated self in the 4 to 6 range (positive) and the other partner rated self in the 1 to 3 range (negative).

The videotape procedure was modeled after the procedure used by Gottman and his associates (e.g., Gottman, 1994). From a list of 15 topics that are sometimes problems or conflict areas for couples, the couple identified one issue that they were willing to discuss in a 10-minute videotape period. The items on the observer rating form were based primarily on major dimensions of interaction that Gottman (1994) identified, arranged in semantic differential and Likert-type rating formats.

All of the observer ratings of the couples' video vignette correlated positively with the ENRICH PCA score with a range of .62 to .51. All of the observer ratings of the couples' video vignette correlated negatively with the ENRICH SPF score with a range of .67 to .57. There was a correlation of .82 between the LovePower Positive Agreement score and the ENRICH PCA score, and .88 between the LovePower Negative Agreement score and the ENRICH SPF score.

As expected, the correlation between the LovePower Positive Agreement score and the Negative Agreement score was $-.92$. The correlations among the eight semantic differential scales ranged between .87 and .98. Correlations among the seven LovePower scales for males ranged from .16 to .89, and for females from .27 to .92.

This study indicates that external raters are able to identify the level of functioning of couples from a brief five- to seven-minute videotape observation. These ratings are significantly related to the partners' own views of their marital quality and to the agreement between partners on this quality.

The high correlations among the videotape ratings suggest that the many possible refined distinctions among specific qualities of individual and couple functioning seem secondary to the overall rating of marital quality or happiness. The overall rating of couple happiness includes nearly all of the variance available.

This suggests that in brief screening settings a very few variables will be just as effective as many additional shades of quality. Therapists can base interventions and coaching on the videotape data with confidence, especially if the partners desire to learn more about possible improvements in their interactions.

Careful reading of the items in both LovePower and ENRICH instruments emphasizes the values for marriage that are contained in these and other instruments. Differences in the amounts and levels of structure seem to be unrelated to marital quality as long as both partners perceive the structure as caring and nurturing.

Transitions

Transitions are to be expected across life (Carter & McGoldrick, 1980; Levinson, 1978). Persons in transition tend to focus more on inner changes and turmoil, leaving less attention to interpersonal concerns (Cantor et al., 1987). Olson (1990) found that couples in transition experience more overall marital dissatisfaction than stable couples. Transitions experienced by either partner produce stress in both partners and lowered satisfaction and affectional expressions. Support for each other, however, enables each partner to have more confidence and less depression (Grossman, 1988; Olson, 1990). Spouses tend to be more dissatisfied with their marriages when one, especially the husband, is in a time of transition in work relationships. Olson's (1990) results suggest that measures of enrichment effects need to consider the life situation of the couple as well as the type of program.

A major challenge to marriage and to its enrichment revolves around the different functions of positive and negative impacts on persons, similar to the classic approach-avoidant behavior patterns that have been researched so thoroughly. Negatives usually indicate danger and pain of some type, thus triggering efforts to avoid the painful circumstances. The avoidance or escape is usually a precise action that separates the partners (physically or emotionally), thus stopping interaction. Conversely, positive approach behaviors not only keep the partners together but also challenge them to maintain the positive patterns indefinitely. This is more work and requires more effort in the face of whatever adaptation effects the partners may experience in their patterns (Gottman, 1994).

Coping well with transitions includes giving major attention to establishing a no-exit commitment approach to marriage (Hendrix, 1988). When both spouses are committed to making the marriage work well for each of them, then they can see transitions, unexpected events, and other changes as opportunities for growing in love and care, not as excuses to escape the marriage (Stanley et al., 1998).

Rampage (1994) conceptualizes marital intimacy as a recurrent transient state in the context of many nonintimate interactions. Achieving the experience of intimacy requires three preconditions: equality between partners, empathy for each other's experience, and a willingness to collaborate around both meaning and action. Rampage defines intimacy as being collaborative, empathic, accepting, intense, and validating of both the relationship and the self. Feminist perspectives on power, the meanings of intimacy, obstacles to marital intimacy, processes relating to intimacy, and assessing intimacy in marriage can offer ways to increase intimacy.

Karney and Bradbury (1995) have proposed an integrated theory of how marriage quality changes, based on their meta-analysis of 115 longitudinal studies representing over 45,000 marriages. They describe four major treatment theories of marriage—social exchange, behavioral, attachment, and crisis—and the advantages and limitations of each theoretical perspective. Their vulnerability-stress-adaptation model of marriage focuses on how the partners apply their adaptive processes to cope with enduring vulnerabilities and stressful events to improve marital quality, which in turn controls marital stability (continuing marriage vs. divorce or other dissolution).

CRITERIA: MARITAL STATUS AND MARITAL QUALITY

Marital outcomes involve two types of variables: marital status (married or divorced) and marital satisfaction or quality of the relationship (Gottman, 1994, pp. 88ff.). As many note in various ways, it is important to distinguish marital status and marital quality. Marital status (whether divorced or not) is related to a variety of demographic and psychological variables (usually at low levels, thus accounting for small percentages of variation). In addition, many couples may stay married in spite of greater distress, whereas other couples divorce under much less distress. Gottman (1994, p. 88ff.) proposes a cascade model for dissolution of marriage in which declines in marital satisfaction lead to separation and eventually divorce. Both logic and research suggest that the quality of the relationship does eventuate into either long-term marriage or dissolution. For enrichment to work more effectively, more information is needed about the systemic processes that lead to either wellness or distress and dissolution.

As part of his comprehensive theory of marital stability, Gottman (1994, chap. 15) uses his cascade model to explain how partners' interactions across behavioral, cognitive, affective, physiological, and other dimensions produce either wellness and stability or distress and dissolution (Babcock et al., 1993). His research shows that marital wellness and stability are related to a continuing ratio of about five positives for each negative, whereas dissolution is associated with a positive-to-negative ratio of one or less.

Gottman's "Four Horsemen of the Apocalypse" (criticism, defensiveness, contempt, and stonewalling) are examples of negatives that eventually drive partners apart. The parallel task is to understand how continuing positive interactions can be maintained and enhanced. On the basis of the systems work of Roland Fivaz, Gottman (1994, chap. 15) proposes a set of conjugate variables (separate types of variables that work together, such as position and momentum) that can account for marital outcomes. Gottman proposes three sets of variables that affect stability of the marriage. Flow or process variables, such as the ratio of positives to negatives, are the moment-to-moment evaluations of interactions that each partner continually makes about current happenings. Well-being or wellness variables form the context in which each partner judges whether the relationship is, in more general terms, either good or bad. The third set of variables includes physiological processes that link cognition, affect, and actions.

Gottman suggests that when each person's indicators of pain and danger cross a certain threshold from positive to negative, that person experiences flooding or being overwhelmed by a sense of distress and non-well-being. This context for evaluating the relationship seems to be related to the person's internal standard for wellness that has developed out of a combination of past experiences in childhood and expectations that each partner has for the marriage.

Several ME programs implicitly incorporate aspects of Gottman's comprehensive model. Process variables, such as the match between the speaker's intent and how that speaker's actions affect the listener, are emphasized in various communication exercises (Guerney, 1977; Hendrix, 1988; Markman et al., 1984; Miller et al., 1991). Well-being variables are represented in the attention that these programs give to commitment to work on the relationship. Nonverbal and physiological variables receive specific attention in the Imago (Hendrix, 1988, 1992) and PAIRS (Gordon, 1988) approaches to marriage and enrichment. These programs include specific ways that couples can measure themselves along many of these variables.

It may be that focusing on issues that couples consider to be most urgent can enable the application of interventions that specifically address the couple's concerns. For example, on the basis of the results from PREPARE, a premarital inventory, Lavee and Olson (1993) identified seven types of couples: devitalized, financially focused, conflicted, traditional, balanced, harmonious, and vitalized. Gottman (1994) describes three types of stable couples (conflict minimizing, volatile, and validating) and two types of unstable hostile couples (defensive engaged and defensive detached).

Precise measurement of key dimensions of a couple's functioning can guide leaders and couples to use appropriate treatments that are validated and standardized, such as those provided in most enrichment programs. This might facilitate matching treatments to couples' needs (Oliver et al., 1993; Worthington, 1992).

However, the commonality in the variety of well-functioning couples suggests that there are common dimensions that underlie changes.

The problem of selecting outcome measures for marital enrichment programs originally came from two sources. First, almost all early psychological outcome research was done with therapy programs in clinical settings, and therefore the outcome measures that were used for ME measurements focused on elimination of symptoms or problematic interactions. The emphasis of ME programs, however, is on improving and enhancing the relationships of nonclinical couples. Effective research on the outcome of ME experiences and skill improvement depend partially on the development of measures that can assess improvements in couples' growth from the adequate (or less than adequate) to the more-than-satisfactory level.

The second source of this measurement problem is the tendency of many to describe the goals of ME in such a global and undifferentiated manner that it is difficult to specify the types of changes that are expected or to make an operational definition of the changes desired. A researcher is in a very difficult position to demonstrate through quantitative measures that a couple has, for example, increased the creative potential for their relationship.

Finally, researchers must recognize and accept that the difficulty of assessing the outcome of ME is due not only to the program developers' failures at operationalizing goals but also to the researchers' failures to design and validate appropriate outcome measures. In particular, measures of marital and individual health and adjustment, as opposed to pathology and maladjustment, need to be developed.

The difficulty of designing the research, however, is only one factor contributing to the scarcity of research on ME. Another major factor is that leaders and programs are usually market driven. Many leaders, well aware of research, then use their best judgment in designing a program that will be attractive to couples. Most leaders have more to do in an event than time permits, and so, every minute of most programs already is utilized. The cost and energy required to publicize and present the best possible program leaves few resources for putting equivalent money and effort into an alternative control-group program that leaders already view as inferior. A waiting-list control group that receives equivalent treatment later often is not easily done unless registrations for a specific event are more than can be accommodated. In addition, it is easy for the positive enthusiasm that most participants express when they conclude an event to further reduce the motivation of leaders to do solid research on their own programs. These elements leave little incentive to leaders to allow time for research evaluation.

These factors need not stand in the way of conducting research on ME. Program leaders with a commitment to empirical validation of their techniques can open their programs to study by researchers. This has been done most clearly by leaders in the PREP, Interpersonal Communication, Relationship Enhancement, PAIRS, Imago Relationship, and PREPARE/ENRICH Growing Together programs. However, those not trained in experimental methods of research understandably may view research as unnecessary, mysterious, or not worth the effort.

The scrutinizing, measuring, and quantifying involved in research does not violate the psychoeducational wellness emphasis of ME. Rather, it expresses the openness to demonstrating the truthfulness and accuracy of legitimate claims for the efficacy of a given program or methodology and reflects the researcher's concern for the whole person and the whole relationship. Accurate communication about needs and perceptions can enable researchers and leaders to cooperate to benefit participants, both current and future, in support of the hard work of ME program development.

Researchers need to be attuned to possible fears and misconceptions about their research in order to be permitted to conduct extensive research on the variety of ME programs. Researchers and leaders need to stress the positive benefit that can result from research that seeks to validate, refine, and better understand the process and outcome of ME. Although a scientific skepticism toward the enthusiastic claims of ME leaders and participants is necessary, the researcher can utilize these claims in researchable hypotheses, not treat claims with hostility or derision. The appropriate scientific attitude is one of neutrality.

To evaluate the outcome at ME programs, researchers must identify and evaluate components of the programs, distinguishing between independent quantifiable observations and the more subjective self-reports. Leaders of ME programs need to know and understand that these actions are based on the nature of the experimental method and do not reflect a rejection on the part of the researchers of either the importance of seeing the program as an integrated whole or the importance of the subjective responses of the participants. Participants' and leaders' subjective responses to program elements can be useful, but they are not sufficient for the demonstration of the effectiveness of ME programs. Good science requires that the outcome of a ME experience be publicly verifiable and replicable and therefore measurable. Thus, creators and leaders of ME programs need to be much more specific and concrete in describing the types of individual and relationship changes that they are trying to produce.

It is only through careful empirical research with appropriate controls and assessment of outcome with reliable and valid measurement techniques that we can learn whether ME programs achieve their stated goals. The participants and leaders of any educational or therapeutic change process cannot know whether changes in their subjective feeling states, perceptions, attitudes, or behaviors are a consequence of the specific technique employed or of nonspecific effects of participation (e.g., expectancy factors, contact with a therapist or leader, contact with other participants' suggestion or demand factors). Nor can those involved in a change process know with any certainty to what extent similar changes might have occurred simply with the passage of time.

PREEVENT TO POSTEVENT CHANGES

Kerschner (1996) analyzed preevent to postevent changes reported by 240 males and 242 females in the study described in chapter 9 (this volume). The primary objective of the study was to create a brief instrument that can tap the primary dimensions of change in couples. He found four major factors that accounted for reported changes: commitment, postevent attitude, communication, and understanding of life experience. The commitment dimension consisted of items from Stanley's (1986) personal dedication to the relationship scale. The postevent attitude factor included changes in reported satisfaction with oneself and one's partner, improved sensitivity and warmth toward one's partner, and perceived improvements in communication skills. The communication factor included perceiving oneself as becoming a better listener, expressing feelings more accurately and appropriately, and perceiving one's partner as also seeing these improvements. The understanding of life factor was composed of items that acknowledged greater awareness of how past experiences affect one's current relationship.

In the Kerschner (1996) study, the single item rating of overall happiness (Goodwin, 1992) was positively related to expressions of love, care, empathy, and understanding between partners (factor loadings of .61 to .78). Lower overall happiness was highly related to thinking more specifically about divorce.

In a related study of 133 couples who attended one of the Imago "Getting the Love You Want" weekend ME workshop, Emerson (1993) found that couples reported increased satisfaction with their marriages both at postevent and three months later. The increase in marital satisfaction from preevent to postevent continued level at the follow-up, suggesting that the increase in satisfaction was maintained. Positive communication also increased at postevent and continued high at follow-up. Commitment initially increased from preevent to postevent, but at follow-up seemed to decrease approximately to preevent levels. Insight into how past experiences affect current relationships also increased. Conflict between partners had decreased at the three-month follow-up. Overall the pattern of increase from preevent to postevent in marital satisfaction, communication, insight, and commitment is typical of enrichment events.

At three months postevent the pattern of change either continues level or begins to drop, which emphasizes again the need for booster sessions and other continuing support for maintaining improvements that begin in the enrichment event.

Hogan (1993) summarizes some common measurement problems in relation to ME. Among these are participants' skewing of rating in the positive direction which, when combined with low ceilings on items, prevent respondents from showing improvement. In addition, participants tend to hide experiences of dissatisfaction when they anticipate needing the specified services again (Lebow, 1983a; Rossi & Freeman, 1989). Hogan also found a tendency for respondents to say that everything is important (47% of 268 respondents) rather than identify components they consider unimportant.

IMPROVING MARITAL ENRICHMENT EFFECTIVENESS MEASURES

Out of the research on measuring outcomes of ME, we can summarize several suggestions for improving the examination and measurement of enrichment effectiveness.

1. For questionnaires of any type,
   a. Use items that directly measure specific components of the event.
   b. Provide a sufficient range of responses, such as a five- or six-point scale.
   c. Consistently use brief scales with known reliabilities and validities.
   d. Use items that have demonstrated sensitivity to changes that are specifically expected from the event.
   e. Distinguish between measures of individual functioning and measures of couple functioning.
2. For interaction between measurement and the program itself,
   a. Build evaluation into every workshop event at the beginning and at the end to allow for preevent to postevent changes.
   b. Use preevent measures that encourage couples to describe the levels of specific skills they have and changes they want to achieve in the workshop, and then, at postevent, couples can evaluate how much change they have accomplished.
3. For follow-up,
   a. Obtain periodic assessment through the use of a brief scale that participants can complete by telephone, e-mail, or in booster sessions as part of follow-up to events.
   b. Use observational measures for both evaluation of the program and feedback to the participants.
4. For research,
   a. Begin research conceptualization by using meta-analyses of studies, such as Giblin (1986) has done, to link proposed research hypotheses and

measures to what has already been done. This was often done in the studies described in these chapters.

b. Give more attention to determining the effectiveness of specific techniques, procedures, and formats for clearly defined populations. For example, Noval et al. (1996) studied ME among church populations. Using Halter's Traits of a Happy Couple program, they found in six groups of couples (total $N = 290$ couples) that the DAS scores increased from preevent (mean $= 102.6$) to postevent (mean $= 119.8$), an overall increase of 17% for effect sizes of 0.97 to 1.20, about twice the average effect sizes that Giblin (1986) found.

c. Perform more studies that attempt to examine cause-effect relationships. For example, Combs et al. (1994) seem to have identified participation in a religious group (church congregation) as a causative factor in achieving greater gains through ME experiences.

d. Perform studies that investigate how intrapersonal and interpersonal processes are related. For example, Lopez (1993) examined how cognitive processes mediate the nature of relationship functioning and relationship satisfaction by activating attention, constraining observational and perceptual processes, and evoking attribution-consistent behavioral and affective responses from both partners. He found that both distressed and nondistressed couples have biased cognitive processes, yet they differ in the ways they focus their attention and attributions.

On the basis of these examinations of change and outcome measures, in chapter 9 we consider research on important factors that make ME events effective.

Chapter 9

Essential Elements for Enrichment Changes in Couples

Various research studies have identified couple commitment, program structure, leader qualities, homework, and involvement in therapy as important factors in effecting change in couples who participate in ME experiences.

OVERVIEW OF MARRIAGE ENRICHMENT TEAM RESEARCH DESIGN

Based on the work of Hof and Miller (1981), Giblin (1986), and Zimpfer (1988), a program of research on marriage assessment and enrichment was begun in 1989 by Hunt and his students at the Graduate School of Psychology of Fuller Theological Seminary. Two research teams have focused on interrelationships between measures of personality, communication skills, marriage quality, and ratings of videotaped vignettes of couple interaction. A third research team has focused on assessing the affect of ME on couple functioning.

The ME research team used a correlational research design with self-report questionnaires from a convenience sampling of couples who participated in ME programs in the United States during the years 1992–1993. Selection of programs was based on overviews of ME by Giblin, Sprenkle, and Sheehan (1985), Hof and Miller (1981), Diskin (1986), Guerney and Maxsom (1990), and Zimpfer (1988). The programs represented a broad spectrum of structure, content, duration, size, religious affiliation, setting, format, and use of leaders.

Names and addresses of directors of well-known ME programs were obtained from Diskin's (1986) article (see Cox, 1995, pp. 7–8; White, 1995, pp. 33–44).

Sarah A. Cox, Ron Kruel, Geraldine T. White, Nancy M. Anderson, Catherine A. Hart Weber, and Johan P. Verseveldt, School of Psychology, Fuller Seminary, contributed extensively to the preparation of this chapter.

The research team either called or wrote to these directors and to other ME leaders requesting their cooperation in this research. The following programs and leaders cooperated in this national research study: Don Dinkmeyer, TIME; Lori Gordon, PAIRS; David Olson and M. Schaefer, Growing Together; Harville Hendrix, Getting the Love You Want; Bernard Guerney, Relationship Enhancement; Howard Markman and Scott Stanley, the Prevention and Relationship Enhancement Program (PREP); Sherod Miller, Couples Communication Programs (CCP); and leaders of the Association of Couples for Marriage Enrichment (ACME), founded by David and Vera Mace.

Three questionnaires were designed for this study. The preevent questionnaire was completed at the beginning of the ME event. On this instrument participants provided information about demographics, relationship quality, communication skills, ME homework use, changes in their relationship, types of marriage therapy received, and commitment to their relationship. Each partner independently completed a questionnaire, placed it in an envelope, and sealed the envelope to ensure confidentiality.

The postevent questionnaire was answered by participants at the end of the ME event. This instrument repeated the preevent sections on relationship quality, changes, and communication, and also asked about topics and activities included in the ME event, program structure, practice outside the ME event, and other responses to the ME event. Again, each partner independently completed a questionnaire, placed it in an envelope, and sealed the envelope to ensure confidentiality.

The follow-up questionnaire was mailed to participants three months after the ME event was completed. As an incentive and an expression of appreciation for participants' involvement in the research effort, the Research Team offered a prize drawing of $500 and $300 for those who completed all three questionnaires.

Copies of these three questionnaires are available in dissertations by Anderson (1994), Cox (1995), Hart-Weber (1995), Verseveldt (1993), and White (1995).

Approximately 600 questionnaires were sent to leaders in these programs, who distributed them to participants in their programs. Of these, 534 participants (267 couples) completed the preevent questionnaire, and 478 completed the postevent questionnaire. A much smaller number completed the follow-up questionnaire.

The demographics of the sample revealed that the majority were currently married (74%) or engaged (13%). The range of years married was 0–37, with 10.6 years the average. Participants were well educated, with 53% having obtained a college degree and 46% having some type of graduate school or professional degree. Slightly less than 50% of the men in the sample earned less than $50,000 annually. Range of income for men was $30,000–$49,000 (24%), $50,000–$74,000 (22%), $75,000 or more (32%); and for women, $30,000–$49,000 (21%), $50,000–$74,000 (12%), $75,000 or more (12%).

Occupations of the male participants included executive/manager (25%), teacher/minister/therapist/professor (14%), physician/attorney/scientist (14%), and homemaker (14%). Occupations of female participants included executive/ manager (15%), teacher/minister/therapist/professor (22%), and homemaker (32%). Occupations represented included bankers, lawyers, accountants, attorneys, nurses, teachers, and skilled tradespersons/technicians. The majority were Caucasian (91%) with the remainder being African American, Asian American, and Hispanic. The majority (71%) had some type of religious affiliation.

The religious preference for men was Protestant (16%), Catholic (14%), other Christian (29%), Jewish (7%); and for women, Protestant (13%), Catholic (15%), other Christian (34%), Jewish (5%). Educational attainment of men included some college/technical education (15%), college degree (28%), graduate/professional (46%), and for women, some college/technical education (24%), college degree (32%), graduate/professional (30%).

Two major essential dimensions of ME are the participating couples and the structure of the event. Research results on these two dimensions are described here. Additional results from this research are reported in chapter 11 on ethnic minority couples.

COUPLE COMMITMENT

Cox (1995) explored commitment in relation to couple satisfaction. Mace and Mace (1982) emphasized that a couple's relationship succeeds or fails depending on the couple's coping system. This coping system is based on three essentials: a joint commitment to ongoing growth in the relationship, an effectively functioning communication system, and the necessary skills to use conflict creatively as raw material for growth.

Similarly to commitment, Conner (1988) described his use of the concept of "permanent love" in a four-month marriage counseling program. Fourteen couples participated in eight sessions in which they considered issues such as the marriage covenant, what a couple can do together, what individuals can do on their own, possible assignments, and making mutual compromises.

Deepening the definition, L'Abate and Rupp (1981) added that ME programs not only encompass these elements but have the additional objective of managing motivations. Among these are clearer communication of one's motives to others; self-determination and commitment; improved functional attitudes toward others (being less rigid and more flexible, taking greater responsibility for interpersonal outcomes); and interdependent behavior (improved interpersonal confidence, competence, cooperation, and leadership).

ME programs give couples the opportunity to define the nature of their commitment to one another, to determine the purpose of their relationship, and to develop the skills, knowledge, and attitudes that are needed to accomplish those purposes (Garland, 1983).

Commitment is a broad dimension that includes the willingness of each partner to work together as a couple, to envision short-term and long-term goals, and to participate in efforts that may bring positive changes and improvements in their relationship. Commitment is the fundamental basis for two persons being identified as a couple. It is the foundation for motivation to learn communication and conflict-resolution skills, behavior exchanges, affection and sexual activities, joint activities, bank accounts, sharing of property and space, and the many other aspects of marriage and other marriage-like relationships.

The level of commitment of partners and their couple happiness and satisfaction constantly interact. Commitment is the partners' decisions and intentions to act in certain ways, and happiness is their judgment of how well the results of their actions match the expectancies they have about their relationship.

Kruel (1995) presented six written scenarios of adverse marital situations to 948 adults (86% Catholic, 12% Protestant) in 15 Roman Catholic churches across the United States. The results showed that the greater the degree that one holds marital commitment to be permanent, the less likelihood that one will choose divorce when facing adverse situations (for $N = 948$, $r = -.61$ across the six scenarios) and the lower one's acceptance of reasons for ending a marriage ($r = -.53$). Commitment includes staying with one's partner in difficult situations. Hendrix (1988) describes this as closing all exits from the marriage in order to grow and learn how to make the relationship work well.

Cox (1995), following Stanley (1986), defined commitment as the desire (as evidenced by associated behaviors) of an individual to maintain or improve the quality of his or her relationship for the joint benefit of the couple and the individual benefit of the participant. Personal dedication is evidenced by an intrinsic desire not only to continue in the relationship but also to work on it, to improve it, to sacrifice for it, to invest in it, to link personal goals to it, and to seek the partner's welfare, not simply one's own.

Similar definitions of commitment as choice, determination, transcendence of alternatives, permanency, and exclusivity are presented by Beach and Broderick (1983), Dean and Spanier (1974), Leik and Leik (1977), Murstein and MacDonald (1983). Adams and Sprenkle (1990) add moral commitment, and Rusbult and Drigotas (1992) emphasize investment. Gorsuch (1989) emphasizes conviction. Stanley (1986) divides commitment into personal (free choice, intrinsic, positive) and constraint (boundaries, externally influenced, limited). More recently, he has emphasized personal commitment (Stanley and Markman, 1992). Johnson (1982, 1991) contrasts personal and structural commitment and notes that definitions of commitment may encourage partners to consider their relationship as conditional and temporary in contrast to unconditional and permanent.

Using the Personal Dedication Commitment (PDC) scale of Stanley (1986) and measures of couple happiness, several associations between commitment and couple functioning were empirically verified using 267 couples (Cox, 1995, pp. 36ff.):

1. A smaller difference between couples' preevent commitment is related to higher happiness at postevent ($r = -.44$, $p < .001$; partial $r = -.18$, $p < .05$ with the influence of preevent happiness removed).
2. Higher personal dedication and commitment scores at preevent is associated with higher postevent couple happiness ($r = .66$, $p < .001$; partial $r = .23$, $p < .001$, with the influence of preevent happiness removed).
3. Higher levels of preevent happiness are negatively associated with the postevent measure of dedication commitment ($r = .32$, $p < .001$), probably due to a ceiling effect in commitment changes.
4. When the preevent level of commitment is added to the preevent difference in commitment, the multiple correlation between these two variables and postevent happiness was $R = .66$, $p < .001$.
5. Hypothesized relationships between couple religious involvement and happiness were not found, perhaps because most of the couples were involved in some type of religious group (overlapping categories of approximately 57% Protestant, 14% Catholic, 23% Christian, 2% Quaker, 7% Jewish, and 20% of women and 25% of men reporting "none") and because of the general/global nature of the religious measure (whether each partner reported a religious preference).
6. The level of couples' commitment increases from preevent to postevent, with couples entering with lower commitment increasing more. This may be due partly to ceiling effects because the measurement procedure has less room for couples whose commitment level is already high to increase further, whereas there is more room for increase in commitment among couples who are below the median at preevent.
7. Skill practice seems to be unrelated to changes in couples' commitment. This may be due to the lag time between learning or improving skills, seeing the effects of these changes, and then incorporating these influences into the overall commitment levels. This could be an example of different levels of observations, with skills being more at a microlevel and commitment being at a macro- or global level.

Participants who had higher commitment to their relationship when they began their enrichment event were more likely to show improved relationship changes at the three-month follow-up ($r = .73$ males, .78 females, $N = 82$ couples). Higher commitment to the relationship is positively related to greater change at the three-month follow-up. Males with higher dedication to the relationship participated in premarital preparation (either PREP or Pre-Cana) whereas males with lower dedication did not (Renick et al., 1992). Commitment and openness to growth is probably a central component in the couple's receptiveness to preventive interventions (Floyd et al., 1995).

These results show that both congruence and level of commitment are related to couple happiness. High commitment probably leads to greater motivation and willingness of both partners to participate in ME activities, yet may be less noticeable than with couples who begin with either lower commitment or with larger discrepancies in commitment between partners. Because commitment probably results from experience with each other in the marriage, thus being translated by them into a happiness or satisfaction judgment, ME programs must address the interaction between commitment and happiness in relation to specific skills and activities of the event.

PROGRAM STRUCTURE

White (1995) explored the structure of ME programs in relation to couple satisfaction. Empirical studies of ME programs suggest that these programs are becoming more carefully structured in the ways that leaders plan and organize the activities, specific skills that are taught and practiced, and in the offering of psychosocial skills that are needed to strengthen marriages.

Although Mace and Mace (1986) originally envisioned ME for couples with satisfying marriages, growing numbers of couples who are more distressed also participate in ME programs in order to learn relationship skills that can change their marriages into more satisfying relationships (Giblin et al., 1985; Guerney, 1977; Powell & Wampler, 1982).

L'Abate and Rupp (1981) note that enrichment's major empirical and technological underpinnings are in the fields of programmed instruction and the social-skills-training movement. By structure, they mean that the program is prearranged and preprogrammed with time-limited sequences of lessons, skills practice, and interaction. Structure is directed toward interpersonal relationships and improvements in dealing with significant others either at home or at work. Across the years, the programs that have emerged as most successful in helping to bring about couples' changes and increased satisfaction are those that have more carefully structured skill practice (Giblin et al., 1985).

Carefully structured conditions help to minimize the fears and anxieties of distressed couples and modulate the reactivity of couples to allow for more positive behavioral experiences (L'Abate & Rupp, 1981). Hof and Miller (1981) noted in their review that the greater the amount of relationship dysfunction, the greater the need for a higher degree of structure, a limited and well-focused agenda, highly skilled and active leadership, conjoint crisis intervention procedures, and structural miniprograms to deal with emerging issues tangential to the enrichment process. Clear, caring structure and control gives couples a greater sense of safety and reduces anxiety (Whitaker & Bumberry, 1988; White, 1995).

Instrumental leaders who were highly active, directive, and calming while being instructive received the highest ratings in Thomas and Tartell's (1991) study of anxious new workers (Thomas & Tartell, 1991). Rohde and Stockton (1994) showed that the lack of structure in the early stages of a group event feeds client distortions, interpersonal fears, and subjective distress. This is more likely to occur for more distressed couples than couples with more satisfying relationships.

Compared to more satisfied couples, distressed couples exchange fewer rewarding (positive) exchanges and more punishing (negative) exchanges, are more reactive to immediate reactions from the partner, are more likely to reciprocate the partner's use of negatives, attend more to negative behaviors, and have higher autonomic arousal during conflict discussions, which causes them to avoid working through conflict (Birchler et al., 1975; Gottman, 1994; Gottman & Levinson, 1985; Jacobson & Margolin, 1979; Margolin & Wampold, 1981).

Compared to higher functioning couples, distressed couples are more likely to feel anxious and uncertain in group ME situations. When the program has clear and flexible structure, warm support, and teaches specific communication and other couple skills, distressed couples are much more likely to make positive changes and benefit from the experience. In addition to providing for skill development, clear group structure assures couples that they can control their relationship. This occurs through the sharing of couples' experiences among couples and through the leaders' providing clear models and giving specific feedback and support to couples.

Clear structure helps couples to cope better with the three major themes that produce distress—alienation, authoritarianism, and inequity (Mirowsky & Ross, 1986). ME programs are especially able to address these themes. Guerney, Brock, and Coufal (1986) state that Relationship Enhancement promotes egalitarianism, closer interpersonal relationships, and an improved ability to communicate personal feelings, thoughts, and wants. These are also the areas that PREP, CCP, PAIRS, Celebrating Marriage, and other enrichment programs address (White, 1995).

White (1995) adapted from Giblin et al. (1985) the items related to structure of ME programs. These nine items contained information about whether the program provided a manual, detailed instructions or descriptions before each exercise, time for practicing skills, handouts, assignments to practice skills outside the sessions, follow-up to check on results of homework, active involvement by the leader(s), and presentations by the leader(s).

White (1995) used a distress index based on the Conflict Tactics Scale (Straus, 1979) and a scale based on the Circumplex model (Olson et al., 1983) that measured cohesion and adaptability. Using this distress index, White found that the more distressed couples are, the more important structure is to them ($r = .25$, $p < .01$, $N = 90$ couples in which both husband and wife reported). When wives and husbands were analyzed separately, this effect held for wives ($r = .34$, $p < .01$, $N = 125$ wives) but not for husbands ($r = .11$, $p < .21$, $N = 131$ husbands).

The higher the level of distress, the more important for wives is the provision of a seminar handbook ($r = .33$, $p < .001$, $N = 90$ wives; $r = .18$, $p < .05$, $N = 90$ husbands), time for practicing in session ($r = .22$, $p < .03$, $N = 90$ wives), and handouts or worksheets ($r = .23$, $p < .03$, $N = 90$ wives). It also was found that, for the most distressed couples, their ratings of the importance of structure correlated positively with changes in their marital satisfaction during the enrichment event ($r = .25$, $p < .05$, $N = 58$ couples).

Both partners of distressed and nondistressed couples gave high ratings to the importance of all seven of the structure items (White, 1995, p. 84). On a Likert scale of 1 to 5, average ratings ranged from 4.20 to 4.89. Thus, in the context of all couples reporting that clear structure and detailed aids are important, distressed couples are more likely to consider this important, and wives more than husbands consider structure to be important. For all couples analyzed, both husbands and wives showed increases from preevent to postevent on the seven-point marital satisfaction scale (3.87 to 4.23, $t = 4.08$, $p < .001$, $N = 101$ husbands; 3.49 to 4.49, $t = 8.75$, $p < .001$, $N = 101$ wives). This extends Giblin's (1986) finding that more highly structured programs tend to have a more positive effect on participant outcomes. This may be understated because most programs are very structured; less structured programs either are not offered or have not been researched.

HOMEWORK IN MARITAL ENRICHMENT

Homework in ME is very important (Anderson, 1994). Guerney and Maxson (1990, p. 1127) define marital and family enrichment as psychoeducational programs designed to "strengthen couples or families so as to promote a high level of present and future family harmony and strength, and hence the long term psychological, emotional, and social well-being of family members." Among the advantages of these programs are their structure and program organization, which make them replicable, economical, and potentially available to a wide segment of the general public. ME programs are therapeutic in attempting to prevent future problems by providing education and enrichment to empower people to solve their own difficulties and use their own resources, and in teaching skills to replace learning deficits. Enrichment comes through developing and building on participants' strengths (Garland, 1983).

Following an educational model, these enrichment programs teach communication skills, conflict negotiation, and decision making. These programs seek to help couples to enhance their relationship by developing their abilities to initiate changes in their relationship through improved interpersonal skills, communication, negotiation, problem solving, and building empathic respect and affirmation (Diskin, 1986; Worthington et al., 1989).

Because some persons have negative associations with the word homework, some programs substitute other terms such as home assignments (Guerney in Relationship Enhancement), between-session practice (Miller, CCP), and home practice. In this chapter, homework is intended to include these and other terms.

Homework in marriage therapy and enrichment contexts includes any assignment given to participants to complete outside of the session (Shelton & Ackerman, 1974). Homework provides the way to extend the practice of newly learned skills and patterns into the participants' daily life. Although little attention has been given to research on specific ME homework, most enrichment programs provide couple practice time during an enrichment event and outside of sessions.

Guerney (1977) emphasized the importance of having clearly specified time, place, and procedures in order to have a higher rate of compliance. L'Abate et al. (1986) described three basic requirements for good homework procedures:

1. Clear structure with an identifiable context of time, place, duration, and description of how participants are to conduct themselves.
2. Opportunity to practice new positive skills that have been learned initially.
3. Ability to transfer what is learned in therapy and enrichment to the home situation.

Holtzworth-Munroe and Jacobson (1991; also Holtzworth-Munroe et al., 1989) summarize studies that indicate that couples who are homework-compliant increase their skill efficacy and interactional competency. Worthington (1986) correlated homework compliance in therapy with leader's preparation of homework, timing of homework, participant's prior history of homework compliance, and leader's follow-up on homework assignments. He found that all of these factors contribute to participants' gaining skills by using homework.

Homework gives specific guidance to participants by translating new knowledge into interactions in daily life. In marriage, each stage of change requires interaction of partners in the context of an effective support system (Mace, 1986). Homework implements the stages of change that Mace and Mace (1986) describe: receiving knowledge, gaining personal insight, taking experimental action based on that insight and learning, changing attitudes, and behavioral change. L'Abate et al. (1986) note that homework affects change by providing the opportunity for participants to practice their new relationship skills daily in their natural environment. They emphasize homework as the vehicle for change in the home environment where change will be most effective. Worthington (1986) also reiterates that it is vital to assign valuable homework to couples and provide directives and support for them to make changes in the context of the home environment.

Guerney and Maxson (1990, p. 1131) showed that ME programs that emphasize practice in skills and behavior yield much better outcomes than those that do not. Guerney (1987) notes that couples need social reinforcement that extends beyond enrichment sessions, and so, homework is a systematic reinforcement of skills learned. The homework must be meaningful to the couple and reviewed by the leader in order to help the couple to be accountable and to provide feedback to the couple.

ME programs vary in the timing of assignments. Although some homework assignments are completed by participants prior to commencing the program, most assignments are to be completed between program sessions. Some leaders also assign homework at the conclusion of the program to encourage participants to maintain and increase their skill gains and efficacy over time.

Homework assignments also differ in type, length, and whether the practice partner is a spouse, relative, or friend. Most assignments consist of reading, writing, and interactional skill practice. Some programs, such as Relationship Enhancement, CCP, and PAIRS, expect couples to spend up to two hours a week on homework assignments. Assignments usually are done with one's spouse or partner. In some programs, other assignments may be done with children, friends, co-workers, relatives, or others. For example, the CCP program includes an assignment for participants to teach the CCP "communication skills mat" procedure to their children.

It is important to ensure success in homework assignments so that couples will have a sense of accomplishment and will avoid failure that leads to discouragement and loss of motivation. For example, Relationship Enhancement does not assign homework skill practice until couples show some success in the group in using the new skill (Guerney et al., 1986).

Providing both verbal and written instructions for homework assignments increases homework compliance and success (Cox et al., 1988). Providing options in homework tasks is also helpful. Leaders may provide several alternative assignments and then assist couples to choose the ones that they are most willing to do. It is important for leaders to monitor homework results to provide systematic reinforcement, answer questions, and give specific feedback on details of the practice.

Anderson (1994) found that having leaders who give reasons for homework is positively correlated with completion of worksheets by participants ($r = .65$) and with homework practice of the listening skills ($r = .50$), self-expression ($r = .40$), conflict-resolution ($r = .56$), and giving feedback to spouse or partner ($r = .51$). Having both oral and written instructions is positively correlated with conflict resolution practice ($r = .31$).

Anderson (1994) related an index of leader adequacy measures to homework compliance. The leader adequacy index consisted of asking participants how often their leader(s) gave reasons for assignments, gave oral instructions, gave written instructions, provided practice examples prior to assigning homework, gave participants choices of homework tasks, and provided review of previously assigned homework. This leader adequacy measure was positively correlated with couples practicing skills of self-expression ($r = .67$) and conflict resolution ($r = .51$).

Anderson (1994) also asked questions about possible homework assignments of writing in a journal, listening to audiotapes, audiotaping of skill practice, viewing videotapes, and maintaining some type of log or record of practice. However, the number of participants answering these questions was fewer than 25 (out of a possible 511 participants) at the three-month follow-up.

In this study, Anderson (1994, pp. 35, 91) found that homework compliance was positively associated with changes in overall ratings of change in marital satisfaction at postevent (with the influence of preevent marital satisfaction partialed out) on 5 of 11 homework measures: reading program texts ($r = .25$), conflict resolution practice ($r = .22$), doing things for self ($r = .38$), doing things for partner ($r = .46$), and doing things as a couple ($r = .34$). The percent of homework compliance also correlated positively with marital satisfaction ($r = .32$). She also found that at the three-month follow-up time, the correlation between homework compliance measures and postevent marital satisfaction, with the influence of preevent marital satisfaction partialed out, continued to be significant ($r = .28$, $p < .01$, $N = 103$).

Although there were correlations of homework compliance with leader adequacy variables and with postevent changes in marital satisfaction, there were no significant correlations between changes in marital satisfaction and leader adequacy variables.

LEADER QUALITIES FOR EFFECTIVE PROGRAMS

Marital stability and subjective marital satisfaction (Hart-Weber, 1995) are seen as determined by the relative frequency of positive-to-negative behavior exchanges between spouses (Jacobson & Holtzworth-Munroe, 1986; Stuart, 1980; Weiss et al., 1973). Gottman (1994) gives evidence for a 5:1 ratio of positive-to-negative exchanges for couples to continue being satisfied, with ratios closer to 1:1 for couples who are dissatisfied and perhaps headed for dissolution.

Guerney (1977) defines ME programs as preventive, therapeutic, and enriching. They are therapeutic in their attempt to prevent future problems by providing education and enrichment to empower persons to solve their own difficulties and to be more resourceful. They are educational in that they teach skills to make up for learning deficits. They are enriching in that they develop and build on participants' strengths (Garland, 1983) and seek to develop and encourage the use of skills needed for effective communication, problem solving, and conflict resolution.

Defining ME as psychoeducational raises many questions about the effectiveness of some types of classroom settings as vehicles for bringing about behavioral and relational changes that seem necessary for the significant improvement of family life. Mace (1981) suggested that, before information can lead to behavioral change, it must pass through a long series of complex processes. These processes are stored knowledge, personal insight, experimental action, attitudinal changes, guided practice with feedback, and behavioral changes sustained over time. It seems necessary with this model that the couple understand the skills they are learning and spend time practicing so that they can continue to use the skills correctly and effectively, finally generalizing them to other areas of their lives. Mace (1981) suggests that this process takes a year or more of practice.

Skill Practice

Couples who receive the most comprehensive skill training and time for practice in a ME program most likely will show an increase in marital satisfaction and relationship skills. Jacobson and Addis (1993) suggest that skill training that includes instructions, practice by the couple, and feedback from the therapist based on the practice sessions is necessary to promote the acquisition of new communication skills.

Enrichment is not just a process of "pumping in" something new from the outside. Rather, it is a matter of drawing out inner resources that the family members already possess, but which they have been unable to use to achieve what they really want in their shared lives (Mace & Mace, 1986). Programs need to encourage couples to create their own relationships within boundaries meaningful to them and to draw marital goals that are internally consistent and congruent with each person's value system and behavioral possibilities (Diskin, 1986).

These couples will find the program most helpful if it addresses topics and skills meaningful to them and builds on existing skills and resources. Some couples have fewer resources to begin with, and a higher score on relationship change can be expected for them. Some couples are unable to learn to use these essential skills because of personality disorders or lack of ability or motivation to make the behavioral changes that ME requires. Significant increases in any of the outcome measures for these couples is much less likely.

Discussion in Groups (Assembly Effect)

In addition to time for skill practice, each stage of change requires two people interacting while having the benefit of an effective support system (Mace, 1981). Worthington et al. (1989) found that discussion in groups improved couples' marriage satisfaction and their sexual and intellectual intimacy. Improvement was thought to be due to the group discussion heightening the couple's attention to how they use their time as a couple.

Zimpfer (1988) suggests that there is benefit from the assembly effect in ME programs that he describes as building cohesiveness and fostering the realization among participants that they are not alone in their struggles. Participants profit from the interaction between and among couples that promotes interpersonal learning, altruism, helper encouragement, and modeling.

Programs differ on whether couples interact with other couples and how much structured information is given. For example, L'Abate's (1985a) Structured Enrichment program emphasizes the leader giving information to individual couples with little interaction between couples. Some ACME programs emphasize discussion among couples with less structured information on topics (Mace & Mace, 1975).

Some programs (Guerney, 1977; Miller et al., 1976) give structured information within a group format. Couples may discuss the information as a group and as a couple and then practice by applying this information to their own situation.

Leader Variables

Guerney and Maxson (1990) recommended further research into such process variables as the interpersonal climate created by leaders (warmth, nonjudgmentalness, genuineness). Jacobson and Addis (1993) suggested that a supportive environment for accelerating positive behaviors will increase behavioral, cognitive, and affective changes. The therapist's ability to establish positive support and rapport with clients is a major factor in positive therapy outcomes (Gurman & Kniskern, 1978). This finding probably also holds for leaders of enrichment programs. A warm, understanding, caring, and genuine supportive relationship is central to leader quality (Floyd et al., 1995).

CCP leaders are not required to be married couples or even male-female couples, though they may be (Miller, Nunnally, & Wackman, 1975). The Relationship Enhancement program (Guerney, 1977) uses individual leaders of either gender as well as leader teams. The Marriage Encounter program uses only married couples working with a trained professional (a clergyman).

Because ME is considered psychoeducational, the literature on adult education and teaching can be very helpful. Cohen's (1981) meta-analysis indicates that teacher ratings are positively associated with student learning. Lowman (1984) outlined a two-dimensional model of effective teaching. Dimension 1 is the skill of creating intellectual excitement, with two important components in teaching: clarity of instructor's communications (presentation) and their positive emotional impact on the students. Dimension 2 considers interpersonal rapport and characteristics such as being warm, open, democratic, genuine, predictable, and approachable.

Of 422 respondents, persons who report that the ME program provided time for skill practice had higher scores for relationship-change skills (Hart-Weber, 1995, pp. 20–30). Participants who had an opportunity for group discussion of marriage issues and skills in couples groups or in separate male and female groups had greater improvement in skills and marital satisfaction (Hart-Weber, 1995). These results are consistent with those of Zimpfer (1988) and Worthington et al. (1989).

Of the 422 participants, 415 (98%) reported that the leader provided structured presentations. Of these 415, 357 (86%) also saw the leader as modeling the skills that were being presented. The perception of the leader as effective in giving presentations and modeling skills is correlated positively with the reporting of positive changes in relationship skills ($r = .23$, $p < .001$, $N = 422$) and higher marital satisfaction ($r = .19$, $p < .001$, $N = 422$).

Perceiving the leader as warm and genuine and as providing a supportive environment is correlated positively with improved relationship skills ($r = .27$, $p < .0001$, $N = 422$) and higher marital satisfaction ($r = .26$, $p < .0001$, $N = 422$).

These findings verify that ME programs are important in providing a safe place where couples can interact, compare notes and talk with other couples. The climate of support and encouragement allows couples to be honest, open, and to recognize that they are not alone as well as to realize that the issues they face are common to other couples. In addition, couples who have faced specific problems can share how they coped with them, providing additional models with which participants can identify and then choose how to apply these insights to themselves.

Developers and leaders of ME programs can link ME to studies of effective teaching (Cohen, 1981; McKeachie, 1994). Most programs use leaders both as participants and as models for the skills they propose to teach. The leader's enthusiasm and values have much to do with the participants' interest and performance.

COUPLES THERAPY AND MARRIAGE ENRICHMENT

From many sources (e.g., Gottman, 1994; Olson, 1990) research results are consistent in identifying poor communication and inadequate problem-solving skills as keys to the quality of marital satisfaction, interaction, and distress. In various ways, both marital therapy and ME seek to enable couples to improve these skills. The primary question is how ME and therapy can work together to benefit the participants, not whether to choose between enrichment or therapy.

In their comprehensive review of marital treatment, Jacobson and Addis (1993) discuss outcome and process research on couple treatment. In general, couples receiving marital treatments achieve significant improvements in comparison to control groups, but there are no reliable differences between different models of treatment. In addition, all treatment approaches still leave too many couples unimproved or at least still somewhat distressed. These reviewers emphasize the need for more basic research, increased prevention efforts, and consideration of the interactions between types of treatment and characteristics of couples.

The importance of coordinating therapy and ME has often been noted (Doherty & Walker, 1982; Ford et al., 1984; Giblin, 1986). Verseveldt (1993) surveyed 267 couples who had participated in some type of ME about their attitudes and experiences with therapy. Of these 267 couples, 175 men (65%) and 211 women (79%) had participated in some type of therapy prior to the ME event. Out of a follow-up sample of 82 couples, 10 additional men and 7 additional women reported that they became involved in therapy after the event. Assuming that 53–64 (65–79%) of the 82 couples who responded at follow-up had been or were in therapy, this suggests that, of couples who are not in therapy at the time of the event, some 10 to 20% will enter therapy after the event.

Among those who attend ME events, there is a positive relationship between commitment and having participated in therapy ($r = .22$ men, .25 women). Having had therapy also is associated with higher relationship changes for women ($r = .29$) and for men ($r = .23$), but the amount of therapy is unrelated to happiness, relationship changes, or commitment level (Verseveldt, 1993, pp. 108ff., 123ff.). Women's scores of relationship change were positively related to their partner being involved in therapy, and the same occurred for men's scores of relationship change in relation to their partners' involvement in therapy ($r = .19$, $p < .01$).

There is some evidence of interactive relationships between therapy and ME (Verseveldt, 1993, pp. 55, 60, 118ff.). Respondents ($N = 267$ couples) indicated that they came to the ME event for reasons similar to their reasons for going to therapy. Among reasons for attending a ME event are "to solve my own problems" (men, 52%; women, 53%), "to solve my partner's problems" (men, 47%; women, 41%), "to learn to communicate" (men, 79%; women, 88%), and "to improve our relationship" (men, 87%; women, 91%). For 25% of men and 30% of women, participation in the ME event was a follow-up to therapy, whereas 12% of men and 16% of women came instead of going to therapy.

Among reasons for going to therapy are "to increase self-awareness" (men, 68%; women, 82%), "to understand and empathize with my partner" (men, 54%; women, 57%), "to identify and affirm positive characteristics" (men, 49%; women, 62%), "to express thoughts and feelings to partner" (men, 57%; women, 61%), "to develop communication skills" (men, 55%; women, 59%), and "to develop problem solving and conflict resolution skills" (men, 47%; women, 51%) (Verseveldt, 1993).

Many participants state that therapy has helped them to accomplish many of the same relationship improvement goals that ME leaders have. Participants clearly see therapy and ME as mutually complementary and beneficial.

Whether persons participate in couples or individual therapy seems to relate to levels of relationship commitment. Among the 39 least happy men in Verseveldt's research analyses, there was a correlation of .33 between participating in couples therapy and commitment, and a negative correlation of $-.28$ with marital satisfaction. For women, participation in individual therapy is negatively related to the female's commitment level ($r = -.44$) and satisfaction ($r = -.31$).

The negative associations between participation in individual therapy and commitment and the positive association between couples therapy and commitment suggest that the commitment levels of each partner to the relationship may be the key factor in decisions about individual vs. couples therapy. Less committed persons may use individual therapy both to address personal concerns and as a way to gain strength to exit an unhappy marriage, whereas more committed partners may see therapy as a way to improve the relationship because they want to stay in an improved marriage.

The negative correlations between satisfaction with the marriage and participation in marital or individual therapy suggest the rather commonsensical principle that partners seek therapy because they are hurting in some way. ME programs may support couples in recognizing that marital distress can be addressed both in the enrichment event and in therapy, just as the effectiveness of individual or couple therapy can be increased by patients' participation in ME. This is also demonstrated by the integrated programs of therapy and enrichment that are becoming available (e.g., Luquet, 1996).

Research on ME seeks to identify and understand the active ingredients of marriage quality, satisfaction, and effectiveness and how these interact with family and other systems. Chapter 7 examined the factors that make ME beneficial to couples. Chapter 8 then considered ways to measure and evaluate program quality. On the basis of these research findings, this chapter has considered interactions between theory, research, and applications along the major dimensions of couple commitment, program structure, leader qualities, use of homework, and interactions between therapy and ME.

ME principles, programs, and research offer theoretical and empirical support for ME effectiveness. We now turn to ways that professionals and couples can apply this knowledge in practical situations.

PART FOUR

STRENGTHENING MARRIAGES: TREATMENT, ENRICHMENT, MENTORING, AND OUTREACH

The four chapters in part 4 describe ways that professionals and couples can take action at primary, secondary, and tertiary outreach to strengthen marriages and families. Although enrichment is certainly preventive in the sense of enabling couples to avoid distress, dysfunctions, and divorce (the "3D" dangers of marriage), we prefer to focus on ways to enable and support positive wellness and well-being of couples and families.

In chapter 10, we refocus on couple treatment by considering how enrichment and therapy are interrelated. Marriage enrichment (ME) and marital therapy ad dress both the individual and the couple levels of intervention. No longer is it a question of therapy or enrichment, but rather the twin questions of how ME strengthens clinical treatments, including individual, couple, family, and group, and how clinical treatments can be more accessible to participants in ME events.

Chapter 11 considers issues in leading and providing ME events to all types of couples, with special attention to ethnic minority couples.

Chapter 12 describes the rapidly emerging couple-to-couple mentor and friend-ship dimensions of ME as a mobile, immediately available support and intervention outreach to couples at their points of need. The Caring Couples Network is an example of how churches, synagogues, and other religious institutions can enable couples and expert leaders to cooperate in making enrichment, mentoring, and other actions for marriage easily available in every community.

Several possibilities for outreach programs that can change the community and the national marriage climate are summarized in chapter 13. Professionals can take action themselves and can encourage others to work on changes from a variety of perspectives. In the concluding chapter, we address social context levels of marriage and family mentoring and support.

The aim of part 4 is to challenge us all to be more proactive for the well-being of couples and families by blending ME philosophy, principles, programs, and research into concerted action that enhances marriages, families, and the general welfare of communities, nations, and the world. The 21st century challenges us all to accomplish this goal.

Chapter 10

Refocusing Marriage Treatments

Conversations such as the following often occur in various ways toward the end of most ME events.

Barbara: This has been a wonderful experience. I wish our friends could have been here and participated also.

Bill: So do I, but how can we reach them? We don't want to intrude in their lives, yet sometimes we see them heading for disaster. Some don't even think much of marriage anymore.

Barbara: It's all so complicated. A couple has to cope with finances, children, jobs, their own parents, as well as try to have some time for themselves. Then when they do have time together, they blow it on television or arguments.

Bill: There are many helps, yet getting couples to be open to enrichment is difficult. So often therapy and enrichment are seen as only for really dysfunctional or crazy persons. With all the complications, if only they could see this fun-loving group, they would certainly change.

As Barbara and Bill note, marriage is both elegantly simple and unfathomably complex. As many have commented before (e.g., Breunlin et al., 1992; Glendon & Blankenhorn, 1995; Gottman, 1994; Jacobson & Addis, 1993), marriage is a far more complicated relationship than most of its participants and nonparticipants realize. Understanding marriage is not unlike the fable of blind persons seeking to understand an elephant, with each attaching a partially accurate interpretation. Added to the many views of marriage itself are the complications of designing and making available a program that can reach the needs of so many different couples.

Theory and research on ME have improved as the social sciences have studied marriage and family from many perspectives, yet much is needed. The urgency of society's problems and the successes of marriages and families encourage us to move ahead, even if it seems to be beyond what can be verified empirically.

Sensitive marriage therapists and enrichment leaders continue to do "*N* of 1" experiments as they work with individuals, couples, and families in enrichment events, clinics, and other settings.

There is not sufficient room in this volume to address in any depth the many perspectives on marriage. Others have done this well (e.g., Breunlin et al., 1992; Fincham & Bradbury, 1990; Glendon & Blankenhorn, 1995; Jacobson & Gurman, 1995, Browning et al., 1997). On the elegantly simple side, marriage involves choices about future, resources, and connections among these in order to produce a desirable balance of positives and negatives.

Some have described marriage as a lifelong journey, which suggests that marriage is one vehicle for traveling through life (e.g., Bowen, 1991; Campbell, 1981; Hendrix, 1988, 1992; Hunt & Rydman, 1979; Luquet, 1996; Whitehead & Whitehead, 1981). An extended metaphor may illustrate some basic questions that all must ask about marriage.

In their pioneering work on flight, the Wright brothers divided the problem of flight by heavier-than-air vehicles into basic components, each with its own solution. In simplest form, these components were how to have a constant source of airflow to accomplish lift, how to obtain a dependable source of power, and how to maintain control of the craft in order to reach a chosen destination. Across the decades of the 20th century, the development of human flight has produced many successes along with some disasters. Aeronautical sciences have continued to improve equipment, navigation, and flight procedures for ensuring safe travel for all types of groups. Training in flight procedures has evolved into flight simulators that can safely produce any flight conditions to train pilots and other personnel in routine and emergency actions for any type of aircraft.

The goal of equipment improvement, speciality training, and regulatory agencies is to enable those who fly safely to get to where they are going when they want to be there, with payoffs to both users and providers. Billions of dollars and centuries of person-years of effort have been and continue to be invested to achieve ever more refined variations of this overall goal. Millions of persons now invest themselves in flying, as passengers, pilots, and support personnel. With all of this, however, some persons still choose not to fly, preferring to travel by other means. Even for those who prefer to fly, other means of travel—walking, elevators, automobiles, trains, and boats—are at times necessary according to one's goals.

The aircraft metaphor illustrates three key issues for those who are concerned about marriage: the goals or purposes of marriage, the resources that can be the means to achieve the goals, and the ways that persons connect resources to goals. Addressing these three issues lays the foundation for choosing how to relate ME, therapy, and other interventions and supports for marriage and family functioning.

WHERE IS MARRIAGE GOING?

Implicit in all marriage supports and interventions, such as ME and therapy, are assumptions about the purposes of marriage. Implicit in assumptions about marriage are assumptions about the purpose of life. If marriage is a journey, then a journey to where and for whom, and when will it be completed? Answers to these types of questions express one's core being, one's choices about life. If the purpose of life is to learn how to love others unconditionally, then in what ways is marriage a laboratory for learning to love another specific person in a variety of situations and conditions?

The many possible purposes of marriage that have emerged in recent centuries (Everett, 1990) can be clustered into three general classes:

1. To socialize sexual desires and to avoid intruding on the rights of others.
2. To assign responsibility for children and socializing the next generation.
3. To provide continuing affection, support, and personal growth.

In deciding which of these purposes to emphasize, each professional also must decide on the system on which to focus. A focus on personal growth in marriage brings an emphasis on individual and couple dynamics, whereas a concern for children may place the focus more on the family or community. In deciding whether to emphasize individual, couple, or family therapy, every professional is making explicit her or his assumptions about the purposes of the couple relationship.

For example, research indicates that commitment includes two major facets: externally imposed constraints and internally chosen personal dedication (Markman et al., 1994; Stanley, 1986; Stanley & Markman, 1992). It seems likely that nearly every couple has times when one or both partners stay in the relationship primarily because of external constraints of some type. Agreeing on a "no exit" commitment (Hendrix, 1988) forms the basis for personal and marital growth, whereas refusing to agree eventually leads to dissolving the relationship. Refining commitment to identify its limits, such as physical abuse or sexually acting out, challenges both couples and therapists. Commitment also forces the questions, commitment to what, to which lifestyle, and to which goals?

The type of therapy that a professional offers expresses assumptions about marriage. A therapist who emphasizes individual therapy may be expressing assumptions that the individual's marriage relationship is less important than personal growth. When individual therapy produces positive changes, then that person will be different in his or her relationships, with impacts on marriage and family. In contrast, emphasis on couple and family therapy will include enabling each individual to consider how his or her actions affect others as well as how their actions affect him or her, placing personal growth in the context of growth and well-being of others in one's household and family.

RESOURCES FOR ACHIEVING MARRIAGE GOALS

Resources offer the means for couples, families, and society to achieve the selected goals of marriage. At the individual level, resources include the character, personality, behavioral patterns, and family background of each partner as well as money, property, and other tangibles that each person brings to the marriage. Resources also include values, education, career possibilities, family relationships, and other potentials of each person, along with the encouragement and support each offers to the other. Resources encompass communication and problem-solving skills, sexual and affection needs and skills, mental and emotional functioning or dysfunctioning, and many additional facets that the partners combine in their ongoing relationship. Among resources are the support systems that each partner has and that the couple extends through their openness to others and their willingness to support others.

In both overt and covert ways, every couple evaluates their resources according to the goals that they have for their marriage journey. One task of both therapy and enrichment is to enable the participants to identify and evaluate their resources in relation to the goals they set for their relationship.

CONNECTIONS AMONG GOALS AND RESOURCES

Choosing goals and finding resources to accomplish them is a continuing process in every relationship. Communication, problem-solving, and conflict-resolution skills have been emphasized heavily in ME and therapy theories and programs. These skills enable the partners to match resources to goals and to plan to increase or obtain additional resources that may be needed for accomplishing specific goals. How partners connect goals and resources has been a major emphasis of many ME programs (e.g., Hendrix, 1988, 1992; Markman et al., 1994; Miller et al., 1988).

There are so many elements among goals and resources and so many ways to connect them that classification systems are inadequate to describe the diversity among couples. Many marital topologies have been proposed to organize them. For example, Cuber and Harroff (1965) described five types of marriage: conflict-habituated, devitalized, passive-congenial, vital, and total. Lavee and Olson (1993) describe seven types of marriages based on ENRICH, and four types of couples based on PREPARE (Fowers & Olson, 1992). Common in these are the vitalized, harmonious, traditional, and conflicted types of couples, with devitalized added as a fifth type for married couples.

Gottman (1994) described three types of functional marriages (conflict avoiders, volatile conflict engagers, and validating conflict engagers) and two types of dysfunctional couples (hostile-defensive engaged and hostile-defensive detached). Gottman has sought to identify how types of marriages are related to marital outcomes. For Gottman, the key to healthy marriage is maximizing positive interactions and minimizing negative interactions in ways that the couple desires.

VALUES AND VALUING

Every marriage is unique in the ways that the partners combine their values, goals, and resources to produce shades of wellness and dysfunction, and then utilize feedback both from within and beyond their marriage to modify their journey. In the couple topologies of both Olson and Gottman are two fundamental couple agreements: First, that both partners know and use constructive goals and patterns; and second, that the two partners agree on these.

One criterion for good communication is the match between the intent and the effect of a message (Gottman, 1994; Markman et al., 1994; Miller et al., 1991). As applied to marriage in general, the intent (goal) is the expression of values of some type. The effect also implies some match between what the receiver desired or expected (a set of values) and the value that the listener assigns to the sender's message and intent. Each partner's values are expressed directly through the effect that each person intends to have on the other. Communication training includes enabling each person to become more aware of his or her effect on the partner (Miller et al., 1991).

Values are expressed in decisions to give priority to certain elements of a system rather than to other elements, such as focusing on communication more than family of origin, or on affect more than cognition. Decisions about the level and timing of interventions also come out of values expressed in goals and assigned to system elements, as well as when the focus on some issues or difficulties is greater than others.

These decisions involve the value systems of the couple, those around them, and the professionals who may be involved. ME and marital therapy need to make contact with the couple at the level of their own perceived needs and values in order for them to consider change. For example, preventive interventions are more effective when applied early in the couple's relationship, such as during engagement and the first years of marriage (Jacobson & Addis, 1993).

INDIVIDUAL AND COUPLE INTERVENTIONS

Bradbury and Fincham (1990, pp. 393ff.) describe three levels of interventions, as seen from the perspective of the individual: First is the individual intrapersonal level that focuses on features of each spouse as a person, including habits, personality, background, skills, and personal resources. Second is the couple or interpersonal level that considers features of interactions between spouses as partners in their marriage system. Third is the contextual or environmental level, which refers to features of the couple's life, such as conflicts between the demand of work and responsibilities at home, external situations that add stress to the couple, relationship, and other environmental factors. These three levels interact to produce the ways that each couple copes with situations and the support for the couple in coping with situations.

A systems approach to therapy assumes that individuals are always in relationship to others. Whether a therapist is working with an individual, a couple, or a family, each individual's current functioning is always in relation to the other family members, to each person's family of origin, and to other experiences that have contributed to each person's current functioning.

Following a holistic approach, many therapists now integrate marital therapy and enrichment by using an educational skill and competence model (Guerney, 1977; Guerney et al., 1986; Jacobson & Gurman, 1995; Luquet, 1996; Stuart, 1979) that teaches individuals and couples the skills they need to maintain healthy relationships. Guerney, for example, draws from psychodynamic, humanistic, learning/cognitive, and systems approaches.

Individual therapy often can be expanded to include the spouse or significant other and close family members. Several types of dysfunctions that traditionally have been seen as individual are more successfully treated when other persons in the individual's living context (or system) are brought into active involvement in the treatment. Among these are agoraphobia, panic disorders, domestic violence, sexual abuse, depression, alcoholism, substance abuse, schizophrenia, borderline conditions, affective and narcissistic disorders, eating disorders, and many disorders of children and adolescents (Jacobson & Gurman, 1986, 1995; Kaslow, 1996b).

Because there are usually two-way effects between the actions of any one member of a household and the other members of that household, involving others in treatment expands the number of facets of the individual's environment that are open to therapeutic interventions. At the marriage/couple level, this certainly argues for involvement of both partners in addressing issues that may seem to be primarily in one of them.

Oliver and Miller (1994) incorporate couple communication skills into marriage counseling. They argue that caring and skilled communication processes are prerequisites to effective problem solving, conflict resolution, and the ability to communicate affection effectively, and they apply Miller's systems-theory approach to couples communication (Miller et al., 1991) to individual couples in counseling.

An excellent example of how ME can inform couple therapy is provided by Luquet (1996), based on Hendrix's enrichment programs for couples (Hendrix, 1988) and for individuals (Hendrix, 1992). Following Hendrix's Imago Relationship Therapy model, Luquet gives therapists clear guidance in designing a 6- to 12-session treatment plan for couples. Luquet's major topics include the couples dialogue communication skill, individual development and childhood wounds, reimaging and empathy, reromanticizing the relationship, restructuring frustrations, and resolving rage. Luquet provides many helpful homework assignments and handouts that a therapist may copy and use with couples. This approach illustrates how the carefully structured work of ME is able to make couples therapy more efficient. Luquet provides clear details for each session, readings, and handouts for couple homework between sessions.

INTERVENTION INVOLVES FIVE STEPS

At each intervention level, moving from knowledge to action involves several essential steps. Mace (1981) noted several steps from information to positive change, and on the basis of the work of Cowen (1986), Bradbury and Fincham (1990, pp. 395ff.) describe the following five steps:

1. Generate a knowledge base of data concerning the causes of (a) competencies and events that relate to positive outcomes and (b) competencies and events that relate to negative outcomes or prevention of positive outcomes.
2. Identify the competencies needed for successful marriage and the circumstances that facilitate or prevent the use of these competencies in order to clarify the concepts that guide the interventions.
3. Translate the guiding concepts into specific interventions.
4. Implement the proposed interventions.
5. Assess whether the intended effect has been achieved and use this information to guide a modification of the interventions.

As many researchers (e.g., Bradbury & Fincham, 1990; Gottman, 1994) have emphasized, there is much to be learned about causes of marital wellness and dysfunction as well as the effectiveness of programs and interventions. Research in these areas must continue. However, the need for wide-scale intervention and prevention efforts is apparent at every stage of a couple's relationship. Although much is yet to be discovered and clarified, research to date suggests that there are several specific steps that practioners can take now.

THERAPY AND ENRICHMENT ACROSS THE CONTINUUM OF COUPLES

In the past, most ME programming was aimed at relatively nondysfunctional couples. Some program leaders restricted participation in ME programs to couples who were not in therapy. Increasingly, however, therapists and enrichment leaders are seeing enrichment programs and therapy as components in a more comprehensive plan of growth for couples (e.g., DeMaria, 1993; Jacobson & Addis, 1993). We now know that, with well-structured formats and trained leaders, many dysfunctional couples can benefit from the ME process.

To make hard and fast distinctions between well-functioning marriages and troubled marriages is not as helpful as approaching the question of who can benefit from which ME programs along a continuum perspective. A description of couples that is based on a continuum of functioning and wellness, ranging from excellent marital relationship function to extreme marital relationship dysfunction, is presented, and we suggest ways in which ME can benefit couples at different points along this continuum.

Early ME literature asserted that programs were designed for and were applicable to couples with a fairly well-functioning relationship who want to make it better and not for couples with serious personal difficulties or troubled relationships (Hof & Miller, 1981; Hopkins & Hopkins, 1975; Hopkins et al., 1978; Mace & Mace, 1976; Miller, Nunnally, & Wackman 1975; Otto, 1976). Programs that utilize leaders who are not clinically trained in marital therapy or counseling are not designed to cope with the potentially disruptive and destructive interactions of more seriously distressed or dysfunctional couples. However, this does not mean that troubled couples cannot or would not benefit from the programs. It only indicates that leaders with minimal training cannot manage the disruptive aspects of their interactions and that the program design is not arranged in such a way as to be able to accommodate the more dysfunctional interactions of couples who do not have a large core of personal competence and marital health on which to build.

Retrouvaille (B. Zwann & P. Zwann, personal communication, April 15, 1997) is a recent example of a program that uses well-trained lay couples to reach seriously troubled couples, working with clergy and other professionals. Probably the reasons that it can do this well is its four-step process of preevent individual interviews with potential participants, the weekend event itself, the three-month postevent follow-up, and the Continuing Our Retrouvaille Experience (CORE). As noted in chapter 5, Retrouvaille is designed for couples having trouble communicating and who realize that they are drifting apart or are already into divorce.

Couples can be placed on a continuum from primarily well-functioning relationships, with a relatively high degree of couple and individual satisfaction and relatively minor problems, to the other extreme of couples who are so severely dysfunctional that they cannot consistently moderate their interactions and thus have high potential for verbally and perhaps physically abusing each other. In the midrange are couples with seriously dysfunctional relationships, a low degree of couple and individual satisfaction, and major problems, yet who are able to control their interactions sufficiently to function adequately in group settings. These midrange couples may be referred to as subclinical. Despite their love for each other and their commitment to the marriage, they are functioning below optimum level and need help with their problems (Guerin et al., 1987; Otto, 1976). These couples may benefit more from a ME program than would the highly functional couples or the seriously disturbed couples. It is hoped that those closer to the dysfunctional end of the continuum will be able to discover their dysfunctional patterns and learn how to relate more effectively before their problems become seriously entrenched pathological symptoms (Jacobson & Addis, 1993; Wright and L'Abate, 1977). At the least, these couples might recognize that they need more help than the program can offer and thus will seek a referral to appropriate counseling or therapy (Dixon & Sciara, 1977).

With this continuum perspective, it becomes not a question of who can or cannot benefit from the ME experience, but of which particular program is best for which particular couple (Worthington, 1992). What type of structure and leadership style would best benefit this couple at their level of development?

For example, in a limited study, Neville (1971) suggests that there is a differential response among various personality types to ME group experiences, and that such groups are more familiar and complementary to some personality types than to others. He concluded that intuitive-feeling-perceptive personality types found their experience in that particular type of program (a marital encounter group) to merge with their lifestyle and were at ease with the process. Although sensing-thinking-judging personality types may have been uncomfortable with some aspects of the process, the results indicated that they responded well to the experience, perhaps because they had thoughtfully analyzed the experience, concluded it was a logical and sensible approach, and thus had committed themselves to the process.

Worthington (1992) suggests that further research on other programs might provide the means to fit an individual with a particular personality type to a particular program. They could be matched in such a way that sufficient cognitive and affective dissonance could be developed for learning and change to take place. The match also would be made in such a way that the program would not be so radically alien to the personality type of the participant as to produce so much anxiety or resistance that he or she would be prevented from accepting the experience and deriving benefit from it.

Another example develops this point further. The Marriage Encounter experience (Bosco, 1973; Demarest et al., 1977; Genovese, 1975) is an intense, highly structured, weekend experience, with the focus almost entirely upon the interaction of the partner with each other (as opposed to interaction with other couples). A specific kind of couple dialogue is practiced throughout the weekend. The leadership team makes several presentations to the total group. Then, in the privacy of their own room, each couple reflects upon what has been said and answers questions related to the presentation, recording them in a notebook. The written self-disclosure then is shared between partners in complete privacy from the others. After each has read the other's self-disclosure, each partner encourages the other to verbally develop and further describe the written feelings, in an attempt to experience each other more fully at an affective level.

Huber (1977) has attempted to evaluate the Marriage Encounter weekend experience. Although his research suffers from several shortcomings (Gurman & Kniskern, 1977), notably the limitation of relying on participant self-evaluation and the lack of long-term follow-up, his findings still may have value. Husbands in the experimental group, in contrast to husbands in the control group, were found to score significantly higher on four major Caring Relationship Inventory (Shostrom, 1967) scales: Affection, Friendship, Eros, and Empathy. Wives in the experimental group showed no significant change when compared to wives in the control group on any of the major scales. Overall positive changes lasted for at least six weeks.

Such results raise some interesting questions. For example, why are men affected in these areas, and not women? Is it possible that the high degree of structure, the rule and norm of self-disclosure, the extreme privacy, and the perception that the experience is logical and sensible (Neville, 1971) interact to provide a safe atmosphere and an environment conducive to change for certain men? Many men are culturally scripted to think logically, to work hard in a disciplined and even compulsive manner, and to be nondemonstrable and nonexpressive with their feelings (Balswick, 1988; Balswick & Peck, 1971). The Marriage Encounter experience may provide the necessary atmosphere and environment for some of the men described above to break the cultural script regarding self-disclosure and affective expression by following the rules of the Encounter experience.

A series of research studies by Gottman (1994, p. 74) indicate that negative physiological affect arousal, especially in husbands, is highly predictive of declines in marital satisfaction. Gottman's cascade model of declines in marital satisfaction (1994, p. 88f) underlies his descriptions of types of marriage in which the key variable is the ability of couples to control and regulate the ways in which they influence each other. The cascade from wellness to criticism, contempt, defensiveness, and stonewalling (1994, pp. 414–416) indicates that every couple has patterns of interaction, which each partner either respects and prefers or dislikes and rejects. When the structure of an enrichment event helps each partner in the couple to gain more control over the hurtful responses and replace them with more positive and caring responses, then men as well as women are enabled to be more caring of each other, which builds the relationship and increases the satisfaction.

DIMENSIONS OF VARIABILITY

There are many dimensions of variability among both couples and programs. As enrichment programs clarify details of the experience, implications for referral to such a program will be obvious. For example, a Marriage Encounter program might be suggested for a relatively well-functioning couple in which it was perceived that the husband (and the relationship) could benefit most directly from experiencing and expressing his feelings and other appropriate self-disclosures. The wife presumably would benefit from the increased friendship, empathy, and so forth from her partner. On the other hand, this program might not be suggested for a couple who already has the ability to share on a significantly affective level but who need to learn specific skills in areas such as conflict resolution or problem solving. Nor would this program be suggested for a couple on the more dysfunctional end of the continuum, where the need for monitoring the couple's interaction is greater than that provided for in the structure of the Marriage Encounter program. A program such as PREP, PAIRS, Getting the Love You Want, or Retrouvaille might be more helpful for addressing conflict-resolution skills.

If ME programs are effective, we need to know with more clarity which particular program, structure, and leadership style would benefit which particular couples. It is hoped that the time will come when enrichment programs can be matched to the couple's intrapersonal and interpersonal needs and socioeconomic and educational levels (Guerney, 1977; L'Abate, 1975; Worthington, 1992).

Hof and Miller (1981) concluded from their own experience and their review of many of the currently available programs (chapter 9, this volume) that the greater the amount of relationship dysfunction, the greater the need for the following:

1. A high degree of structure;
2. A limited and well-focused agenda;

3. Highly skilled and active leadership trained in marital and individual therapy and group dynamics;
4. Some conjoint crisis-intervention therapy during the experience, or branching, which is the use of structured miniprograms to deal with emerging issues tangential to the enrichment process (L'Abate, 1977);
5. Close attention to screening (Guerney, 1977; L'Abate, 1977; Liberman et al., 1976; Smith & Alexander, 1974);
6. Group size that allows leaders and couples to pace the group according to the needs of the couples and to provide sufficient coaching and feedback.

The greater the amount of relationship function in all couples involved, the less need there is for these six factors to be present in the program. This is not to imply that thoughtfully designed programs, with clear goals, specific objectives, and appropriately trained and skilled leadership are not needed at the more functional end of the continuum. They most certainly are. Nor should it imply that couples at the more functional end of the continuum could not benefit from a highly structured, limited-agenda program, with highly skilled leaders trained in marriage and individual therapy and group dynamics. These couples most certainly can. With programs developed for these couples, there is also the possibility for greater flexibility with structure, a more varied agenda, less forced and repetitive skill practice (because couples can and will practice on their own); less close monitoring of the interactions of participants; greater use of small leadership-sharing groups composed of participant couples, and a greater reliance on peer leadership, that has been appropriately prepared and trained in the design and leadership of these ME programs.

Experience among ME leaders suggests that there are advantages to having an enrichment group with couples at various points along the wellness–dysfunction continuum, with the lower limit excluding couples who are unable to function in a group setting. Higher functioning couples provide real-life models of healthier marriages as well as encourage those who are in greater distress. With these principles in mind, we turn to apply them in various settings.

Chapter 11

Leading Marriage Enrichment Events

Susan and Sam, both professionals with doctoral degrees, have been married to each other for over 20 years. As a therapist, Susan works primarily with adolescent patients with eating disorders. Sam is vice-principal of a large high school. Being well aware of the many ways that family dynamics affect adolescents, they are discussing whether and in what ways they may become more involved in ME.

Susan: Its obvious that many of the young women I see would not have such harmful patterns if their parents were functioning better in their marriage. I would like to offer an enrichment program for marriages as one way to reach parents before their marital system draws their kids into dysfunctions.

Sam: That's a great idea, but it seems like a tall order. I've often thought about that when I see some of the acting-out problems in our student body. Now that our own children are older, maybe we could organize a one-day enrichment for parents once or twice a year.

Susan: We could lead it ourselves, or maybe we could get some others to become trained as leaders. I also like the marriage enrichment weekend we attended last year.

Sam: So did I. Let's get more information about training requirements of the programs that seem to fit us best. Then we can decide the best way to proceed in our community. With our focus on adolescents, we could offer something for midlife couples.

Deciding where to be most effective with couples involves several issues. This chapter focuses on professionals leading or consulting with leaders of ME events

---

Ronald Smith and Elizabeth Koo, School of Psychology, Fuller Seminary, contributed extensively to the preparation of this section on marriage enrichment in ethnic churches.

and on examples of ME with specific populations. Based on the principles for leading ME events (chapter 4, this volume), the sample of currently available programs (chapter 5, this volume) and the examples of enrichment resources (chapter 6, this volume), some perspectives on training are offered. Further details of specific programs can be found in Berger and Hannah (1998).

L'Abate (1990) reminds us that family problems usually reach a crisis state before professionals are called in. Primary and secondary prevention strategies are effective for reaching couples and families early at their times of initial perceived needs. Practitioners need to be trained in marriage and family assessment and diagnosis, treatment techniques, and prevention methods. On the basis of this training and experience, practitioners also may consult with agencies and programs concerning ways to strengthen enrichment services for couples as well as being available for referrals.

LEADER TRAINING

Therapists, counselors, and other professionals may become leaders or consultants to ME programs. The initial step is to get well acquainted with the specific one or two programs that seem most compatible with your own theoretical perspectives, values, and lifestyle, as well as whether one intends to lead as an individual or as a couple. After reading about the program and obtaining additional information about it, usually the next step is to participate as a couple in a program. In this way one experiences the program as "naive" participating couples do, before knowing its theoretical details.

Most programs have some type of basic leader training (see chapter 5, this volume; also see Berger & Hannah, 1998). Some programs, such as the Association of Couples for Marriage Enrichment (ACME), have short workshops, whereas others, such as Getting the Love You Want (Hendrix, 1988, 1992; Luquet, 1996), the Prevention and Relationship Enhancement (PREP) program (Renick et al., 1992), and PAIRS (Gordon, 1988) require extended training in the theory and methodology before advancing to training for workshop leadership. After basic training the potential leader then leads one or more events under supervision of an experienced leader.

Even if one does not intend to lead workshops, leader training is very helpful to professionals who are willing to serve as specialists or consultants to enrichment leaders. These roles may involve being available for referrals or giving speciality-issue training to leaders (such as in sexual functioning, group dynamics, or community resources).

Although some programs may not require that all leaders be trained in a mental health or counseling discipline, such training is highly desirable. Even among ACME leader couples, most have at least one partner who has professional training in some type of helping profession. Professional training gives leaders the theoretical and practioner-experience foundation that becomes a basic context for understanding the program principles as well as issues of professional ethics, boundaries, and other aspects of leadership.

ETHNIC COUPLES

African-Americans

Ronald Smith (1995) has clearly demonstrated that ME programs are effective with African-American couples. The information in this section is based on his dissertation research.

The effectiveness of African American churches as a support system for families and couples often is taken for granted, yet few African American churches provide ME programs specifically designed for African American couples. Many African American couples are hesitant to use marriage therapy and enrichment opportunities because of misconceptions about their value for African American couples and how to benefit from them (Smith, 1995, p. 3).

As of 1989, of the 7 million African American families in the United States, only 4 million had both husband and wife present; 3 million had only one parent raising children under age 18 (Schaefer, 1993). In addition to factors affecting all types of families, African American families often have greater economic challenges from poverty and less interaction with male role models for family functioning (Smith, 1995, p. 10).

There are many ways that local churches and other religious groups can offer ME and other family services to meet these challenges (Garland & Pancoast, 1990). However, little research has been done on the effectiveness of ME among African American couples as one way to improve the quality of African American families.

Smith (1995) notes that the psychoeducational components of ME provide role models for positive male-female relationships:

> Some [African Americans] have been raised in single-parent homes without a model for marital interactions that work. Others have grown up in situations in which they have witnessed angry, hostile verbal or physical exchanges as their only model of male-female interaction. Some Black men and women who have grown up in two-parent, intact families have initially reported a "good" relationship between their

parents, but have later admitted that they had only a vague sense of how their parents interact as a couple. (Smith, 1995, p. 14).

In Smith's study, 60 African American couples in a predominantly Black Seventh Day Adventist church volunteered to participate in a ME weekend event held at a mountain retreat center from Friday evening through Sunday. In addition to fellowship and interaction among couples, the weekend consisted of seven work segments on these topics, phrased as they were in the workshop.

1. Love and power as your decision to use your resources to care for each other as partners at many choice points in your marriage journey.
2. The power of commitment is in choosing your future and building a solid foundation for your marriage.
3. Increasing your positives by enhancing fulfilled expectations that multiply good times.
4. Evaluating your resources through the power of teamwork in managing your abilities and strengths.
5. The power of conflict resolution that decreases negatives by replacing hurtful patterns with healthy skills.
6. The power of communication that connects the four love-power dimensions (future, resources, positives, negatives) to increase love.
7. Reaching out to other couples in church and community.

Smith used presentations, illustrations, exercises, and private discussion between spouses in the weekend workshop, and often utilized experiences and history specific to the experiences of African Americans and enabled couples to apply ME skills to their own marriages.

From the 60 African American couples, Smith randomly selected 30 couples to attend one weekend event and the other 30 couples to attend an identical event the following weekend. All couples responded to a LovePower 75-item quality-of-marriage inventory at three time points—before attending the enrichment event (time 1), at the end of the first event (time 2, when one group had completed the event but the other group had not), and after the second event (time 3, when both groups had completed the ME event.

There were no differences between the two groups at time 1. At time 2, the LovePower measures for the group of couples who had experienced ME increased over their time-1 measures as well as being higher than those of the group of couples who had not yet attended the enrichment weekend. At time 3, both groups had improved over their time-1 levels, with no differences between the two groups at time 3.

The design of this study made it clear that the ME experience was the intervention that produced the marriage improvements that these couples reported across these three times. Smith also notes that religiously based enrichment programs often are more accepted by African American couples.

> Religion plays a vital role in the lives of many Black families, yet some family problems stem from a family's interpretation and rigid adherence to certain religious beliefs. One who conveys no acceptance of the family's religious beliefs may find he or she is not respected by the Black family or couple. (Smith, 1995, p. 24)

The same elements of ME that have been found to be effective in ME with White couples also applies to ethnic couples. In addition, these elements are especially crucial for ME among ethnic couples:

1. The leaders must be known and trusted by the couples who participate.
2. The event must be clearly affirmed and supported by persons in authority who are respected by the couples.
3. A focus on recruitment of husbands is especially important because many ethnic couples are likely to assume a patriarchal structure for marriage. Men may see ME as reducing their power and control in marriage.
4. Especially among couples with limited incomes, provision for child care during the enrichment event may be essential to allow couples to attend the event.
5. Follow-up supportive contacts and booster sessions are more essential because couples may come from contexts that are less supportive of the new skills and patterns that the ME workshop teaches.

Chinese Americans

Elizabeth Koo (1997) has demonstrated that ME programs are effective with Chinese American couples. The information in this section is based on her dissertation research.

Although ME programs are widely available, most participating couples are from the Anglo or Caucasian ethnic groups. Churches have been major providers of ME opportunities (Dinkmeyer & Carlson, 1986a,b; Garland, 1983; Mace & Mace, 1984; Noval et al., 1996), yet enrichment programs need to be adapted to the needs of Chinese American couples and families. The increase in marital discord among Chinese Americans, resulting in part from acculturation (Loew, 1990), challenges ME leaders to develop programs that are appropriate for Chinese American populations.

Mak (1994) summarizes how Confucian values have molded Chinese character and behavior with tenets of harmony, hierarchy, kinship, affiliation, and development of one's potential. The emphases are on humility, modesty, obligation to family, conformity, obedience and subordination to authority, and treating oneself strictly while treating others leniently (Mak, 1994; Koo, 1997). Traditionally, Chinese families have been patriarchal with emphasis on the father-son relationship more than on the husband-wife relationship. Verbal expression of emotions are predominantly somatically oriented (Koo, 1997).

The ambiguity and lack of agreement among researchers concerning concepts of marital quality, satisfaction, adjustment, and happiness extends also to Chinese families. As suggested by Fincham and Bradbury (1990), one solution is to treat marital quality as the global evaluation of one's marriage. Applying this insider's perspective to Chinese couples is more difficult because of Chinese emphasis on maintaining public respect for one's family rather than disclose information that would bring disrespect to them (Koo, 1997).

Given cultural parameters such as these, a didactic, recreative, and experimental ME seminar can be effective among Chinese American couples. As Chinese couples become more acculturated, conflicts increase between Chinese and Western expectations about marriage. Conflicts also increase between older and younger generations concerning how much allegiance should be given to parents vs. spouse (Koo, 1997). Koo sees increasing education and Western influences as encouraging Chinese women to move toward more equalitarian expectations for shared decisions in marriage. These changes also challenge men to move from male-dominated to equalitarian power in marriage and families.

Koo (1997) obtained 68 Chinese American couples from 10 Chinese churches in the greater Los Angeles area. Initially, couples were randomly assigned to a seminar treatment or no-treatment waiting-list group. The treatment group attended one of two LovePower one-day (Saturday) enrichment events. However, the assignment procedure had to be modified because of the unavailability of some couples for specific seminar dates. Perhaps as a result, the overall marital satisfaction level of the treatment group was lower than that of the no-treatment group (average overall LovePower, 4.0 vs. 4.4 for nonattenders, $t = 4.19$, $p < .001$). Measures at the preevent point showed that, compared to those who did not attend, the couples who participated were older (mean $= 38.9$ vs. 35.7) with fewer having previously attended an enrichment event (39% vs. 48% for nonattenders).

At the end-of-event and one week after the event measurement, the nontreatment group was still higher than the treatment groups on their subjective evaluation of marital quality (mean $= 8.3$ vs. 7.8 end-of-event, $p < .001$; mean $= 8.3$ vs. 7.8 one week later, $p < .001$). To control for initial differences, Koo calculated scores of within-group change from preevent to end of event and postevent follow-up. Across nearly all measures, the treatment groups showed an increase whereas the no-treatment group showed either the same or decreased marital quality and LovePower scores (usually at the $p < .001$ levels).

Koo (1997) found that acculturation was related negatively to couples' reported marital quality at the preevent measurement time but, for the treatment group, changes in marital quality and in LovePower skills were not related to acculturation levels. Although social desirability is related to the LovePower measures ($r = .18$, $p < .05$ to .26, $p < .005$), all changes in these measures are unrelated to social desirability levels. This suggests that the cultural concern to present oneself in a favorable way may be related to Chinese American couples' reporting of higher marital quality. Conversely, greater acculturation of Chinese American couples may enable them to be more candid about their levels of marital quality, thus producing apparently lower marital quality prior to the event. Even so, there were no differences between men and women in the relationship between marital quality and acculturation level, and treatment couples did show gains in LovePower skills and marital quality at end of event and postevent.

These results (Koo, 1997) demonstrate that Chinese American couples are responsive to ME in ways similar to other U.S. couples. Once couples commit to participate in an event, their marital quality does increase. However, one important anecdotal finding in her study concerned the issue of having a woman recruit couples in Chinese American settings. Initially Ms. Koo made direct invitations to couples in various churches, but received few responses. As an outsider to the churches, she changed her strategy to contacting influential men in the churches who in turn invited couples to participate. As a result, response from couples was much greater. Whether this was due to gender differences or to status or friendship factors with a person known to the potential participants is not clear. It does, however, suggest that greater attention must be given to the ways in which couples are recruited for ME events. This may be even more significant among ethnic groups who are less familiar with enrichment programs.

Koo's study demonstrates that Chinese men as well as women are capable of responding to relationship education and enrichment, contrary to traditional Chinese norms (Bradshaw, 1994). This may represent a gender factor across cultures as well. Understanding the couple's personal cultural values and challenges of immigration is critical to establishing sufficient trust and rapport to involve them in enrichment or therapy (Lee, 1989).

Koo (1997) also urges Chinese churches and other religious groups to become more proactive in reaching couples with ME, without ignoring more generalized family programs that may be in place. The values of ME do transcend cultures in their emphases on unconditional commitment, flexible and forgiving family relationships, shared power and decision making, and intimacy based on caring and concern (Balswick & Balswick, 1995).

PRISON POPULATIONS

There are opportunities for offering ME programs in prison settings. Among felons who are married at the time of conviction, the majority will experience separation or divorce within a year of confinement. Because of the strain that imprisonment makes on marriage and families, ME can be offered as one way to address both the usual couple issues as well as issues related directly to conviction and imprisonment.

The opportunity to provide ME events in a prison setting depends heavily upon the support of prison authorities. Cooperation with the prison chaplain, warden, and other authorities is essential. Special permission may be necessary to have extended visiting hours and other arrangements for the event. R. A. Hunt and J. A. F. Hunt (personal communication, July 15, 1984) have led ME events in prison settings. Arrangements for the event were made primarily by the chaplain. In moderate-security situations, guards are usually present during the events to guarantee that all prisoners are accounted for and that spouses have appropriate access to the events. In minimum-security prisons, security may be guaranteed by the chaplain through a system of prisoner counts and curfew hours. The program is basically the same as in other settings. In one prison situation with 25 participating couples, both spouses in 7 couples were inmates.

COMBINING ENRICHMENT AND VIDEO

ME has been delivered with the aid of television and videotape presentations. A series of videotape presentations are available from John Gray, Gary Smalley, and Barbara de Angelo.

Shorter enrichment events with a large number of participating couples can be effective when they are properly prepared, organized, and led. In a statewide family enrichment program with some 500 United Methodist clergy and their spouses in Florida, couples met in district settings led by a facilitator couple for a half-day enrichment. Live presentations that included prerecorded couple vignettes illustrating couple interactions were televised to seven district locations where facilitators led participants to consider specific exercises that were described in the telecast

(R. A. Hunt & J. A. F. Hunt, personal communication, April 5, 1991). Follow-up counseling and support then was provided by district and conference resource personnel.

OTHER POPULATIONS

Floyd and Floyd (1987) outline ways to integrate cognitive, emotional, and behavioral principles into ME. They provide an outline that explains the overall structure and content of each session. They emphasize intrapersonal communication, conflict negotiation, interpersonal communication, life stages, and futuring exercises. They also recommend ways to use reading materials, films, and videotapes.

Avis (1986) designed a ME program to respond to the particular needs and stresses of dual-career couples. Their program includes renegotiating roles and responsibilities, structuring and managing time, meeting emotional needs, dealing with competition, and sharing control and power with seven $2\frac{1}{2}$-hour weekly sessions.

Zimpfer (1986) discusses the use of the small-group method in religiously based helping relationships and the use of religious-spiritual content in small helping groups. Group therapy, marriage therapy, ME, growth groups, and assertion training are considered. The philosophy and implementation of various types of services are discussed. Recommendations are made for training and practice session for clergy involved in religiously oriented helping relationships.

This sampling of program applications illustrates the wide range of possible populations to which ME can be offered effectively. Program formats, activities, settings, and methods need to be adapted to the socioeconomic, ethnic, and other parameters of the potential participants. Mentor couples can provide much greater flexibility in addressing the needs of specific couples and populations. The possibilities with mentor couples are addressed in the next chapter.

Chapter 12

Mentors—Have Enrichment, Will Travel

Ken and Joy have been asked to be a mentor couple as part of a marriage preparation program. The reservations they describe here are probably typical of most mentors.

Ken: I feel complimented to be asked to be mentors to other couples, yet I'm not sure we are the ones to do it. We still have some problems of our own that we haven't yet resolved.

Joy: It is a bit scary to think that we might not have some needed answers, or worse, that we might guide a couple in a wrong direction.

Ken: But, like our leader said, couples need to see a real marriage up close, both the good and the difficult times, and how we cope, keep romance going, and deal with real-life issues.

Joy: Ours is a "real marriage," of course, yet I don't want to have to tell everything to another couple we hardly know.

Ken: Nor do I. I think the mentor training should help us on these as well as on ways to encourage another couple at the points of their need more than ours.

Joy: Our own experiences in marriage enrichment are a good start. Having professionals leading the training and being available as consultants gives me confidence that we won't be in over our heads. I'm willing to try if you are.

Professionals can offer prevention by training mentor couples as well as by leading marriage enrichment (ME) events (chapter 11, this volume) and consulting with programs for couples and families. This chapter focuses on training mentor couples and consulting with marriage programs. Then, the Caring Couples Network is described as one example of how these three professional areas can be implemented through religious groups. Chapter 13 on outreach addresses some broader changes that are needed now and in the future.

Trained mentor couples make many of the benefits of ME available to couples at any time, tailored to the couples' specific needs. Mentor couples can provide a mobile couple enrichment network capable of reaching virtually all couples in a community. Through the outreach of mentor couples, marriage resources can be made available to those who otherwise would never hear of them. Mentor couples can link couples in need to therapy services and support networks. Informal mentor and support networks have long existed through relatives, neighbors, and religious and other community groups. Programs using carefully trained mentor couples are very recent but they are an exciting wave of the future for enabling hundreds of thousands of healthy couples to offer support, encouragement, mentoring, modeling, and other networking to all types of couples.

Finding effective and efficient ways to increase marriage and family wellness is emphasized increasingly by leaders in most marriage and family areas (Jacobson & Addis, 1993; L'Abate, 1990). Prevention of marital dysfunction is essential for healthy families who can sustain a healthy society (Popenoe et al., 1996). Among others, Giblin (1986) encouraged clinicians to give time to preventive work.

In a sense, prevention keeps something bad from happening, whereas wellness sustains and enhances something good. The long-term maintenance of positive conditions and outcomes typically is less noticed than the highly profiled bad news. To highlight the positive dimensions of prevention, we prefer the phrase, "prevention/wellness," or better, "wellness" and "well-being," although these are not as widely used.

The quality of the marital dyad is central to the quality of the family. It is helpful to differentiate between primary, secondary, and tertiary prevention (Fincham & Bradbury, 1990; L'Abate, 1990). Usually, prevention refers to primary prevention, the goal of reducing the number of new cases of marital distress and dysfunction by reaching marriages before distress begins. Secondary prevention seeks to reach couples who are at risk of increasing difficulties if their current patterns are not modified. Tertiary prevention focuses on treating marriages that are already dysfunctional. Bradbury and Fincham (1990, p. 376) paraphrase L'Abate and distinguish these levels of prevention according to when the intervention occurs in the course of dysfunction: "before it happens, before it gets worse, and before it is too late."

These distinctions among levels of prevention are helpful but the basic question concerning any couple remains: In what realistic ways can we enable this couple to grow from where they are to the well-being and joy that they can experience? To do this involves not only skill training and commitment, but a deeper systemic appreciation of the vital role of marriage in family and society. If marriage is so important to the spouses, their families and relatives, and to all of us in every community, then strengthening and supporting marriage become vital tasks for us all.

The distinctions among levels of prevention are related to the concepts of first- and second-order change (Watzlawick et al., 1974). First-order change refers to gradual, quantitative, continuous changes that are made within an existing system. Second-order change refers to qualitative, abrupt, and discontinuous changes— paradigm shifts that modify the system itself by changing its rules to produce health and avoid dysfunctions—that the current system may produce. Interactions between these orders of change and the family life cycle have been explored by Breunlin et al. (1992). One can consider third-order change as metasystemic ways of changing how we attempt to change systems, which is the focus of chapter 13.

As applied to marriage and family enrichment, many corrective and preventive interventions express first-order changes by addressing communication, commitment, and other facets of the marriage system. One typical assumption is that the two partners are committed to working on the issues by closing off exits from the relationship (Hendrix, 1988). Second-order change occurs when one or both partners make changes in themselves or in their relationship rules, which then precipitate new ways of looking at issues. Examples of such second-order changes would be partners agreeing on having a time to work on problems, or one partner deciding not to put up with abuse, or partners entering into Alcoholics Anonymous or other self-help support group, or partners deciding to exit the relationship.

Although mentors usually address prevention and first-order changes in a couple, mentoring is more a second-order change because the presence of mentors shifts the network in which a couple operates and seeks to encourage partners to find fresh perspectives, revised assumptions, and reordered values. Where a couple may have been surrounded by examples of distressed or dysfunctional marriage, the mentor couple brings a real-life example of a healthier marriage. Where one or both partners in a couple may have had some examples of healthy couple and family functioning, the mentor couple may enable the couples that they are mentoring to consider anew some of the strengths that couples in their family and friendship networks demonstrate.

SIGNIFICANCE OF MENTORING

Greeley (1991), drawing data from Gallop polls, demonstrates that the percentage of happy, successful marriages is much higher than often is assumed, suggesting that there are many healthy married couples who could be mobilized to share their stories of success with others. Even if the percentage of healthy couples is assumed to be only half of all married couples, with some 48 million married couples in the United States, approximately 24 million couples would be at the healthier end of the marital wellness spectrum, equivalent to approximately 10% of the total U.S. population.

McManus (1995, pp. 215, 295) emphasizes the vast resource of potential mentors for couples that is available among the married couples in churches and synagogues. To illustrate this point, if we assume that a denomination's demographics are similar to the general U.S. distribution, then the number of married couples who might serve as mentors would approximate at least 10% of the membership (depending upon whether the denomination reports all children as members). If we assume that only 1 out of 10 of these couples would be willing and able to mentor other couples, the number of potentially available mentor couples would approximate 1 to 2% of the total reported membership. Applied to a denomination, for every one million members, there are approximately 200,000 couples, some 10,000 to 20,000 of whom could become mentors to other couples. A typical church of 1,000 members (with 200 couples) could have 10 to 20 couples who could serve as mentors. McManus (1995) also asserts that every church has many couples who are willing to be mentors to other couples. He insists that these potential mentor couples "are the greatest untapped resource for saving marriages in the United States" (McManus, 1995, p. 134).

Who Mentor Couples Are

Mentor couples have a healthy marriage in which there are more positives than negatives. Spouses in these couples are committed to each other and to long-term growth in their relationship skills. They agree on positive values and are coping adequately with conflicts and differences. They see problems as challenges to be solved rather than excuses for divorce. These couples are open to feedback from others and seek professional help when needed.

Although mentor couples have a variety of family lifestyles, interests, and involvements, they usually would be in the upper levels of any of the marriage wellness continua. For example, in the Gottman (1994) classifications, they could be in any of the stable categories (conflict-minimizing, volatile, and validating). In the Olson categories (Fowers & Olson, 1992), these couples could be vitalized, harmonious, or traditional. In the Dyadic Adjustment Scale measurements, they would be above the 110 or so overall score that often is used to separate satisfied couples from dysfunctional ones. Mentor couples are well aware of their own marriage strengths and growth areas and know that there are many ways to have a happy, healthy marriage.

Mentor couples also know the fundamentals of making marriage work. Among the basic skills that all successful couples must have are mutual agreement on positive values, respect, affection, and goal setting. These successful couples are aware of and regularly use expressions of support and affirmation. Their ratio of positives to negatives is at least five to one (Gottman, 1994). These couples use problem-solving and conflict-resolution methods that support both partners and move toward realistic solutions. They have made long-term commitments to each other to make their marriage work well, having closed off all possible exits from the marriage (Hendrix, 1988). Put another way, they continue in their marriages because they enjoy each other, not because they are afraid to divorce.

Mentor couples would be the first to say that their own marriages are not perfect. Rather, these couples typically say that they are enjoying their marriages and still have some issues and patterns on which they are working. These partners covenant with each other to work on issues and to use any appropriate resources to continue to strengthen and renew their relationships.

Skills for Mentoring

In addition to having sufficient wellness in their own marriages, mentor couples need to have the necessary skills for effectively helping others (Carkhuff, 1969, 1972; Egan, 1986; Tan, 1991, especially chap. 6). Mentor couples need at least two sets of skills. First are the personal qualities that facilitate helping relationships with others. Among these are warmth, empathy, genuineness, respect, common sense, competence in living, integrity, openness, and other qualities that make both partners in the couple attractive and accessible to others.

There is a considerable literature on skills for supportive friendship, lay counseling, and mentoring (Tan, 1991). Persons with sufficient levels of these personal qualities can improve their abilities with training in being more aware and sensitive, on how to listen, and on how to communicate well (Brammer, 1973; Carkhuff, 1972; Egan, 1986; Miller et al., 1991; Tan, 1991). Through training and evaluation, all mentor couples need to demonstrate sufficient levels of these rapport and support skills. Among several programs for training caregivers in nurture and support skills is the Stephen Ministries (Haugk, 1984). The caregiving principles and skills that are organized in this program can be adapted by couples who mentor. Where this or similar support ministries are established, couples mentoring couples could be an expansion of this religious-based support system.

The second set of skills is specific to the type of mentoring. For example, if a couple is to lead an enrichment event, appropriate training and skill development must be done. If a couple will be giving feedback on a marriage inventory such as PREPARE, training in using that instrument is essential. This set of skills is built upon the basic personal qualities and communication skills of each partner.

TRAINING MENTOR COUPLES—SOME EXAMPLES

Marriage preparation and early marriage mentoring are urgently needed both for marriage wellness and for dysfunction/divorce prevention. McManus (1995) describes several examples of mentor couples working with other couples at several stages of their relationships. His emphasis is on churches and synagogues enabling couples to provide mentoring to other couples. He describes "evenings for the engaged" in which a mentor couple and one or more engaged couples meet over four or more evenings in a home. McManus emphasizes the opportunities that religious groups have to strengthen marriage through premarital and marital enrichment work, preparation of adolescents and adults for marriage and family living, working with stepfamilies, and enabling couples to avoid divorce.

Couple-to-Couple (Giles et al., 1996) is a program for training and supervising lay couples as support couples to provide friendship support and mentoring to engaged couples in Asbury United Methodist Church in Tulsa, OK. Begun in 1993, some 200 engaged couples have received friendship and mentoring from 25 support couples. In this program, support couples are trained to facilitate discussion of critical marriage areas with engaged couples. The contacts are intended to be friendship among equals, where support couples are not presented as superior to the engaged couples and friendship is not used as a substitute for therapy.

In this program, training coordinators are responsible for recruiting potential support couples. Basic training is done in 10 sessions, and child care for participants is provided at no cost. Training includes learning to use the PREPARE/ENRICH inventories and textbooks on marriage. Among key training topics are guidelines for confidentiality and self-disclosure; assertiveness; clarification of the roles of the support couples, ministers, and counselors; referral procedures; active listening; gender perspectives and differences; and ways to enable couples to explore issues that are important to them. Teamwork is emphasized, and supervision and training of support couples is provided continuously. Through supervision the program ensures the quality of mentoring provided by support couples and tracks the status of engaged couples who are receiving support.

The program originators have created a Couple-to-Couple training manual to guide in setting up a program and provide training for support couples (Giles et al., 1996). The manual also includes samples of forms, publicity, and other resource materials.

Great Start is a promising church-based program for premarital and recently married couples that involves mentor couples. This program combines the communication training programs of Sherod Miller (Miller et al., 1991; Miller, 1997) and the PREPARE/ENRICH marriage assessment systems of David Olson (Fowers & Olson, 1992; Olson & Fowers, 1986) into a premarriage and early marriage series. This program is being developed in cooperation with Country Club Christian Church in Kansas City, MO.

The Great Start program has three phases. In the premarital phase, couples utilize the PREPARE inventory and are trained in basic listening and speaking skills. In the second phase, couples married one to three years use the ENRICH inventory. If couples have not already completed the basic communication training, they can do it during this phase. In the third phase, around the time of the first wedding anniversary, the couples participate in advanced communication training and use Olson's Coping and Stress Profile. Approximately 150 couples participated in this program in its first year.

Parrott and Parrott (1995a) encourage mentoring with engaged and newlywed couples that emphasizes positive relationship skills that can "save your marriage before it starts" (SYMBIS). They offer a training program for mentor couples (Parrott and Parrott, 1997). Resources for their program include a participant's guide for each partner, a leader's guide, and videotape resources. Included in this program are questions to help potential mentor couples evaluate how well they embody the positive qualities needed, as well as several tools and questionnaires to use with couples. Training models are suggested, and mentor couples are guided in encouraging couples with whom they are working to explore a wide range of marriage issues. Private times for the couple to reflect and discuss issues are interleaved with times for couple-to-couple discussions. Group enrichment sessions are also part of this program.

CARING COUPLES NETWORK—BLENDING ENRICHMENT, MENTORING, OUTREACH

The need for better preventive and family wellness support has been emphasized by many (for example, L'Abate, 1990; Council on Families in America, 1995; Popenoe et al., 1996). One important solution to family crises and failures is linking healthy couples to couples who need help. The Caring Couples Network is a way for churches to reach couples and families in their communities.

The Caring Couples Network (Hunt & Hunt, 1996a) is a denominationwide network to facilitate cooperation between couples, pastors, and professionals in marriage and family areas. Many couples return from ME events with new growth in their own marriages and a vision of how other couples could benefit from similar enrichment opportunities. Many religious leaders support marriages through pastoral care, education, and other efforts of churches, synagogues, and other religious parareligious agencies. Professionals in marriage- and family-related fields apply their skills in many ways to the needs of couples and families. These three types of persons want to support better marriages and families, yet often they work somewhat independently for the same goals.

The focus of the Caring Couples Network is on reaching couples and families at their points of need. Mentor couples are available to couples considering marriage, to engaged and newly married couples, and to couples at any time along their marital journey. Mentor couples who themselves have coped well with difficult situations can be especially helpful to other couples who are facing issues such as financial crises, chronic illness, major accidents, or the death of a child or other close relative. Couples who have successfully overcome domestic violence, alcoholism or other substance dependencies, or extramarital sexual affairs may be more able to reach out to other couples who are in denial or are avoiding these issues.

One assumption of Caring Couples Network is that marriage expresses the spouses' faith and values. All other areas of living (children, work, leisure, education, health, etc.) are affected by the ways that each spouse lives his or her values on a daily basis. Marriage is both a way to enable two persons to grow in their love for each other and a key social unit of the community. The quality of marriages affects everyone through the values that parents give to their children; the participation of families in churches, schools, and neighborhoods; work and family interfaces; intergenerational relationships; and other ways.

As essential members of the Caring Couples Network teams, professionals in marriage- and family-related areas can provide consultation, training, and leadership to mentor couples. A team needs to consult with professionals about the possibilities and limitations they may have in providing mentoring and other services to couples and families. When issues in mentoring arise that seem beyond the competence of the mentor couple, they need opportunities to consult easily with professionals on the situation. Professionals in mental health disciplines can assist mentor couples to find emergency services, encourage persons to seek therapy, and find other support services in the community in addition to continuing their support as mentor couples.

Professionals can provide training of mentor couples in ways similar to those that typically are provided for volunteers on telephone hot lines and in lay counseling programs. Training should include information about mental health conditions, diagnostic guidelines, and community services. Training also should include practice for mentors in being aware of their strengths and limits, building rapport, sensitivity to dynamics of the couple, ethical considerations, and communication skills.

A major emphasis of the Caring Couples Network is training couples as mentors to other couples. The Caring Couples Network team may sponsor a variety of ME events, parenting classes, and other educational efforts that are open to anyone in the community. Professionals may be the leaders and presenters for these events, or may train leaders and consult for them.

CONSULTING WITH GROUPS

The importance of couples relating to each other has been emphasized by several ME programs, such as ACME, since their beginning. More recently, Denton (1986b) described ways that marriage and family enrichment programs can be established in communities in which enrichment leaders are not available. He suggests training couples who may have some experience with enrichment to serve as facilitators in groups of couples who then can discover their own resources. His approach includes selecting leader couples who have basically strong marriages and who can empathize with others and avoid advice giving. These couple support groups provide both group and private couple discussion time, using resource materials designed for enrichment purposes.

Local ongoing support groups for couples are increasingly emphasized by ME programs. Research suggests that husbands and wives who have support networks that overlap express greater satisfaction with their marriages (Hansen et al., 1991). The ACME newsletter and various internet web sites provide information, guidance for organizing groups, and many helpful resources that can stimulate discussion and exploration.

This vision of couples reaching other couples is embodied especially in the ACME and Marriage Encounter approaches. The desire of professionals to emphasize systemic marriage and family therapies is expressed through the American Association for Marriage and Family Therapy (AAMFT), the Family Psychology Division of the American Psychological Association (Division 43), and other professional associations. There are many instances of professionals, religious leaders, and couples working together in specific situations, but these often depend on the cooperative attitudes and energies of persons who know each other. Because churches and synagogues are major leaders in lifting up the importance of marriage and family, there is a need for churches and synagogues to mobilize a comprehensive approach to marriage and family wellness. The Caring Couples Network represents an ecumenical effort to do this.

Programs that utilize mentor couples with other couples seem to be better received when participating couples perceive the program as voluntary and carefully designed. For example, Stucky, Eggeman, Eggeman, and Moxley (1986) surveyed

10 couples (ages 19–28) from a ME program for newlyweds and 68 female graduates (ages 17–23) who had taken a high school course on family life. They found that respondents perceive premarital counseling more favorably when it is voluntary and includes more information and guided exercises.

Our survey of mentoring as a new frontier for ME and support illustrates that professionals have an essential role to play in the mentor couple movement. Professionals are needed to provide many types of information, training, and referral resources to mentor couples. Professionals can multiply their impact in a community through consultation with mentor couple programs.

In this chapter we have seen how mentoring with couples can be a second-order change in the rules and networks that surround couples. It is likely that the use of mentor couples will continue to increase. We now turn to a variety of what may be called third-order changes in society through which ME principles and programs can reach many more couples and families by affecting their institutions and general society.

Chapter 13

Active Consulting to Improve
the Marriage Climate

This concluding chapter focuses on the big picture of second- and third-order changes that can affect all couples and families. Popenoe et al. (1996) urge all citizens to become activists on behalf of better marriages and families in order to improve parenting and provide stable, healthy environments for all children. Earlier chapters in part 4 invite professionals to become more involved with marriage by providing and enabling therapy, leading enrichment events, training leaders for ME events, and training and consulting with mentor couples. We encourage professionals and others to become activists in the ways that are available and seem most appropriate to them.

Many community leaders, researchers, and members of various professions are interested in prevention as a major direction for promoting individual health, marital fitness, and family wellness (Gottman, 1994; L'Abate, 1990). McManus (1995, p. 51) reminds us that too often those who stand for marriage and family wellness fail to challenge media portrayals of irresponsible and hurtful family relationships.

Community leaders, researchers, and members of various professions need to join with mental health workers in emphasizing prevention as the key factor in the field of individual health promotion, marital fitness, and family wellness (L'Abate, 1990). Training professionals to implement effective prevention techniques and using programmed materials are effective tools.

CHANGING THE MARRIAGE CLIMATE

The marriage climate refers to the overall ways in which society views marriage, as expressed through policies, laws, regulations, media, and other avenues. In a strong call for action, the Council on Families in America (1995) addresses us all through one or more of these ways:

- Religious leaders and organizations;
- Civic leaders and community organizers;
- Employers and the business community;
- Social work, health care, and other human service professionals;
- Marriage and family therapists, family life educators;
- Pregnancy health care providers;
- Family law attorneys, judges, and children's advocates;
- Teachers, principals, and leaders in education;
- Foundation executives and philanthropic leaders;
- Family scholars, print and broadcast media journalists and editors;
- Entertainment industry writers, producers, and executives;
- Local, state, and federal legislators;
- General public.

This large view gives much support to the work of professionals and volunteers in ME and outreach. Because it places ME as a major expanding approach to strengthening marriages, it encourages all ME programs to see marriage as fundamentally essential to society rather than merely as a private matter between partners.

Among implications for changing the marriage and family climate are these:

1. Keep doing what your program is doing, research it, and find ways to do it better.
2. Expand programs to all segments of society, through creating flexible formats, seeking financial support for couples who cannot afford costs, and seeking child-care support for children while their parents attend enrichment events.
3. Encourage other sectors of society (as in the preceding list) in outreach efforts in your community.
4. Become clear and convinced of the differences between marriage as a public long-term commitment and unmarried cohabiting couples as a private, short-term, limited relationship.
5. Seek to support "one woman–one man" marriage as the norm for two-parent families. Other family structures may become alternatives when persons are either unwilling or unable to do the hard work of maintaining marriage.
6. Find ways to foster cooperation among the many sections of society that are concerned for healthy families, with each sector seeing the unique contributions it can make to the overall strengthening of marriage as the key to families.

7. Enable couples to be connected to some type of continuing support group based in community, church, synagogue, school, and other organizations. Fidelity and commitment are essential as the basis for openness and growth. Then, as spouses grow, they are more able to parent children, maintain the well-being of their household and family, and participate as citizens in society. The principles and goals of ME are shared among many community, educational, and religious institutions. Informal and intentional support groups for couples need to be expanded.

There is much to be done, yet there are many possibilities for expanding ME variations to make them available to every couple. We encourage you to begin with what comes "natural" to you as an activist who seeks to support marriage and family health and well-being.

Imagine what would happen if only 10% of all married couples—about 5 million couples—participated in a ME event this coming year. This still would be more than the numbers who are estimated to have participated in ME since the movement began in the 1960s. Try to calculate the many improvements that would happen to these couples, to their children, and to our society.

The following are a few possible actions for strengthening families, in addition to clinical practice, leading enrichment events, training mentors and others, and extending research:

- Teaching in high school, college;
- Being members of boards of community agencies;
- Being active in church, synagogue, or other group concerned for families;
- Working with courts, police, family members;
- Being hot-line consultants;
- Lobbying at governmental, business, and industrial levels;
- Providing leadership in professional associations at local, state, and federal levels;
- Enabling, sponsoring, and/or volunteering in employee assistance programs;
- Consulting with attorneys, physicians, and health care providers;
- Shaping marriage and family policies in health maintenance organizations;
- Mediating divorces and promoting efforts for positive marriage dissolution practices;
- Participating in post divorce recovery programs;
- Providing better support for public servants (e.g., police) who work with families;
- Changing laws and policies concerning family violence, substance abuse.

As you review earlier chapters, which issues most captured your attention, energy, and desire to do something more? Consider persons that you know (or could contact) who will be able to have positive influence in these areas. Which realistic goals will you set for yourself in these areas? Some possibilities are described in the following sections.

SCHOOLS AND COLLEGES

Family life education in schools, colleges, and community agencies offers both outreach and professional opportunities related to ME. Stahmann and Salts (1993) critically review literature and methods for educating for marriage, including forming, maintaining, and ending relationships. They cluster these into three approaches: general education, premarital counseling, and marital enrichment. For decades, many colleges have offered courses on marriage through social science departments. Depending on the department orientation, instructor, and textbook materials, these courses often emphasize relationship communication skills, problem solving, parenting, prevention of domestic abuse, and family system issues.

Education in personal relationships for people of all ages is essential as part of a holistic emphasis in a complex postindustrial society. Gammage (1991) describes how churches, community agencies, and schools can work together to educate persons for marriage. Educators must advocate more strongly for cooperative marriage and family education and enrichment in all sectors.

Lee and Brage (1989) outline development of more positive approaches in six important areas of family life education: clarification of factors that contribute to strong, healthy families; improved parent education techniques; ways to build self-esteem in relation to family; improvements in ME; lifetime development in the context of the family life cycle; and increased support for families with special needs.

ME can be included at several places in college settings. Many colleges offer courses in marriage, family, sexuality, and relationships. In addition to these, student-life organizations offer workshops and other programs concerning dating and marriage. Catron and Catron (1989) report a program to meet parents' needs for information and reassurance concerning the transition of their children to college. This provides an opportunity for parents to reassess their own long-range plans for the future. The program helps parents move through the transition from empty nest toward a fuller, more intimate and purposeful relationship as a couple. Catron and Catron demonstrate how concepts and experiential approaches used in ME can be applied effectively in other settings.

Many courses and programs for marriage and parenting education are used successfully in high schools and colleges across the nation. Following are a few examples.

The State of Utah established the Governor's Initiative on Families Today (GIFT) program in 1988 to reach and help as many Utah families as possible with parenting and communication skills. There is an annual conference held at the Salt Lake City Convention Center with many local speakers and presenters. The program is held around the state as well. The community response has grown dramatically from hundreds to thousands who attend the program each year.

PARTNERS for Students is a self-contained, 10-week course developed by the American Bar Association, Family Law Section, under the leadership in Lynne Z. Gold-Bikin, Esq. PARTNERS is a curriculum designed to teach students basic family law concepts and relationships skills.

Connections: Relationships and Marriage is a curriculum for teaching students in grades 11 and 12 how to have healthy relationships and successful marriages. The content includes self-understanding and building self-esteem, healthy relationships and the importance of values, effective communication and conflict-resolution skills, and preparation for marriage and anticipating the realities of family life. Written by Charlene Kamper, the curriculum is appropriate for schools, youth groups, and youth organizations and was developed with financial assistance from the Dibble Fund.

The PAIRS Foundation has adapted the PAIRS course for secondary school students to teach the art and science of effective human relationships. Titled PAIRS for PEERS, the curriculum has been designed by Dr. Lori Gordon to emphasize communication, conflict resolution, and self-esteem building in language appropriate for adolescents and adapted to fit their life stage and developmental needs.

Family life educators have developed curricula and workbooks that can be used by mental health professionals, clergy, youth group leaders, and teachers. The list is increasing, but one example is the Training in Marriage Enrichment (TIME) program. Developed by Dinkmeyer and Carlson (1986a,b), TIME gives practical aids for enriching marriages, including detachable Daily Focus and Marriage Skills cards.

EMPLOYEE ASSISTANCE AND HEALTH PROGRAMS

Bowen (1985) initially researched the family relationships of 664 U.S. Air Force married couples (husbands' mean age, 34.1 years; wives' mean age, 33.1 years) and their attitudes toward and knowledge of family enrichment and support programs. He found that the majority of them had satisfying marital and parent-child relationships. Most respondents described their families as self-reliant. Spouses reported that their parents were the most important source of support for their marriages, emphasizing the roles of extended family networks for service personnel.

Although many respondents were aware of parenting education, ME, and marital counseling programs, few had heard of couple-communication training or family cluster programs, and few families had taken advantage of any of these programs. Bowen (1985) interprets these findings as demonstrating a need for more publicity for existing programs as well as for developing programs that can be offered through business, industrial, and military workplaces. He suggests that professionals can provide marriage and family enrichment speciality services through these workplace channels.

On the basis of that research, Bowen (1991) developed the Marital Assessment Profile (MAP) as a corporate support program for employees and their spouses, grounded in theoretical principles and empirical research. Similar to other marriage enrichment programs, MAP enables employees and their spouses to improve their marriage through values clarification, self-development, and cooperation. MAP focuses on dynamics of relationships and on enabling partners to maintain a relationship that encourages both individual and relational growth through personal empowerment.

Tailored to the corporate sector, Bowen's MAP assumes an ecosystem perspective with a focus on helping couples to examine the nature of work and family interfaces and how these affect their marital and family relationships. In addition to direct benefits to participants, this program also works to establish a more productive and supportive work and family partnership with win-win benefits for both the company sponsor and the program participants. Bowen (1991) has field-tested the MAP program and sees marriage and family enrichment and support programs being increasingly supported by corporations. He shows how enrichment programs benefit companies by reducing absenteeism and substance abuse, increasing employee morale, and creating more cooperation and flexibility between families and employers.

Utilizing social work, social exchange, and system principles, Bowen (1991) orients his approach to senior managers and human resource professionals in the private and public sectors who want ways to strengthen their employees by assisting them in their marriage and family relationships. In corporate environments it is essential to clarify boundaries between work and family life. Bowen describes a value-behavior congruency model for marriage and offers ways to cope with disparities between expectancies and actualities in marriage in the context of work and in lifelong human development. He provides a solid rationale for the model and illustrates applications in military and industrial situations.

With the expansion of employee assistance programs and business and corporate leaders' increasing awareness of demographic and social trends and linkages between personal well-being, marital quality, family, and work, programs such as

Bowen's can reach many couples and families who would not otherwise be aware of traditional enrichment programs.

For example, Larson, Wilson, and Beley (1988) found that employees want career, family, and marriage counseling and enrichment services. As part of identifying services that the Employee Wellness Program at Montana State University needed, they conducted a comprehensive needs assessment on family wellness of 150 employees. They found that 25% of respondents were experiencing family problems. On the basis of their research, they developed a comprehensive set of programs to address these needs.

The important interactions between health and marriage quality have been documented by many (e.g., Fincham & Bradbury, 1990; Gottman, 1994; Jacobson & Gurman, 1986, 1995; O'Leary, 1987), with suggestions for ways that ME and therapy can make positive contributions to general health functioning.

The Duke Center for Living at the Duke University Medical Center promotes good health and disease prevention by combining the latest advances in medicine with comprehensive lifestyle programs that emphasize preventive medicine, proper nutrition, fitness, and emotional well-being. Under the leadership of Martin Sullivan, M.D., the staff of the Healing the Heart Program have integrated materials from the PAIRS Program into their curriculum.

COMMUNITY MARRIAGE POLICIES

The research on ME and marital therapy that we have reported clearly indicates that persons can increase their competence in marriage. Programs are needed at premarital and every stage thereafter in the marriage. These competence factors include increasing spouses' mutual commitment, relationship skills, agreement on values and goals, interactions among family members, and encouraging support from friends and relatives. These factors are also vital elements of healthy parenting, because spouses in healthy marriages are more likely to be able to provide the conditions for raising children who will help rather than harm their communities and the world, which includes us all.

McManus (1995) describes many excellent examples of ME, education, and outreach programs for a variety of populations. He emphasizes ways in which churches, synagogues, and other religious groups can take action to change the marriage climate. Churches and synagogues, through their pastors, priests, and rabbis, bless some 73% of all first marriages (McManus, 1995, pp. 50, 294), or some 1.6 million couples out of approximately 2.3 million marriages performed each year.

Because religious institutions are involved in so many marriages, they have a major opportunity to encourage couples to examine their competence for marriage and to learn the best ways for making their marriage work well. To do this, communities can cooperatively establish a marriage policy that sets clear standards that couples must meet before the church or synagogue representatives will solomize their marriage.

McManus (1995, p. 326ff.) describes ways to implement a community marriage policy. The first step is to induce a diverse group of leading clergy and lay persons from all religious groups—Catholic, mainline Protestant, evangelical, Jewish, minority, and other groups in the community—to meet to agree on having a policy and to identify the common elements. It is better to agree on some issues, such as minimum premarital preparation, than to allow disagreement on other issues to prevent any action at all. Examples of policies are available from the Marriage Savers Institute (McManus, 1995) and some national church organizations (such as the Caring Couples Network [Hunt & Hunt, 1996a]). This group can then draft a policy and obtain support and ratification for it through its constituent congregations.

The community marriage policy is only as good as the willingness of judges, justices of the peace, pastors, and community and religious groups to support and implement it. Among important steps in this cooperative effort is support from community leaders, agencies, churches, and synagogues. Widespread media coverage that describes the positive benefits of premarital preparation, mentoring, and enrichment helps to encourage both pastors and couples to participate. Flexible premarital preparation programs for couples in both individual and group settings are essential. To meet standards, leaders must be prepared and offer preparation programs in ways that can be utilized easily by couples.

The central element in community marriage policies is premarital preparation. The policy should state minimum requirements that must be met in order to have any of the participating ministers, priests, or rabbis perform the wedding. A minimum number of hours of preparation should be specified with suggested content and types of activities. Within this framework, different churches can offer their own emphases. These may include a variety of enrichment formats for couples, some of which may focus on certain types of couples, such as first-time married, remarried, blended families, and other situations.

These preparation programs may be offered by clergy, professionals, and lay couples working together in ways that seem best for their situation, as suggested in the Caring Couple Network approach (Hunt & Hunt, 1996a). Provisions for training mentor couples, obtaining resources, and informing prospective couples must be maintained. Follow-up support during the initial postwedding establishment phase also may be offered even if not required in the policy. If there are expenses involved, some financial aid or free services need to be available for those who may not be able to afford the costs. Once implemented, leaders need to provide for ways to monitor the policy, ensure quality in the supporting programs, and make modifications as needed.

SHOULD PREPARATION FOR MARRIAGE BE REQUIRED BY LAW?

Marriage is a public health and safety issue because the behaviors of the partners affect themselves and their children, their work, and their community. Requiring appropriate preparation for marriage is one step toward increasing family wellness and thus decreasing family dysfunction and divorce. Some churches, synagogues, and other groups require premarital counseling and education, as indicated in the above discussion of community marriage policies. However, in many communities, standards for marriage preparation are neither uniform nor evenly enforced across a community or a denomination.

Requiring preparation for entering marriage gives widespread support to couples in making their marriages work as well as signifying that society considers marriage to be a very important foundation for a civil society (Glendon & Blankenhorn, 1995). Although some might object that this intrudes upon a couple's freedom, it is clearly in line with the right of society to prohibit, ignore, or encourage specific behaviors that are known to affect us all. This applies in all areas of life. For example, persons who drive vehicles on public streets are required to study traffic laws, meet vision standards, and demonstrate that they can operate the type of vehicle for which they are being licensed. Persons who handle food in public eating places must meet certain health requirements. At the public health levels, these regulations do not prevent all accidents and food poisonings, but they certainly reduce such incidents. Continuing education programs, such as defensive driving courses and periodic inspections of restaurants, further help to maintain the safety and wellness of us all.

Some may claim that they already know how to have a good marriage and therefore should not be required to participate in any premarital preparation. The claim of driving competence does not exempt one from a driver's examination, nor should the claim of knowledge about how to make a good marriage exempt a couple from a premarital preparation program, especially if that program is tailored to the needs of these "gifted" couples. In fact, having such gifted couples participate with others who have more work areas would help to model positive patterns of relationships. Couples who have the basic skills can easily demonstrate them.

Marriage and family education for children and adolescents, premarital preparation, and ME programs have been shown repeatedly to reduce the incidences of family disruption and divorce (Arcus et al., 1993a,b; McManus, 1995). At present, most civil marriage license regulations only involve meeting minimum age requirements, some blood test results, and payment of a fee. However, in some communities, judges require some type of preparation for marriage as part of the waiting period between applying for a marriage license and performing the wedding service. In several states, lawmakers are actively considering statutory requirements for marriage preparation prior to obtaining a marriage license.

Requiring preparation in order to obtain a marriage license could benefit from the principles used with driver's license regulations. Typically a driver's license includes three examinations: a vision test, a knowledge test of rules required for operating a vehicle on public roads, and a behind-the-wheel demonstration of one's ability to operate a vehicle properly. Additional regulations apply according to whether one will drive buses or other commercial vehicles. In addition, most public schools now offer driver's education courses, and remedial work (such as driver's school) for persons with poor driving records.

The body of knowledge we now have about marriage assessment and enrichment makes feasible analogous education and examinations for a marriage license. It is possible to test how well each partner "can see" (i.e., perceives) marriage and family relationships (both current and family of origin) and how much each knows about the principles of commitment, goal-setting, communication, and problem solving, and then to simulate marriage situations and issues through paper/pencil inventories and computer simulations. Psychoeducation to improve a person's competencies for marriage is the central objective of premarital and ME programs. These objectives form the core of premarital preparation programs as suggested by Markman et al. (1994), McManus (1995), and others. The longer time between obtaining a marriage license and the wedding (such as four months in some community marriage contracts) can be used to strengthen marriage and prevent divorce only if partners participate in some type of premarital preparation.

Marriage assessment and enrichment technologies increasingly make it possible to test the marriage competencies of the partners with considerable accuracy. As with the behind-the-wheel drivers exam, we can predict whether the couple will succeed in their marriage (e.g., Fowers & Olson, 1992; Gottman, 1994; Markman et al., 1994; Olson & Fowers, 1986). A realistic examination of marriage competencies could be done through simulation and other assessment techniques.

A couple cannot adequately "test" marriage as long as exits from it are possible. This is the reason that typical nonmarried cohabitation (living together) arrangements either contribute nothing to, or negatively affect, the future marriage success. However, in another sense, every couple in every year of their marriage is continually examining their relationship and deciding whether to continue. The idea of reality checking in actual living underlies proposals for some type of two-step marriage. In these proposals spouses initially would enter marriage for a limited time (such as a year or more), and would not have children. On or before the time limit they could exit with few negative consequences (other than their investment of a year of their lives). At the time limit they then would enter a lifelong marriage commitment, including the right to have children (by birth or adoption).

The rationale for stronger regulations for entering marriage is that the partners not only affect each other but also affect society by the ways that they parent their children, just as operating a vehicle on public roads affects all drivers. The reality, of course, is that one third or more of all couples are pregnant or already have children at the time of their wedding. Nevertheless, marriage and parenting education, including demonstration of basic competencies, also could be applied in situations in which couples already have children.

Discussion of the values of requiring some type of premarital preparation are appearing with more frequency in the media news, special reports, and talk shows. In a few states, proposals for a more restrictive "covenant marriage" have appeared (e.g., Arkansas in 1997 and California in 1998). Although well intentioned, a covenant marriage approach has some problems. "Covenant" is both a legal and a religious term, thus mixing church and state in complicated ways. The couples who are at highest risk for domestic violence, divorce, and dysfunctions are least likely to enter into a more restrictive "covenant" marriage. In addition, having two or more "types of marriage" opens the door to additional interpretations of marriage that would eventually make the sanctions for marriages less meaningful. Finally, research shows that the positive effects of marriage preparation need to be renewed through booster sessions every two or three years to sustain improved levels of healthy family functioning. Problems such as adultery, domestic abuse, and desertion are symptons of dysfunctional relationships. Healthy marriages come from positive incentives for learning and practicing relationship skills in a network of supportive relatives and friends.

A more effective approach is to provide to all couples financial incentives that would encourage them to participate in premarital preparation and later in marriage education or enrichment, which research shows to be a major factor in keeping marriages intact and healthy. Couples could receive a discount or credit on the marriage license fee for participation in a premarital education/preparation program. This could be done by increasing the marriage license fee by the amount of the discount and then discounting it (back to the original fee) for those who give evidence of having completed a marriage preparation program. An alternative would be to give couples a tax deduction (up to a ceiling amount) for costs of premarital preparation and for ME or marriage counseling in any year in which they participate in a marriage enhancement event, similar to tax deductions for required participation in continuing education for a profession or trade. These provisions would apply to all marriages. Standards for marriage education programs could be established, similar to standards for continuing education providers. These incentives also would encourage professionals to offer marriage preparation, education, and enrichment programs.

MARRIAGE- AND FAMILY-RELATED LAWS AND PROCEDURES

In many ways, values and virtue involve the functioning of marriages and families and give rise to the laws and regulations that a society establishes or ignores (Glendon & Blankenhorn, 1995). Weitzman (1981) explored in depth the unwritten assumptions about marriage that are embedded in common law and then gave suggestions for ways that any couple can structure their relationship in the context of current law. Contributors to the Popenoe et al. (1996) symposium on society and marriage explore how laws may either support marriage or encourage disruptions. Schneider (1996) considers the pros and cons of supporting family wellness by restricting entry into marriage, confining family life to a committed marriage, making divorce more difficult, protecting children from the effects of divorce, and changing the language of family law. Although Schneider acknowledges the difficulties of regulating family functioning through law, Gallagher (1996) is more optimistic in pointing to family dysfunctioning as being expressed in the ways in which laws are made, implemented, and abused.

Schneider (1996) notes how economic factors in the form of tax structures affect family resources and eventually affect family functioning. The recent change in the tax laws allowing nonworking spouses to place into IRA accounts the same amount as working spouses is one example of ways in which laws affect families. Schneider (1996, p. 242) asks what would happen if American law failed to enforce business contracts in the ways that it fails to support family functioning. Galston (1996) suggests a multifaceted public agenda to change policy and law to encourage and support quality family functioning rather than encourage abandonment and divorce.

These brief comments indicate that there is much that can be done by law and political policy to support marriage and family functioning. The challenge is to professionals to involve themselves in these issues and to encourage those whom they know to have competence and motivation to address these issues as major tertiary ways to support marriage enrichment and its contributions to family wellness.

Among examples of how laws relating to marriage and family shape the ways in which spouses work with each other is divorce. The need to be honest about divorce as being caused by both parties to the marriage led both to no-fault divorce provisions and to a rise in the divorce rate. Originally, no-fault referred to either spouse being able to obtain a divorce without having to prove that the other partner was at fault and the petitioning party had no blame. However, too often no-fault has been interpreted as an easy and convenient way to leave the responsibilities of marriage and family. In recognition of these issues, Gallagher (1996, p. 242) describes no-fault as "unilateral" divorce.

McManus (1995, pp. 265–291) and Regan (1996) summarize recent arguments against this no-fault attitude. They describe efforts to make changes in divorce laws that will encourage couples to work at making their marriages better instead of quitting when the going gets rough. Premarital marriage preparation and continuing ME acknowledge that marriage takes commitment to work and that with appropriate help most couples can grow through difficulties to a satisfying marriage. Divorce needs to be available when couples have made long-term serious attempts to create a good marriage, but not as an easy way out of a marriage in order to enter another convenient relationship. Divorce is better than murdering one's spouse, but even the most amiable divorce leaves permanent damage to the spouses and their children.

Popenoe et al. (1996) document how divorce changes in the roles of men in families and offers suggestions for changes to strengthen marriage and encourage more men to participate in family life at deeper levels of service and involvement. They address the need to change the marriage climate in America. Regan (1996, p. 165) describes ways that family law can "vindicate not the acontextual but the relational self." A postmodern movement from the individual self to the relationship self is needed. Regan argues that shared norms of responsibility can inform marriage and family law because the status of marriage includes trust, fairness, sacrifice, loyalty, care, and other elements of what the partners consider to be the best life they can possibly create. Divorce represents not only the loss of this status but also points to the ways in which each partner has failed to be sufficiently responsible and active in creating the desired home environment. Regan emphasizes that marriage and divorce law not only regulates but also constitutes marriage by creating images of what marriage is intended to be and can be.

Schneider (1996, p. 189) affirms marriage and family as social institutions that shape the lives of individuals and help to organize society. As such, the law can help to promote marriage and family stability in many ways. He indicates that no other relationship, such as domestic partners or unmarried cohabiting partners, is equivalent to marriage. Creating sanctions and incentives for marriage would clearly signify that these other relationships cannot be considered as the functional equivalence of marriage, thus strengthening marriage. Among other ways that law can strengthen marriage, Schneider suggests a longer period of waiting between application for a marriage license and the wedding, strengthening laws against domestic abuse, and changes in alimony, community property, and child support laws, regulations, sanctions and requirements.

Perhaps the most creative solution that Schneider proposes is the "marriage commitment fund" (Schneider, 1996, p. 201). In this plan the state would require every couple at the time of their wedding to place an amount (perhaps 10% of their income) into a marriage commitment fund, and then to pay into that fund (perhaps 1 to 3% of income) throughout their marriage. If they are still married when they retire, the couple would receive back all of their contributions, somewhat like an IRA (Individual Retirement Account), perhaps with interest and tax-free. If they divorce, money from the fund would go to help cushion their children from the negative economic consequences of the divorce, and the couple would not receive any money.

Gallagher (1996) notes that, today, up to 65% of marriages will eventually fail (depending on socioeconomic, religious, and preparation levels), and that one third to two thirds of all children are born out of wedlock. Although these rates vary considerably according to socioeconomic, ethnic, religious, and marriage preparation factors, Gallagher emphasizes that our society must "re-create" marriage. She suggests that the social climate can be changed to provide positive support for marriage through changes in tax laws, enforcement of marriage contracts, provision of effective psychoeducation, and an increase in the waiting period between applying for and obtaining a divorce. She also notes that "the freedom to flee and the freedom to commit are opposite and contradictory freedoms" (Gallagher, 1996, p. 245).

Galston (1996) describes three civic functions of the two-parent family: development of civic character and competence, linkages between the family members and the community as citizens, and essential economic well-being. He suggests ways to continue the gains that the United States has made in liberty and equality by consciously establishing a promarriage agenda. Basic to this agenda are creating economic incentives for staying in school and preparing for a career, job-training, welfare revisions, giving more tax relief to families with children, and cooperation between business and government to make work settings more supportive to parents with children.

At cultural levels, Galston (1996) urges a national public policy in which the U.S. government seeks to give high priority to the stability and well-being of families, something that is now given to policies that promote the stability and health of the economy, including many types of economic indicators. Indicators of marriage and family health need to have high visibility with decisions that seek to correct negatives and enhance positives concerning families.

Galston (1996) especially notes how television and internet media affect families by giving examples and models of good marriage and family, as well as negative examples. For example, over 90% of some 10,000 sexual incidents depicted in 1991 prime time by the three major television networks were outside of marriage (Galston, 1996, p. 288). He argues strongly for finding a balance between moral laissez-faire and tyrannical censorship by encouraging positive programming that crowds out violence and inappropriate sexuality.

ON BECOMING ACTIVISTS FOR MARRIAGE

Many positive changes have occurred in ME programs, research, and extensions since Hof and Miller (1981). However, if ME is to become a significant factor in preventive marital health that affects a broad spectrum of the population, more improvements will have to be made within and outside the movement. People within the movement will need to actively open their programs to the careful scrutiny of appropriate empirical research, so that the effective components of each program can be identified, and, as a result, more effective and efficient programs can be created. Increasingly, programs are doing this important research (e.g., Relationship Enhancement, PREP, PAIRS, Getting the Love You Want, and Couples Communication Program).

For research to improve, proponents of ME will have to realize that the enthusiastic testimonies of participants and leaders are important but not sufficient to sustain a program. Explicit, carefully defined theoretical frameworks for the various programs and techniques need to be developed. The competitive "ours is the best program" enthusiasm needs to be replaced with a more open and flexible attitude that is based on cooperative efforts to match programs to the specific needs and abilities of specific individuals and couples. The need for appropriate and ongoing training of nonprofessional and professional leaders must continue to be addressed, with an emphasis on the cognitive and theoretical areas as well as the experiential and interpersonal relations areas.

The professional community of marital and family counselors, therapists, researchers, and educators will need to work more closely with lay persons and paraprofessional in training and consulting capacities. This networking will allow mutual supporting of the important and unique contributions of both sides to couple and family health and wellness. Increasingly, professionals acknowledge that significant learning, change, and growth can occur within a learning experience led by (and even created by) nonprofessionals. With that acceptance can come open support of such programs and a specific and planned effort to utilize professional skills in the development and training of appropriate nonprofessional leaders (Bradbury & Fincham, 1990; Floyd et al., 1995; L'Abate, 1977; McManus, 1995; Tan, 1991).

The helping professions have been slow to accept the viability of a marital health or ME systems approach to dyadic interactions and relationships (Kaslow, 1996b). Part of the reason may lie in the failure of many proponents of systems-based interventions such as ME to have been seriously concerned with appropriate research and theoretical considerations. However, that is possibly only part of the reason. The fears described by Vincent (1973, 1977), such as diminished professional stature (i.e., "If they can really help themselves so much, or can be helped by someone with much less training than I have, then what will happen to me and my practice?"), probably still exist. There also could be fears that if people can be helped by marital enrichment, all that will be left for the trained professional therapist will be the very difficult cases (Vincent, 1973).

There always will be a need for highly skilled, trained, and qualified professionals in the field of marital and relationship therapy. Some people simply do not benefit from ME experiences, or at least not as much as from conjoint or individual therapy. Sometimes therapists do not look at the condition of their own marriages or other intimate relationships that may affect their professional work. In addition to providing direct services to couples, professionals can multiply their positive influence by becoming more involved in second- and third-order changes that in turn positively affect families and marriages.

Can the trained professional be content with offering only individual services? We think not, especially if research continues to demonstrate that ME and other forms of preventive marital health are as helpful and efficient, perhaps at times more so, than traditional individual therapy methods. It is clear that enrichment and therapy are not in competition. Rather, each type of intervention has its unique contribution to improving the wellness and mental health of couples and families. This being the case, then, there is a need for the trained professional therapist to learn and develop specific skills in preventive marital health and ME in order to help couples to develop their potential for effective relationships (Floyd et al., 1995; Jacobson & Addis, 1993; Wright and L'Abate, 1977).

Managed health care continues to bring widespread changes in all areas of physical and behavioral health, especially in requiring more precise accountability and efficient brief treatments (Goodman et al., 1992). In these changes in the mental health delivery system, there is great potential for marriage and family enrichment programs to be a significant resource in wellness and prevention as well as in treatment of many physical health conditions. Programs such as those developed by Bowen (1991), Larson et al. (1988), and Luquet (1996) integrate the best from both ME and marriage and family therapy approaches. The emerging efforts toward relational diagnoses and systems-sensitive treatments (Kaslow, 1996a) increase opportunities for ME leaders to help to create the next generation of comprehensive wellness and preventive care for families and their members and for marriages.

A major expression of the acceptance of a philosophy of systemic approaches to individual, marriage, and family well-being, wellness, health, prevention, and enrichment by the professional community is the creation of the Coalition on Family Diagnosis. Kaslow (1996b) has documented the long and difficult road to wider consensus on systemic diagnoses and treatment of persons involved in marriage, family, parenting, and other intimate relationships. Descriptions of the essential need to attend to marriage and family dynamics in treating many conditions that formerly have been seen only as individual problems are available in O'Leary (1987) and Jacobson and Gurman (1986, 1995).

The hope that marital health could be developed as a multidisciplinary and interprofessional specialty field was expressed by Vincent (1973, 1977). Trainees need to be exposed to growth-oriented and preventive approaches and models as well as to models that focus on the treatment of dysfunctional relationships or systems. That exposure needs to include appropriate theory and practical experiences, with couples in therapy as well as those from the broader community (cf. Guldner, 1978). Since that time, professional groups such as American Association for Marriage and Family Therapy (AAMFT) and the National Council on Family Relations (NCFR) have included marriage and family enrichment as a required areas of study for persons in graduate professional education and training programs. Family-life-education degree programs are closer to the goal of specialization in the area of enrichment as proposed and consistently urged by L'Abate (L'Abate 1977, 1981, 1985a, 1990; L'Abate & O'Callaghan, 1977). Even without the establishment of a separate specialty field or degree programs, there is still the need for the training programs in marriage and family therapy and counseling to focus on marital enrichment and preventive marital health.

Agencies that serve the family continually need to be encouraged to include positive and preventive programming in their services to clinical and nonclinical populations. ME programming needs to be extended to those preparing for marriage and to senior citizens (Mace and Mace, 1977). The need to give specific attention to affection and sexuality in ME programs (Otto, 1975) has been done by some programs, such as PREP, PAIRS, and Passionate Marriage (Schnarch, 1997).

The various proponents and practitioners of ME (professional and nonprofessional) and marital counselors, therapists, researchers, and educators need to join in a truly collaborative and concerted effort to make the potential benefits of ME available to all couples who could benefit from such a service. A united effort, welcomed and sought by all groups, conceivably could exert significant political pressure, could encourage governments to develop a focused emphasis and policy on marriage, and could tap the financial and personnel resources of various government agencies to provide positive, growth-oriented services (Mace and Mace, 1975; McManus, 1995; Popenoe et al., 1996). The lack of consensus on some issues should not blind us to the larger gains from uniting on the widespread consensus that marriage and the family relationships are the crucible for a virtuous and a democratic society (Glendon & Blankenhorn, 1995; Browning et al., 1997).

As some of these hopes and dreams become realities, preventive marital health and ME will achieve a new and deeper level of significance in our society. The development, implementation, and assimilation of a growth-oriented marital philosophy throughout our society can have a significant effect on marital and family life in the future. In the final analysis, it will take commitment on the part of individual couples to the ongoing process of ME for themselves and for others. For most couples that will mean a disciplined involvement in a personally meaningful program designed to enable the participants to fulfill their potential as individuals and as married couples. For professionals that will mean finding the places and doing the constant tough work for first-, second-, and third-order changes. Becoming activists for marriage and family wellness is also enrichment at its best.

Epilogue

MESSAGE FROM DR. DAVID R. MACE

Authors' note: David R. Mace wrote this Epilogue for the Hof and Miller (1981) book. To introduce the epilogue to this current volume, we include it here, in its original form, because it so well expresses the deep conviction and wonderful spirit of Dr. Mace who for so many years sought to spread the good news of marriage enrichment. Among their many accomplishments for couples and families throughout the world, David and Vera Mace founded ACME in 1972 as part of their 40th wedding anniversary celebration in their effort to encourage cooperation among programs and increase availability of ME to couples around the world. Dr. Mace died in December 1990. We think that he would concur with this update of the Hof and Miller volume.

I gladly accept the invitation of the authors to contribute an epilogue to this book. I do so because, in my judgment, what it presents is accurate, sound, and convincing. No other publication has, to my knowledge, put together as yet such a felicitous combination of material concerning the new and very promising field of ME. Beginning with a broad and well-balanced survey of the entire field, it then describes, in great detail, an actual ME program* which in my opinion must be ranked with the best that have so far been developed.

The book therefore provides the reader with a clear and full picture. If you have read it with attention, you now know most of what anyone at present knows about the subject. And I would further add that this is a subject in which, in my opinion, a great number of people are going to want to be well informed during the next 10 years. Let me try to explain why I take that view.

Human society is, in a sense that has never been so true in time past, at a point of crisis. Vast cultural changes have, in our lifetime, opened up prospects that

---

*The "Creative Marriage Enrichment Program" to which Dr. Mace refers was developed by Hof and Miller and presented in detail in their 1981 book. It is summarized in chapter 5.

engender in us, as we look to the future, both dazzling hopes and numbing fears. Science and technology have opened up revolutionary possibilities that boggle the mind. We are in fact no longer talking about "the future," but about "futures"—a vast array of options that now confront us. Of the many directions in which we can now go, which shall we take? The making of that choice wisely could lead us to the fulfillment of humanity's most ambitious hopes. Unwisely made, the choice could lead to stark disaster.

Can we act wisely? Yes, surely, if we go forward together hand in hand, achieving our human destiny in harmonious cooperation, mutually trusting and supporting each other. To do this, however, we must achieve one goal above all others—we must improve the quality of our relationships.

In this century we have harnessed the power of the atom and probed the inner secrets of the cell. We have penetrated outer space. We have made giant strides toward the conquest of disease. We have seen the possibility of improving living standards beyond the wildest dreams of our forefathers. Yet with all these achievements, we have so far failed dismally to improve the quality of human relationships. Hate, suspicion, and greed are with us as they have always been—and their destructive power—has been exponentially increased. Now the last frontier confronts us. Unless we can find a way for human beings to live together in peace and harmony, all the glittering prizes we have won may be lost.

My professional life began in a London slum in the 1930s, in the depths of the Depression. I saw widespread suffering and misery and was compelled to look for answers. A few years later I witnessed the horrors of war as the bombs rained down and helpless, innocent people were murdered and mutilated through "man's inhumanity to man." Still I was looking for answers. Amid all the destruction and hate I kept meeting beautiful people who loved and cared. But there were not enough of them to take over and fashion a society that would be based on mutual cooperation and integrity.

How can we greatly increase the number of caring and loving people? That was, and still is, the critical question.

For myself, I found the answer. I saw clearly that human families were the factories where people are made—or marred. As a counselor, I saw how people were twisted and hardened, early in life, when they lived in loveless homes— loveless because men and women who sought joy and intimacy and tenderness in marriage failed to find what they sought, for all their earnest striving. I tried to help such people by establishing counseling services. I opened the first continuing marriage counseling agency in Europe, and saw it grow and multiply. As the years passed, I saw knowledge increase as the behavioral sciences, though still far behind the physical and biological sciences, gradually developed and came of age. I began to cherish the hope that a long last we might focus our attention on the most vital goal of all—the understanding of close, intimate relationships, and the discovery of how to nourish and support such relationships so that they could produce loving, caring people—the kind of people we need so desperately.

Progress has been slow, but we are getting nearer and nearer to our goal. We are finally beginning to learn the art of teaching men and women to achieve their goals—not goals we want to impose upon them, but goals they deeply and earnestly long for and strive for themselves. If only we can make that possible, and then multiply the process on an ever-increasing scale, a vast transformation of human relationships could result in time, and we would release a positive power that could be more revolutionary than any previous revolution in human history.

Too long have we clung to the illusion that the basic unit of human society is the individual. An individual does not develop identity in isolation. Our children begin life with an inheritance of undeveloped and undifferentiated potential—for good or for evil—and they become persons through continuous interaction with other individuals with whom they meet and mingle. The true unit of human society is therefore the dyad—two individuals, interacting with each other, and in the process, making and molding each other's identity.

I see this book as a harbinger of new beginnings. It tells the story of how at last we are digging down to the very roots of human society—close dyadic relationships—and helping them to become, by the flowering of the rich potential for love that is within them, the best that they are capable of becoming.

The cynics may dismiss all this as starry-eyed idealism, just as they did long ago when men of faith looked out over the desert and glimpsed the shimmering outlines of the Promised Land. I am content to say to the unbelieving, "Ten years from now, I predict that marriage and family enrichment will have developed resources that will make possible, for the many, relationships of a quality now experienced only by the few. And when that time comes, it may indeed be possible, on such a broad-based foundation, to begin the task of building a better and a happier world."

Dr. David Mace
(As of 1981) Director of Marriage Enrichment and Training,
Department of Human Enrichment and Development,
North Carolina Baptist Hospitals, Inc.,
Winston-Salem, North Carolina

SOME TOUGH ISSUES

In order to we build on Dr. Mace's vision to the next millennium, we want to address several tough issues that ME brings. Our basic assumption is that our readers are competent both to raise their own questions and to utilize this volume as an aid in finding their own answers and engaging others in a mutual quest for better research, program, and supports for using enrichment resources to sustain better marriages and families. Thus we have tried to lay out principles, techniques, and research with a minimum of specific answers. However, our viewpoints at times may have been unclear, inferred, or lacking. As an invitation to continuing dialogue, we want to address some issues with the desire of stimulating our readers and their colleagues, students, and couples to take action wherever they have opportunities.

1. What are the relative merits of skill-based, experiential, or other models? We see marriage as a complex system composed of a man and a woman, each of whom is already a complex bio/psycho/socio/spiritual person-system, with both persons deeply affected by genetic, environmental, and choice dimensions, and both the spouses and their marriage set in the context of family, work, community, and world systems (e.g., Breunlin et al., 1992). From this multisystems perspective, we see the basic elements of social learning (Stuart, 1980) as underlying the positive changes that enrichment approaches seek. Both spouses have models, habits, resources, and goals that involve social skills and experiences.

   As we noted in earlier chapters, enrichment programs need to include, as much as possible, models, demonstrations, and examples of positive outcomes along with details of the specific skills involved. Participants then need sufficient guided practice in applying these skills to their own situation so that they can actually continue developing the new patterns on their own. It is not a question of which element is most important or essential, but rather a matter of understanding how each of the components fits together to produce desired changes and sustain them across the couple's marital and life journey.

2. How do cognitive, emotional, sexual, motivational, developmental, health, ethical, moral, economic, educational, family-of-origin, environmental, and other dimensions of human functioning relate to marriage? We have seen how both ME and marital therapy have moved from a narrow emphasis on one or another of these dimensions to recognize how essential all of these elements are to marriage and family wellness. Again the multi- and meta-systems perspectives are essential. We know that the atmosphere and dynamics in a home, controlled in major ways by the married couple, has profound influences on all in the home. Each family member influences others and is influenced by them. No program can hope to make major changes in even one or two of these dimensions in one-day, one-weekend, or even one-session-a-week formats, yet we also see individuals and couples, in both research and program applications, who are able to change salient elements in their relationship and achieve surprising and exciting changes

in a brief period of time. We need to understand these phenomena more adequately as we seek to expand service and provide enrichment to all types of couples.

3. What models of marriage are implied by ME? As described in part 1, enrichment programs always have, both expressly and implicitly, some set of values and priorities concerning marriage. Among the values that we have assumed in this volume are that (a) marriage always involves one woman and one man as spouses; (b) the spouses should be coequal in terms of power, control, and decision making (i.e., neither spouse automatically has authority or roles solely on the basis of gender, physical strength, or other factors); (c) within this coequal balance, spouses are to arrange their roles, power, and control in ways that they desire, as long as the results do not impinge negatively on themselves or others; (d) marriage is a lifelong journey based on mutual commitment; and (e) divorce is possible but not necessary if the marriage is working well for both participants. These are just a few examples of assumptions about marriage that every enrichment program and couple need to clarify, illustrating the need to be more explicit about marriage assumptions so that couples can choose programs that fit their own goals, and program leaders can be clear about the goals of the program.

4. What meanings may be attached in the relationship of many ME programs to religious groups? Religious groups vary widely along many dimensions, such as theological beliefs and creeds; marriage, family, and parenting models; and standards for behavior and social action. The initial step is to identify which religious groups are included. The values and models for marriage and family described above can be found in many, but not all, religious groups. Where value perspectives are similar, religious groups and ME programs can be very important allies. We cannot automatically assume that enrichment should or should not be related to religious groups or to other nonreligious agencies. Only as we clarify the values, goals, and assumptions of both can a judgment be made. For these reasons we point first to the qualities of enrichment programs and leaders so that we then can examine how these match a sponsoring or cooperating religious or nonreligious group.

Most marriage and family enrichment programs have grown out of religious sources, usually because of the concern for marriage and family quality that has motivated leaders to seek better ways of nurturing and enhancing home and family relationships. Although some ME programs are directly controlled by religious groups (such as Marriage Encounter, Celebrating Marriage), most have emerged through the efforts of gifted and energetic professional and lay persons who are activated by a combination of religious and humanitarian motivations to reach out and try to help couples.

5. How shall we balance paid professional and volunteer ME leadership? To do enrichment programs and services well requires much training, time, and marketing skill as well as leadership qualities. The economics of enrichment programs must be faced honestly. Although we hope that few leaders and programs are motivated primarily by greed and economic gain, we also know that good programs seldom happen if they are not self-supporting. This means that either the participants themselves must pay sufficient fees to cover their own expenses and those of the leadership or these must be covered in some other way. Although higher pay does not necessarily mean better leadership, it does enable persons of high quality and ethical standards to be able to devote themselves to expanding and improving their enrichment programs and services.

   The other end of the economic dimension is that many couples at risk who most need ME are unable or unlikely to pay the costs of participating in enrichment. When economic disincentives are added to an already low motivation for change, ME too often becomes limited to those who are willing to pay, typically the higher socioeconomic groups. Some ME leaders may try to address this situation through a variety of scholarship grants, pro bono efforts, or facilitating sponsorship by community agencies, businesses, or religious groups.

   One aspect of this dilemma is emerging evidence that dysfunctional marriages affect not only the partners but also their children, extended families, neighborhoods, schools, and society (e.g., Blankenhorn, 1995; Glendon & Blankenhorn, 1995). Whether individuals are married or not, they are affected by the general marriage quality of all couples. As these effects are increasingly demonstrated empirically, perhaps realistic marriage insurance plans, tax credits and deductions for preventive enrichment, and other financial incentives will become available. If marriage improvement could become as profitable as the factors that destroy families, economic incentives would help to make marriage and family enrichment better and more widely available. It appears that a few leaders in ME seem to be learning these lessons. The challenge is to combine well-researched programs, wide availability, competent leadership, and economic viability.

6. How can society use its power to sanction or prohibit to encourage better functioning marriages and families? In chapter 13, we considered several aspects of licensing as applied to marriage. As the marriage and family enrichment movements continue to expand and mature, one challenge is to find ways to make a marriage license signify competence to "practice" marriage in ways that benefit the spouses, families, and society. As more couples benefit from enrichment and therapy services and as society begins to see

the effects of marriage preparation and continuing enrichment programs, realistic and validated "tests" of marriage and parenting competencies may become part of the marriage license procedure. This may place new perspectives on issues of "conception" or "reproduction" control. Perhaps society will need to distinguish a marriage license from a "reproduction and parenting" license.

TOWARD A MILLENIUM VISION

It has now been 18 years since Dr. Mace wrote his epilogue for the original Hof and Miller (1981) volume on which this book is based. As we conclude this update and expansion, we think that comments on several points made by Dr. Mace are in order.

First, marriage and family enrichment have come of age in the sense of being better grounded in research, clearer about their principles and assumptions, more easily available to more persons, and more flexibly and cooperatively related to therapy and intervention efforts. This volume has reconfirmed basic ME principles and presented evidence that ME does produce positive results in couples. The question of whether ME is effective has been answered affirmatively. Now, the next questions involve identifying which tools work best for which specific needs of specific types of couples and under which circumstances for specific goals.

Second, marriage is a lifelong journey with challenges, changes, and choices concerning daily interactions as well as in times of major life transitions. Marriage, parenting, and values interact in major significant ways (Fowler, 1990, 1996). It is clearer that long-term marital improvement requires not only an initial "one-time" ME event but also periodic booster sessions. We now know that marriage support groups, follow-up events, newsletter reminders, and other "continuing education" for marriage are essential for sustaining higher levels of marital success. We know that the mutual commitment (a continually reaffirmed choice) of both partners to a long-term successful relationship is a key element in successful marriage. The next questions concern the roots of commitment, the ways in which extrinsic constraints and internal dedication work together to sustain marriage, how the ratios of positives to negatives produce marital outcomes, and how the factors may operate uniquely in different marriages.

Third, a wider variety of enrichment programs for specific needs is emerging. Programs are now available for premarital education, for couples facing divorce, for couples where one or both partners have children, for couples with addictions or other serious problems, as well as for marriage education in high schools. Some enrichment programs are now available for same-sex couples. Programs are being delivered via internet, videotape, televised news specials, and other channels. Continuing research is needed to evaluate content and methods as well as delivery and support channels for all types of couples.

Fourth, ME is moving into the mainstream of society in several ways. The national convention initiated in May 1997 by the Coalition for Marriage, Family, and Couple Education (CMFCE), and repeated in July, 1998, has become an annual event with many varieties of programs displayed. Through the CMFCE network, so ably guided by Diane Sollee and a committee of consultants, much media coverage of marriage continues throughout the year with enrichment leaders appearing on television talk shows, special reports, and on news and other media. Schools are seeking well-designed programs for marriage and family education. In an increasing number of communities, clergy and civil leaders have instituted some type of community marriage policy that requires pre-wedding marriage education and preparation.

Fifth, from many sources new tools and techniques are available that professionals can use in enrichment, therapy, and other settings. No longer are tools and activities considered to be only for therapy or enrichment, and the earlier sharp distinctions between therapy and enrichment have given way to blending tools, settings, and programs into a cooperative process that emphasizes what is best for the couple involved.

Sixth, couple mentors are providing a major expansion of ME availability to more couples. Professionals are learning how to train and work with lay mentor couples. Couples who themselves are learning to cope better with issues in their own marriages can often, with training, become very effective as part of ME programs and support systems. Although much informal mentoring occurs between couples and their relatives and friends, well-trained couples can serve well as mentors in many ways. The key is training, and there is now a need to specify standards for mentors and increase the cooperation between professionals and mentor couples.

Seventh, the economic benefits of ME are increasingly being acknowledged. Much more research is needed to demonstrate the efficiency of preventive education so that couples can "get it right, or better, the first time" rather than waiting until they crash and then seeking help. Both types of services are needed. Attention to understanding how motivation for ME can be increased is needed. Well-functioning marriages are a major key to well-functioning families, which in turn reduce the need for society to pay for rehabilitation, foster families, police, and other community services needed to address the effects of dysfunctional families. As the economic benefits are more clearly demonstrated, continuous political action is needed to encourage government, business, insurance, and other sectors of society to modify structures to support and encourage funding of marriage and family education.

Eighth, marriage and family education and enrichment have appeared as part of professional training programs. Well-trained professionals in the human services disciplines that involve marriage and family relationships need to know how to provide enrichment programs, how to encourage and train lay couple mentors, and how to facilitate outreach to couples who have not been reached with the encouraging possibilities that ME offers.

With all of these advances, we are still at the beginning of the possibilities that the enrichment movement holds for improving family quality and extending peace. More professionals are needed who value preventive methodologies. More leaders are needed in business and government who will institute enrichment opportunities. New ways to reach couples who are most at risk yet least able to pay for enrichment need to be established by community agencies, business and professional groups, and education and religious organizations.

With all the encouraging advances, we still have a society that, as David Mace stated, clings to "the illusion that the basic unit of human society is the individual." Although the systems view seems obvious to those in marriage and family enrichment, it is especially dramatic in human families, "the factories where people are made—or marred" from birth (or prenatally) to adulthood. ME has made many gains, yet much work is still ahead. In this volume we have pointed to some of these directions with the hope that you, our readers, will continue to achieve the potentials for marriages and families envisoned here and reach beyond to possibilities now only dimly seen. These are some of the difficult yet exciting and rewarding challenges of the new millennium. We hope that this volume has moved you and your colleagues into actions to enable better marriages and families, and through them to a more peaceful world.

Contact Information for Specific Programs

Current information on many enrichment programs, services, and conferences is available from the Coalition for Marriage, Family, and Couples Education:

Coalition for Marriage, Family and Couples Education, LLC (CMFCE)
5310 Belt Road, NW
Washington, DC 20015-1961
202-966-5376
202-362-3332
FAX: 202-362-0973
Website: http://www.smartmarriages.com
E-mail: CMFCE@smartmarriages.com
Diane Sollee, Director

"Around the Coalition" shares a wide range of information on educational and enrichment approaches to marriage, family, divorce, and related issues. Opinions expressed are not necessarily shared by members of the Coalition. To add or delete your name from the "Around the Coalition" updates list, "subscribe" or "unsubscribe" by return email. An archive of past newsletter updates may be obtained at: http://archives.his.com/smartmarriages/index.html#start

Specific programs and addresses as of mid-1998:

American Bar Association
Partners
610-272-5555
FAX: 610-272-6976
E-mail: lynnezgb@aol.com
Lynn Gold-Biken

Association for Couples in Marriage Enrichment (ACME)
502 N. Broad Street
P.O. Box 10596
Winston Salem, NC 27108
800-634-8325
910-724-1526
FAX: 910-721-4746
E-mail: wsacme@aol.com
(founded by David & Vera Mace)

Caring Couples Network
Family Unit, General Board of Discipleship
The United Methodist Church
P.O. Box 840
Nashville, TN 37202-0940
615-340-7119
FAX: 615-340-7565
mnorton@gbod.org
Richard A. Hunt
626-584-5553
E-mail: rahunt@fuller.edu

Center for Marriage & Family Intimacy
800-881-8008

Compassionate Family
2109 Derby Ridge
Silver Spring, MD 20910
301-588-2297
FAX: 301-587-0766
E-mail: Stosny@iname.com
Steven Stosny, PhD

Connections: Relationships and Marriage
The Dibble Fund
P.O. Box 7881
Berkeley, CA 94707-0881
800-695-7975
E-mail: KayReed@aol.com
Kay Reed

Couples Communication
7201 S. Broadway, Suite 11
Littleton, CO 80122
800-328-5099
303-794-1764
FAX: 303-798-3392
E-mail: Sherodmil@aol.com
Sherod Miller, PhD

Couples Health Program
76 Bedford Street #19
Lexington, MA 02173
617-863-5600
E-mail: Janice Levine@fso.com
Janice Levine, PhD

Couples Place Internet Site
Promising Partnerships, Inc.
1040 Broadway
South Portland, ME 04106
207-799-8012
E-mail: dsanford@couples-place.com
David Sanford, MSW, PhD

Couples School
The Choche Center/Academy House, #410
1420 Locust Street
Philadelphia, PA 19102
215-735-1908
Judith Coche, PhD

Divorce Busting; Keeping Love Alive
P.O. Box 197
Woodstock, IL 60098
800-6 Michele (664-2435)
815-337-8000
FAX: 815-337-8014
Michele Weiner-Davis, MSW

Family Wellness Associates
P.O. Box 7869
Santa Cruz, CA 95061
408-426-5588
FAX: 408-426-5588
E-mail: familywell@aol.com
George Doub & Virginia Morgan Scott

Getting the Love You Want (IRT)
335 N. Knowles Avenue
Winter Park, FL 407-644-3537
800-729-1121
FAX: 407-645-1315
E-mail: IIRT@aol.com
Rick Brown, Wayne Luquet, Harville Hendrix

GIFT (Governor's Initiative on Families Today)
120 N. 200 West, P.O. Box 45500
Salt Lake City, UT 84145-0500
801-538-4105
FAX: 801-538-3993
Margaret Jones, Conference Coordinator

Healing the Heart Program
Duke University Medical Center
DUMC 3022
Durham, NC 27710
919-660-6600
919-660-6681 - Office
FAX: 919-681-8376
E-mail: sulli003@mc.duke.edu
Martin Sullivan, MD

Hot Monogamy Training Workshops
(based on Image Relationship theory)
512-891-0610
Pat Love, PhD

IDEALS (Institute for the Development of Emotional and Life Skills, Inc.)
12500 Blake Road

Silver Spring, MD 20904-2956
301-986-1479
301-986-1479
Bernard Guerney, Jr., PhD

Imago Workshops
Box 759
Abique, NM 87510
505-685-4430
FAX: 505-685-4570
Harville Hendrix, PhD

Interpersonal Communication Programs, Inc.
7201 S. Broadway
Littleton, CO 80122
800-328-5099
303-794-1764
Sherod Miller, PhD

Life Innovations
Prepare/Enrich and Growing Together
Family Social Science University of Minnesota
290 McNeal Hall
St. Paul, MN 55108
612-625-5289
800-331-1661 - Prepare/Enrich
612-625-7250 - FACES
FAX: 612-625-4227
David Olson, PhD

Maintaining a Loving Relationship
Ackerman Institute
149 E. 78th Street
New York, NY 10021
212-679-7310
212-744-0206 - At Ackerman
E-mail: fraenkel@nyc.pipeline.com
Peter Fraenkel, PhD

Making Marriage Work
University of Judaism
15600 Mulholland Drive
Los Angeles, CA 90077
310-476-9777 Ext. 233
E-mail: dr4cpls@aol.com
Sylvia Weishaus, PhD

Making Marriage Work
502-852-7611
E-mail: jhbrown01@ulkyvm.louisville.edu
Joe Brown

Marriage Alive and The Second Half of Marriage
P.O. Box 31408
Knoxville, TN 37930
423-691-8505
E-mail: mailine97@aol.com

Marriage Coming of Age
200 Sheridan Road
Highland Park, IL 60035-5330
847-433-0154
FAX: 847-433-0153
E-mail: wordmbeg@interaccess.com
Mercy & Ed Gilpatric, Partners

Marriage Encounter
50 N. Maple Hill Road
Havertown, PA 19083
800-795-LOVE
800-559-AMOR
800-456-8330
800-334-8920
405-672-0177

Marriage Savers
9500 Michael's Court
Bethesda, MD 20817
301-469-5870

E-mail: 74723.3507@compuserve.com
Mike & Harriet McManus

Marriage Survival Kit
Seattle Marital and Family Institute, Inc.
P.O. Box 15644
Seattle, WA 98115-0644
888-523-9042
206-729-0787 (in Washington state)
John Gottman, PhD

Married and Loving It
283 S. Butler Road
Mt. Gretna, PA 17064
800-327-2590
E-mail: mjm@philhaven.com

Mars and Venus Counseling Center
12711 Ventura Boulevard #190
Studio City, CA 91604
818-508-3318
FAX: 818-508-3319

Mars and Venus Institute
20 Sunnyside Avenue #A120
Mill Valley, CA 94941
888-463-6684
415-389-6851
415-389-6857
FAX: 415-381-2147
E-mail: bmb@nbn.com
John Gray, Merril Bevins, Bart Bevins

National Institute for Relationship Enhancement (NIRE)
4400 East West Highway, Suite 28
Bethesda, MD 20814-4501
301-986-1479
301-231-6162 - home
FAX: 301-986-1233
E-mail: niremd@nire.org
Bernard Guerney, Jr., PhD

New Beginnings
Families Intern, Inc.
414-359-1040
FAX: 414-359-1074
E-mail: chidwic@ibm.net
Ann Chidwick

Northwest Media, Inc.
326 W. 12th Avenue
Eugene, OR 97401
800-777-6636
FAX: 541-343-0177
E-mail: nwm@northwestmedia.com

PAIRS
1152 N. University Drive
Pembroke Pines, FL 33084
888-PAIRS4U
FAX: 703-998-8517
E-mail: Lori - pairsline@aol.com
E-mail: Office - www.pairs.com
Lori Gordon, PhD

PREP—Fighting for Your Marriage
1780 S. Bellaire St., Suite 621
Denver, CO 80222
800-366-0166
303-871-3370
303-871-3829
303-750-8798
FAX: 303-440-4335
E-mail: hmarkman@du.edu
Howard Markman, PhD

Christian PREP
303-692-8932
E-mail: 75103.1655@compuserve.com
Scott Stanley, PhD
Susan Blumberg, PhD

PREP, Inc.
1780 S. Bellaire Suite 621
Denver, CO 80222
800-366-0166 - Product Orders
E-mail: PREPInc@aol.com

Prepare/Enrich
Life Innovations, Inc.
P.O. Box 190
Minneapolis, MN 55440-0190
612-331-1661
FAX: 612-331-2318
E-mail: Lifeinno@aol.com

Recovery of Hope Network
800-327-2590

Relationship (RE) Enhancement Program
4400 East-West Hwy.
Bethesda, MD 20904-4501
301-986-1479
E-mail: niremd@nire.org

Retrouvaille International, Inc.
P.O. Box 25
Kelton, PA 19346-0025
610-869-9230
FAX: 610-869-9214
E-mail: BillPeg@aol.com
Bill & Peg Zwaan

Saving Your Marriage Before It Starts (SYMBIS)
Seattle Pacific University
3307 Third Avenue West
Seattle, WA 98119
206-281-2178
800-286-9333 - Catalog Orders
FAX: 206-285-3790
E-mail: LPiii@spu.edu
Les & Leslie Parrott

Stepfamily Association of America, Inc. (SAA)
599 Sky Hy Circle
Lafayette, CA 94549
510-284-1524
510-284-5204-Home
FAX: 510-284-9586
E-mail: JohnV66488@aol.com
John Visher, MD
Emily Visher, PhD

Stepfamily Association of America, Inc. (SAA)
215 Centennial Mall South #212
Lincoln, NE 68508-1834
800-735-0329
FAX: 402-477-8317

To Love and To Cherish (TLC)
(adaptation of Relationship Enhancement for church settings)
Bill Nordling, PhD

Today's Family
1482 Lakeshore Dr.
Branson, MO 65616
E-mail: Honorgts@aol.com
Gary Smalley, Director

Training in Marriage Enrichment (TIME)
Systematic Training for Effective Parenting (STEP)
101 Broad Street
Lake Geneva, WI 53147
414-248-7942
800-584-1733 - Order books & materials
FAX: 414-248-1202
Jon Carlson, PhD

Training in Marriage Enrichment (TIME)
4010 NW 99th Avenue
Coral Springs, FL 33065
954-752-0793
FAX: 954-345-2052
Don Dinkmeyer, PhD

We Can Work It Out
Center for Family Psychology
Department of Psychology, O'Boyle Hall
Catholic University of America
Washington, DC 20064
Private Practice Office:
5310 Wisconsin Avenue #220
Washington, DC 20015
202-319-5750 (CUA Office)
202-319-4474 - Direct Line for classes, etc.
414-363-8477 - Wisconsin Office
Cliff Notarius, PhD

References

Ackerman, N. W. (1954). *The Psychodynamics of Family Life*. New York: Basic Books.

Adam, D., & Gingras, M. (1982). Short and long-term effects of a marital enrichment program upon couple functioning. *Journal of Sex and Marital Therapy, 8*, 97–118.

Adams, J. F., & Sprenkle, D. H. (1990). Self-perception and personal commitment: A challenge to current theory of marital dissolution and stability and implications for marital therapy. *American Journal of Family Therapy, 18*, 131–140.

Alexander, (1973). Defensive and supportive communication in formal and deviant families. *Journal of Consulting and Clinical Psychology, 40*, 223–231.

Anderson, N. M. (1994). *The relation of homework compliance, marital satisfaction, and leader adequacy for couples in marital enrichment programs*. Unpublished doctoral dissertation, Graduate School of Psychology, Fuller Theological Seminary, Pasadena, CA.

Arcus, M. E., Schvaneveldt, J. D., & Moss, J. J. (Eds.). (1993a). *Handbook of family life education: Vol. 1. Foundations of family life education*. Newbury Park, CA: Sage.

Arcus, M. E., Schvaneveldt, J. D., & Moss, J. J. (Eds.). (1993b). *Handbook of family life education: Vol. 2. The practice of family life education*. Newbury Park, CA: Sage.

Augsburger, D. (1988). *Sustaining love*. Ventura, CA: Regal Books.

Avis, J. M. (1986). Working together: An enrichment program for dual-career couples. *Journal of Psychotherapy and the Family, 2*, 29–45.

Babcock, J. C., Waltz, J., Jacobson, N. S., & Gottman, J. M. (1993). Power and violence: The relation between communication patterns, power discrepancies, and domestic violence. *Journal of Consulting and Clinical Psychology, 61*, 40–50.

Bader, E., Microys, G., Sinclair, C., Willet, E., and Conway, B. (1980). Do marriage preparation programs really work? A Canadian experiment. *Journal of Marital and Family Therapy, 6*, 171–179.

Bader, E., Riddle, R., & Sinclair, L. (1981). Do marriage preparation programs really help? A five year study. *Family Therapy News, 2*, 3–4.

Balswick, J. O. (1988). *The inexpressive male*. Lexington, MA: Lexington Press.

Balswick, J. O., & Balswick, J. (1995). *The dual-earner marriage: The elaborate balancing act*. Grand Rapids, MI: Revell.

Balswick, J. O., & Peck C. W. (1971). The unexpressive male: An American tragedy. *The Family Coordinator, 20*, 363–368.

Bassoff, E. (1985). The memory board: A therapeutic activity for married couples. *Journal of Counseling and Development, 64*, 70–71.

Baucom, D. H., & Adams, A. N. (1987). Assessing communication in marital interaction. In K. D. O'Leary (Ed.), *Assessment of marital discord: An integration for research and clinical practice* (pp. 139–181). Mahwah, NJ: Erlbaum.

Beach, S. R. H., & Bauserman, S. A. K. (1990). Enhancing the effectiveness of marital therapy. In F. D. Fincham & T. N. Bradbury (Eds.), *The psychology of marriage* (pp. 349–401). New York: Guilford Press.

Beach, S. H. R., & Broderick, J. E. (1983). Commitment: A variable in women's response to marital therapy. *The American Journal of Family Therapy, 11*(4), 16–24.

Beaver, W. A. (1978). *Conjoint and pseudo-disjunctive treatment in communication skills for relationship improvement with marital couples.* Unpublished doctoral dissertation, Marquette University, Milwaukee, WI.

Beck, D. F. (1975). Research findings on the outcome of marital counseling. *Social Casework, 56,* 153–181.

Becnel, H., & Levy, L. (1983). A marriage enrichment program as a facilitator of focusing and finding meaning in life. *Family Therapy, 10,* 275–282.

Berger, R., & Hannah, M. T. (1998). *Handbook of preventive approaches in couple therapy.* New York: Brunner/Mazel.

Bergin, A. E., & Garfield, S. L. (Eds.). (1976). *Handbook of psychotherapy and behavior change* (ed.). New York: Wiley.

Bergin, A. E., & Garfield, S. L. (Eds.). (1994). *Handbook of psychotherapy and behavior change* (4th ed.). New York: Wiley.

Berne, (1964). *Games People Play.* New York: Grove Press.

Berne, E. (1968). *Principles of group treatment.* New York: Grove Press.

Birchler, G. R., Weiss, R. I., & Vincent, J. P. (1975). A multimethod analysis of social reinforcement exchange between maritally distressed and nondistressed spouse and stranger dyads. *Journal of Personality and Social Psychology, 31,* 349–360.

Blankenhorn, D. (1995). *Fatherless America: Confronting our most urgent social problem.* New York: Harper & Row.

Bolles, R. N. (1981). *The three boxes of life and how to get out of them.* Berkeley, CA: Ten Speed Press.

Bolte, G. L. (1975). A communication approach to marital counseling. In A. S. Gurman & D. G. Rice (Eds.), *Couples in conflict.* New York: Aronson.

Bosco, A. (1973). *Marriage Encounter, a rediscovery of love.* St. Meinrad, IN: Abbey Press.

Bowen, M. (1978). *Family therapy in clinical practice.* New York: Aronson.

Bowen, G. L. (1985). Families in blue: Insights from Air Force families. *Social Casework, 66,* 459–466.

Bowen, G. L. (1991). *Navigating the marital journey: MAP, A corporate support program for couples.* New York: Praeger.

Bowman, M. A. (1992). *Physiological linkage in recovering alcoholic couples.* Unpublished doctoral dissertation, Graduate School of Psychology, Fuller Theological Seminary, Pasadena, CA.

Bradbury, T. N., & Fincham, F. D. (1987). Assessment of affect in marriage. In K. D. O'Leary (Eds.), *Assessment of marital discord: An integration for research and clinical practice* (pp. 59–108). Mahwah, NJ: Erlbaum.

Bradshaw, C. K. (1994). Asian and American women: Historical and political considerations in psychotherapy. In L. Comas-Diaz & B. Green (Eds.), *Women of color: Integrating ethnic and gender identities in psychotherapy* (pp. 72–113). New York: Guilford Press.

Brammer, L. M. (1973). *The helping relationship.* Englewood Cliffs, NJ: Prentice-Hall.

Bray, J. H., & Jouriles, E. N. (1995). Treatment of marital conflict and prevention of divorce. *Journal of Marital and Family Therapy, 21,* 461–473.

Brenneman, T. J. P. (1991). *Religiousness, purpose in life, and marital quality.* Unpublished doctoral dissertation, Graduate School of Psychology, Fuller Theological Seminary, Pasadena, CA.

Breunlin, D. C., Schwartz, R. C., & Kune-Karrer, B. M. (1992). *Metaframeworks: Transcending the models of family therapy.* San Francisco: Jossey-Bass.

Brody, G. H., Arias, I., & Fincham, F. I. (1996). Linking marital and child attributions to family processes and parent-child relationships. *Journal of Family Psychology, 10,* 408–421.

Brown, R. (1976). *The effects of couple communication training on traditional sex stereotypes of husbands and wives.* Unpublished master's thesis, Appalachian State University, Boone, NC.

Browning, D. S. (1996). Altruism, civic virtue, and religion. In M. A. Glendon & D. Blankenhorn (Eds.), *Seedbeds of virtue: Sources of competence, character, and citizenship in American Society.* Lanham, MD: Madison Books.

Browning, D. S., Miller-McLemore, B. J., Couture, P. D., Lyon, K. B., & Franklin, R. M. (1997). *From culture wars to common ground.* Louisville, KY: Westminister John Knox Press.

Bruder, A. H. (1972). *Effects of a marriage enrichment program upon marital communication and adjustment.* Unpublished doctoral dissertation, Purdue University, West Lafayette, IN.

Buber, M. (1923). *I and Thou* (translated by R. G. Smith). New York: Scribner.

Burns, C. W. (1972). *Effectiveness of the basic encounter group in marriage counseling.* Unpublished doctoral dissertation, University of Oklahoma, Norman, OK.

Campbell, E. E. (1974). *The effects of couple communication training on married couples in the child-rearing years.* Unpublished doctoral dissertation, Arizona State University, Tempe, AZ.

Campbell, S. (1981). *The couple's journey: Intimacy as a path to wholeness.* San Luis Obispo, CA: Impact Press.

Cantor, N., Norem, J. K., Niedentahl, P. M., Langston, C. A., & Brower, A. M. (1987). Life tasks, self-concept ideals, and cognitive strategies in a life transition. *Journal of Personality and Social Psychology, 53,* 1178–1191.

Carkhuff, R. R. (1969). *Helping and human relationships* (Vols. 1, 2). New York: Holt, Rinehart, & Winston.

Carkhuff, R. R. (1972). *The art of helping.* Amherst, MA: Human Resources Development Press.

Carter, E. A., & McGoldrick, M. (1980). *The family life cycle: A framework for family therapy.* New York: Gardner Press.

Catron, D. W., & Catron, S. S. (1989). Helping parents let go: A program for the parents of college freshmen. *Journal of College Student Development, 30,* 463–464.

Cattell, R. B., Eber, H. W., & Tatsuoka, M. M. (1970). *Handbook for the Sixteen Personality Factor Questionnaire (16PF).* Champaign, IL: Institute for Personality and Ability Testing.

Clairmont, P., Swindall, L., Meberg, M., & Johnson, B. (1997a). *The joyful journey book.* Grand Rapids, MI: Zondervan Press.

Clairmont, P., Swindall, L., Meberg, M., & Johnson, B. (1997b). *Joy breaks*. Grand Rapids, MI: Zondervan Press.

Clarke, C. (1970). Group procedures for increasing positive feedback between married partners. *The family coordinator, 19*, 324–328.

Cleaver, G. (1987). Marriage enrichment by means of a structured communication programme. *Family Relations Journal of Applied Family and Child Studies, 36*, 49–54.

Clinebell, H. (1976). Cassette programs for training and enrichment. In H. Otto (Ed.), *Marriage and family enrichment: New perspectives and programs* (pp. 254–265). Nashville, TN: Abingdon Press.

Cohen, P. A. (1981). Student ratings of instruction and student achievement: A meta-analysis of multi-section validity studies. *Review of Educational Research, 51*, 281–309.

Cole, C. L. (1988). Family and couples therapy with nonmarital cohabiting couples: Treatment issues and case studies. In C. S. Chilman, E. W. Nunnally, & F. M. Cox (Eds.), *Variant family forms: Vol. 5. Families in trouble series* (pp. 73–95). Newbury Park, CA: Sage.

Collins, J. D. (1971). *The effects of the Conjugal Relationship modification method on marital communication and adjustment*. Unpublished doctoral dissertation, Pennsylvania State University, University Park, PA.

Collins, J. D. (1977). Experimental evaluation of a six-month conjugal therapy and relationship enhancement program. In B. G. Guerney, Jr. (Ed.), *Relationship enhancement*. San Francisco: Jossey–Bass.

Collins, G. R. (Ed.). (1991). *Case studies in Christian counseling*. Dallas, TX: Word Press.

Combs, C. W. (1994). *Effects of cognitive-behavioral marriage enrichment on marital adjustment of church couples*. Unpublished doctoral dissertation, George Fox College, Newberg, OR.

Conner, R. W. (1988). Applying reality therapy to troubled marriages through the concept of permanent love. *Journal of Reality Therapy, 8*, 13–17.

Cookerly, J. R. (1977). Evaluating different approaches to marriage counseling. In D. H. L. Olson (Ed.), *Treating Relationships*. Lake Mills, IA: Graphic Publishing, pp. 475–498.

Council on Families in America. (1995). *Marriage in America: A report to the nation*. New York: Institute for American Values (also published as chapter 13 in Popenoe et al., 1996).

Cowen, E. L. (1986). Primary prevention in mental health: Ten years of retrospect and ten years of prospect. In M. Kessler & S. E. Goldston (Eds.), *A decade of progress in primary prevention* (pp. 3–45). Hanover, PA: University Press of New England.

Cox, D. J., Tisdelle, D., & Culbert, J. (1988). Increasing adherence to behavioral homework assignments. *Journal of Behavioral Medicine, 11*, 519–522.

Cox, S. A. (1995). *Commitment and couple happiness among marriage enrichment participants*. Unpublished doctoral dissertation, Graduate School of Psychology, Fuller Theological Seminary, Pasadena, CA.

Cozby, P. S. (1973). Self disclosure: A literative review. *Psychological Bulletin, 79*, 73–91.

Cromwell, R. E., Olson, D. H., & Fournier, D. G. (1976). Diagnosis and evaluation in marital and family counseling. In D. H. Olson (Ed.), *Treating relationships* (pp. 517–562). Lake Mills, IA: Graphic Publishing.

Crow, G. A., & Crow, L. I. (1988). *The functioning of the family system: An educational approach to positive procedures within areas of family life*. Springfield, IL: Charles C Thomas.

Cuber, J. F., & Harroff, P. B. (1965). *The significant Americans: A study of sexual behavior among the affluent*. New York: Appleton–Century–Crofts.

D'Angelli, A. R., Deyss, D. S., Guerney, B. G., Jr., Hershenberg, J. L., & Shorofsky, B. A. (1974). Interpersonal skill training for dating couples: An evaluation of an educational mental health service. *Journal of Counseling Psychology, 21*, 385–389.

Dean, D. G., & Spanier, G. B. (1974). Commitment—An overlooked variable in marital adjustment? *Sociological Focus, 7*, 113–118.

deGuzman, S. (Ed.). (1996, May/June). Types of marriage enrichment events. *Marriage Enrichment, 24*, 7.

Demarest, D., Sexton, J., & Sexton, M. (1977). *Marriage Encounter.* St. Paul, MN: Carillon.

DeMaria, R. (1993). Integrating marriage enrichment and marital therapy: A case study of PAIRS, a contemporary psychoeducational marital intervention program. *Families, 6*, 42–59.

Denton, W. (1986a). Introduction to marriage and family enrichment: A shift in paradigm. *Journal of Psychotherapy and the Family, 2*, 79–96.

Denton, W. (1986b). Starting a local enrichment group. *Journal of Psychotherapy and the Family, 2*, 69–77.

Denton, W. (1986c). *Marriage and family enrichment.* New York: Haworth Press.

Derlega, V., & Chaikin, A. (1975). *Sharing intimacy: What we reveal to others and why.* Englewood Cliffs, NJ: Prentice–Hall.

DeYoung, A. J. (1979). Marriage Encounter: A critical examination. *Journal of Marital and Family Therapy, 5*, 27–34.

Dicks, H. V. (1967). *Marital tensions.* New York: Basic Books.

Dillon, J. (1975). *Marital communication and its relation to self-esteem.* Unpublished doctoral dissertation, United States International University, San Diego, CA.

Dinkmeyer, D., & Carlson, J. (1985). TIME for a better marriage. *Individual Psychology Journal of Adlerian Theory, Research and Practice, 41*, 444–452.

Dinkmeyer, D., & Carlson, J. (1986a). TIME for a better marriage. *Journal of Psychotherapy and the Family, 2*, 69–77.

Dinkmeyer, D., & Carlson, J. (1986b). A systematic approach to marital enrichment. *American Journal of Family Therapy, 14*, 139–144.

Diskin, S. (1986). Marriage enrichment: Rationale and resources. *Journal of Psychotherapy and the Family, 2*, 111–125.

Dixon, D. N., & Sciara, A. D. (1977). Effectiveness of group reciprocity counseling with married couples. *Journal of Marriage and Family Counseling, 3*(3), 77–83.

Doherty, W. J. (1997). *The intentional family.* New York: Addison-Wesley.

Doherty, W. J., & Boss, P. G. (1991). Values and ethics in family therapy. In A. S. Gurman and D. P. Kniskern (Eds.), *Handbook of family therapy* (Vol. 2, pp. 606–637). New York: Brunner/Mazel.

Doherty, W. J., & Walker, B. J. (1982). Marriage Encounter casualties: A preliminary investigation. *American Journal of Family Therapy, 10*, 15–25.

Dowrick, P. W., & Biggs, S. J. (Eds.). (1983). *Using video: Psychological and social applications.* New York: Wiley.

Dunn, D. (1993). *Willing to try again: Steps toward blending a family.* Valley Forge, PA: Judson Press.

Durana, C. (1994). The use of bonding and emotional expressiveness in the PAIRS training: A psychoeducational approach for couples. *Journal of Family Psychotherapy, 24*, 269–280.

Egan, G. (1986). *The skilled helper: A systematic approach to effective helping* (3rd ed.). Monterey, CA: Brooks/Cole.

Ely, A. L., Guerney, B. G., & Storer, L. (1973). Efficacy of the training phase of conjugal therapy. *Psychotherapy: Theory, Research, and Practice, 10,* 201–207.

Emerson, D. E. (1993). *Evaluating the effectiveness of "Getting the Love You Want" marital enrichment seminars.* Unpublished doctoral dissertation, Graduate School of Psychology, Fuller Theological Seminary, Pasadena, CA.

Ennis, P. (1989). *The third option: A ministry to hurting marriages manual.* Syracuse, NY: Roman Catholic Diocese of Syracuse.

Epstein, N., & Jackson, E. (1978). An outcome study of short-term communication training with married couples. *Journal of Consulting and Clinical Psychology, 46,* 207–212.

Everett, W. J. (1990). *Blessed be the bond.* Lanham, MD: University Press.

Everts, J. F. (1988). Marriage enrichment in the antipodes: Evaluation of a New Zealand-based program. *Australian Journal of Sex, Marriage, and Family, 9,* 30–36.

Fichten, C., & Wright, J. (1983). Videotape and verbal feedback in behavioral couple therapy: A review. *Journal of Clinical Psychology, 39,* 216–221.

Fincham, F. D., & Bradbury, T. N. (Eds.). (1990). *The psychology of marriage.* New York: Guilford Press.

Fisher, R. E. (1973). *The effect of two group counseling methods on perceptual congruence in married pairs.* Unpublished doctoral dissertation, University of Hawaii, Honolulu, HA.

Flather, D. R. (Ed.). (1996). *The resource guide for Christian counselors.* Grand Rapids, MI: Baker Book House.

Floyd, D. S., & Floyd, W. A. (1987). A cognitive emotional behavioral enrichment retreat weekend. *Australian Journal of Sex, Marriage, and Family, 8,* 184–193.

Floyd, F. J., Markman, H. J., Kelly, S., Blumberg, S., & Stanley, S. (1995). Preventive intervention and relationship enhancement. In N. S. Jacobson & A. S. Gurman (Eds.), *Clinical handbook of couple therapy* (pp. 212–226). New York: Guilford Press.

Ford, J. D., Bashford, M. B., & DeWitt, K. N. (1984). Three approaches to marital enrichment: Toward optimal matching of participants and interventions. *Journal of Sex and Marital Therapy, 10,* 41–48.

Fowers, B. J., & Olson, D. H. (1992). Four types of premarital couples: An empirical typology based on PREPARE. *Journal of Family Psychology, 6,* 10–21.

Fowler, J. W. (1990). Faith development through the family life cycle. In J. Roberto (Ed.). (1990). *Growing in faith: A Catholic family sourcebook.* New Rochelle, NY: Don Bosco Multimedia.

Fowler, J. W. (1996). *Faithful change: The personal and public challenges of postmodern life.* Nashville, TN: Abingdon Press.

Freeman, K. (1992). *The effect of biofeedback on couples' physiological responses during conflict resolution.* Unpublished doctoral dissertation, Graduate School of Psychology, Fuller Theological Seminary, Pasadena, CA.

Friedman, E. H. (1985). *Generation to generation: Family process in church and synagogue.* New York: Guilford Press.

Friedman, E. H. (1991). Bowen theory and therapy. In A. S. Gurman & D. P. Kniskern (Eds.), *Handbook of family therapy* (Vol. 2, pp. 134–170). New York: Brunner/Mazel.

Gallagher, C. (1975). *The marriage encounter: As I have loved you.* Garden City, NY: Doubleday.

Gallagher, M. (1996). Re-creating marriage. In D. Popenoe, J. B. Elshtain, and D. Blankenhorn (Eds.), *Promises to keep: Decline and renewal of marriage in America* (pp. 233–246). Lanham, MD: Bowman & Littlefield.

Galston, W. A. (1996). The reinstitutionalization of marriage: Political theory and public policy. In D. Popenoe, J. B. Elshtain, and D. Blankenhorn (Eds.), *Promises to keep: Decline and renewal of marriage in America* (pp. 271–291). Lanham, MD: Bowman & Littlefield.

Gammage, S. (1991). Working with couples: Educational interventions. In D. Hooper & W. Dryden (Eds.), *Couple therapy: A handbook* (pp. 241–256). Milton Keynes, England: Open University Press.

Garland, D. S. (1983). *Working with couples for marriage enrichment: A guide for developing, conducting, and evaluating programs.* San Francisco: Jossey-Bass.

Garland, D. S., & Pancoast, D. L. (1990). *The church's ministry with families.* Dallas, TX: Word Publishing.

General Board of Discipleship (1982). *Celebrating Marriage.* Nashville: General Board of Discipleship, The United Methodist Church.

Genovese, R. J. (1975). Marriage Encounter. *Small Group Behavior, 6,* 45–56.

Gesten, E. L., & Jason, L. A. (1987). Social and community interventions. *Annual Review of Psychology, 38,* 427–460.

Giblin, P. (1986). Research and assessment in marriage and family enrichment: A meta-analysis study. *Journal of Psychotherapy and the Family, 2,* 79–92.

Giblin, P. (1993). Research: Marriage and marital therapy. *The Family Journal: Counseling and Therapy for Couples and Families, 1,* 339–341.

Giblin, P., Sprenkle, D. H., & Sheehan, R. (1985). Enrichment outcome research: A meta-analysis of premarital, marital, and family interventions. *Journal of Marital and Family Therapy, 11,* 257–271.

Gilbert, S. J. (1976). Self disclosure, intimacy and communication in families. *Family Coordinator, 25,* 221–231.

Giles, C., Giles, J., McKay, J., & McKay, P. (1996). *Couple-to-couple: A manual for training lay mentor couples.* Tulsa, OK: Couple-to-Couple Press.

Gillis, H. L., & Gass, M. A. (1993). Bringing adventure into marriage and family therapy: An innovative experiential approach. *Journal of Marital and Family Therapy, 19,* 273–286.

Glendon, M. A., & Blankenhorn, D. (1995). *Seedbeds of virtue: Sources of competence, character, & citizenship in American society.* Lanham, MD: Madison Books.

Goldberg, J. R. (1993, October). The business of preventing and treating troubled marriages. *Family Therapy News, 24,* 3–6.

Goldstein, A. P. (1969). Domains and dilemmas. *International Journal of Psychiatry, 7,* 128–134.

Goldstein, A. P. (1973). *Structured learnings therapy.* New York: Academic Press.

Goodman, M., Brown, J., & Dietz, P. (1992). *Managing managed care: A mental health practitioner's survival guide.* Washington, DC: American Psychiatric Press.

Goodwin, R. (1992). Overall, just how happy are you? The magical question 31 of the Spanier Dyadic Adjustment Scale. *Family Therapy, 19,* 273–275.

Gordon, L. H. (1988). *PAIRS curriculum guide and training manual* (annual updates). Falls Church, VA: PAIRS Foundation.

Gordon, L. H. (1990). *Love knots.* New York: Bantam Books.

Gordon, L. H. (1993). *Passage to intimacy.* New York: Simon & Schuster.

Gordon, T. (1970). *Parent effectiveness training.* New York: Wyden.

Gorsuch, R. L. (1989). Conviction and commitment. *American Psychologist, 44,* 1158–1159.

Gorsuch, K. E. (1992). The predictability of violence in marital relationships. Unpublished doctoral dissertation, Graduate School of Psychology, Fuller Theological Seminary, Pasadena, CA.

Gottman, J. M. (1994). *What predicts divorce? The relationship between marital processes and marital outcomes*. Hillsdale, NJ: Erlbaum.

Gottman, J. M., & Levinson, R. W. (1985). A valid procedure for obtaining self-report of affect in marital interaction. *Journal of Consulting and Clinical Psychology, 53,* 151–160.

Gottman, J. M., & Levinson, R. W. (1986). Assessing the role of emotion in marriage. *Behavioral Assessment, 8,* 31–48.

Gottman, J. M., Notarius, C., Gonso, J., & Markman, H. (1976). *A couples guide to communication*. Champaign, IL: Research Press.

Gould, R. (1993). *An overview of the therapeutic learning program: Short-term computer-assisted psychotherapy*. Santa Monica, CA: Interactive Health Systems.

Gray, J. (1984). *What you feel you can heal: A Guide for enriching relationships*. Mill Valley, CA Heart Publishing Co.

Gray, J. (1992). *Men are from Mars, women are from Venus*. New York: Harper/Collins.

Greeley, A. M. (1991). *Faithful attraction: Discovering intimacy, love, and fidelity in American marriage*. New York: Doherty.

Grossman, F. K. (1988). Strain in the transition to parenthood. *Marriage and Family Review, 12,* 85–104.

Guerin, P. J., Fay, L. F., Burden, S. L., & Kautto, J. G. (1987). *The evaluation and treatment of marital conflict*. New York: Basic Books.

Guerney, B. G. (1969). *Psychotherapeutic agents: New roles for nonprofessionals, parents, and teachers*. New York: Holt, Rinehart & Winston.

Guerney, B. G., Jr. (1977). *Relationship Enhancement*. San Francisco: Jossey-Bass.

Guerney, B., Jr. (1987). *Relationship enhancement marital/family therapist's manual*. State College, PA: Ideals.

Guerney, B. G., Jr., Brock, G., & Coufal, J. (1986). Integrating marital therapy and enrichment: The Relationship Enhancement approach. In N. S. Jacobson & A. S. Gurman (Eds.). *Clinical handbook of marital therapy* (pp. 151–171). New York: Guilford Press.

Guerney, B. G., Jr., Guerney, L., & Cooney, T. (1985). Marital and family problem prevention and enrichment programs. In L. L'Abate (Ed.), *Handbook of family psychology and therapy* (pp. 1179–1217). Homewood, IL: Dorsey Press.

Guerney, B. G., Jr., & Maxson, P. (1990). Marital and family enrichment research: A decade review and look ahead. *Journal of Marriage and the Family, 52,* 1127–1135.

Guldner, C. A. (1978). Family therapy for the trainee. *Journal of Marriage and Family Counseling, 4,* 127–132.

Gurman, A. S., & Kniskern, D. P. (1977). Enriching research on marital enrichment programs. *Journal of Marital and Family Therapy, 3,* 3–11.

Gurman, A. S., and Kniskern, D. P. (1978). Deterioration in marital and family therapy: Empirical, clinical and conceptual issues. *Family Process, 17,* 3–20.

Hahlweg, K., Baucom, D. H., & Markman, H. J. (1988). Recent advances in therapy and prevention. In I. R. H. Falloon (Ed.), *Handbook of behavioral family therapy* (pp. 413–448). New York: Guilford Press.

Hahlweg, K., & Markman, H. J. (1988). Effectiveness of behavioral marital therapy: Empirical status of behavioral techniques in preventing and alleviating marital distress. *Journal of Consulting and Clinical Psychology, 56,* 440–447.

Hansen, F. J., Fallon, A. E., & Novotny, S. L. (1991). The relationship between social network structure and marital satisfaction in distressed and nondistressed couples: A pilot study. *Family Therapy, 18*(2), 101–114.

Harrell, J., & Guerney, B. G., Jr. (1976). Training married couples in conflict negotiation skills. In D. H. L. Olson (Ed.), *Treating relationships* (pp. 151–166). Lake Mills, IA: Graphic Publishing.

Hart-Weber, C. A. (1995). *Leadership variables and type of activities included in marital enrichment programs.* Unpublished doctoral dissertation, Graduate School of Psychology, Fuller Theological Seminary, Pasadena, CA.

Haugk, K. C. (1984). *Christian caregiving.* Minneapolis: Augsburg.

Heitland, W. (1986). An experimental communication program for premarital dating couples. *School Counselor, 15,* 57–61.

Hendrix, H. (1988). *Getting the love you want.* New York: Harper and Row.

Hendrix, H. (1992). *Keeping the love you find.* New York: Pocket Books.

Hendrix, H., & Hunt, H. (1994). *The couples companion: Meditations and exercises.* New York: Pocket Books.

Henss, R., & Boning, U. (1984). Auswirkungen cines Kommunikationstrainings für Paargruppen aus der Sicht unterschiedlicher Beurteiler [The effect of a communication training program for couples]. *Psychologische Beiträge, 26,* 224–238.

Hill, E. W. (1991). Marital enrichment and couple decision-making. *Australian Journal of Marriage and Family, 12,* 77–91.

Hines, G. A. (1976). *Efficacy of communication skills training with married partners where no marital counseling has been sought.* Unpublished doctoral dissertation, University of South Dakota, Vermillion, SD.

Hof, L., & Miller, W. R. (1981). *Marriage enrichment: Philosophy, process, and program.* Bowie, MD: Brady.

Hogan, T. F. (1993). *An evaluation of client satisfaction with the "Getting the Love You Want" workshop.* Unpublished doctoral dissertation, Graduate School of Psychology, Fuller Theological Seminary, Pasadena, CA.

Holtzworth-Munroe, A., & Jacobson, N. S. (1991). Behavioral marital therapy. In A. S. Gurman & D. P. Kniskern (Eds.), *Handbook of family therapy* (Vol. 2, pp. 96–133). New York: Brunner/Mazel.

Holtzworth-Munroe, A., Jacobson, N. S., Deklyen, M., & Whisman, M. A. (1989). Relationship between behavioral marital therapy outcome and process variables. *Journal of Consulting and Clinical Psychology, 57,* 658–662.

Hopkins, L., & Hopkins, P. (1975). Marriage enrichment and the churches. *Spectrum, 51,* 16–19.

Hopkins, L., Hopkins, P., Mace, D., & Mace, V. (1978). *Toward better marriages.* Winston-Salem, NC: ACME.

Huber, J. W. (1977). *Measuring the effects of Marriage Encounter experience with the caring relationship inventory.* Unpublished manuscript.

Hunt, J. A., & Hunt, R. A. (1981). *Growing love in Christian marriage* (Couples book). Nashville, TN: United Methodist Publishing House.

Hunt, R. A. (1987). Marriage as dramatizing theology. *Journal of Pastoral Care, 41,* 119–131.

Hunt, R. A., & Chia, D. (1996, April). *Video ratings and couple functioning: Love-Power in marriage.* Paper presented at the Christian Association for Psychological Studies Conference, St. Louis, MO.

Hunt, R. A., & Hunt, J. A. F. (1976). *Ministry and marriage*. Dallas, TX: Ministry Studies Board.

Hunt, R. A., & Rydman, E. J. (1979). *Creative marriage* (2nd ed.). Boston: Allyn & Bacon.

Hunt, R. A., & Hunt, J. A. F. (1994). *Awaken your power to love*. Nashville, TN: Nelson Press.

Hunt, R. A., & Hunt, J. A. F. (1996a). *Caring couples network handbook*. Nashville, TN: Discipleship Resources.

Hunt, R. A., & Hunt, J. A. F. (1996b). *Caring couples network: A team in action* [Videotape]. Available from United Methodist Communications, Nashville, TN.

Hunt, R. A., & King, M. B. (1978). Religiosity and marriage. *Journal for the Scientific Study of Religion, 17*, 399–406.

Huppert, N. M. (1984). Communicating for better or for worse. *Australian Journal of Sex, Marriage, & Family, 5*(1), 25–35.

Jackson, D. D. (Ed.). (1968a). *Communication, family, and marriage: Human communication* (Vol. 1). Palo Alto, CA: Science and Behavior Books.

Jackson, D. D. (Ed.). (1968b). *Therapy, communication, and change: Human communication* (Vol. 2). Palo Alto, CA: Science and Behavior Books.

Jacobson, N. S., & Addis, M. E. (1993). Research on couples and couples therapy: What do we know? Where are we going? *Journal of Consulting and Clinical Psychology, 61*, 85–93.

Jacobson, N. S., & Christensen, A. (1996). *Integrative couple therapy: Promoting acceptance and change*. New York: Norton.

Jacobson, N. S., & Gurman, A. S. (Eds.). (1986). *Clinical handbook of marital therapy*. New York: Guilford Press.

Jacobson, N. S., & Gurman, A. S. (Eds.). (1995). *Clinical handbook of couple therapy*. New York: Guilford Press.

Jacobson, N. S., & Holtzworth-Munroe, A. (1986). Marital therapy: A social learning-cognitive perspective. In N. S. Jacobson & A. S. Gurman (Eds.), *Clinical handbook of marital therapy* (pp. 29–70). New York: Guilford Press.

Jacobson, N. S., & Margolin, G. (1979). *Marital therapy: Strategies based on social learning and behavior exchange principles*. New York: Brunner/Mazel.

Jacobson, N. S., & Martin, B. (1976). Behavioral marital therapy: Current status. *Psychological Bulletin, 83*, 540–556.

Jessee, R., & Guerney, B. E. (1981). A comparison of gestalt and relationship enhancement treatments with married couples. *American Journal of Family Therapy, 9*, 31–41.

Joanning, H. (1982). The long term effects of couple communication program. *Journal of Marital and Family Therapy, 8*, 463–468.

Johnson, M. P. (1982). The social and cognitive features of the dissolution of commitment to relationships. In S. Duck (Ed.), *Personal relationships: Dissolving personal relationships*. New York: Academic Press.

Johnson, M. P. (1991). Commitment to personal relationships. In W. H. Jones & D. W. Perlman (Eds.), *Advances in personal relationships* (Vol. 3). London: Kingsley.

Johnson, S. M., & Greenberg, L. S. (1984). The differential effects of cognitive, behavioral, and experiential interventions in marital therapy. *Journal of Consulting and Clinical Psychology, 53*, 175–184.

Johnson, W. E. (1990). *Blessed be the bond*. Lanham, MD: University Press of America.

Jourard, S. M. (1964). *The transparent self.* New York: Van Nostrand.

Jourard, S. M. (1971). *Self disclosure.* New York: Van Nostrand.

Jourard, S. M., & Richman, P. (1963). Factors in the self-disclosure input of college students. *Merrill-Palmer Quarterly, 9,* 141–148.

Kaplan, H. S. (1974). *The new sex therapy.* New York: Brunner/Mazel.

Karney, B. R., & Bradbury, T. N. (1995). The longitudinal course of marital quality and stability: A review of theory, method, and research. *Psychological Bulletin, 118,* 3–34.

Kaslow, F. W. (Ed.). (1996a). *Handbook of relational diagnosis and dysfunctional family patterns.* New York: Wiley.

Kaslow, F. W. (1996b). History, rationale, and philosophic overview of issues and assumptions about relational diagnosis. In F. W. Kaslow (Ed.), *Handbook of relational diagnosis and dysfunctional family patterns* (pp. 1–18). New York: Wiley.

Kerschner, M. (1996). *Item selection of the Hunt Assessment of Marital Program outcome instrument.* Unpublished doctoral dissertation, Graduate School of Psychology, Fuller Theological Seminary, Pasadena, CA.

Kilmann, P. R., Julian, A., & Moreault, D. (1978). The impact of a marriage enrichment program on relationship factors. *Journal of Sexual and Marital Therapy, 4,* 298–303.

Kilmann, P. R., Moreault, D., & Robinson, E. A. (1978). Effects of a marriage enrichment program: An outcome study. *Journal of Sexual and Marital Therapy, 4,* 54–57.

Koo, E. (1997). *Assessing the impact of the "Love-Power Marriage Enrichment Seminar" on marital quality of couples in Chinese-American churches.* Unpublished doctoral dissertation, Graduate School of Psychology, Fuller Theological Seminary, Pasadena, CA.

Kruel, R. (1995). *Permanence in marital commitment.* Unpublished doctoral dissertation, Graduate School of Psychology, Fuller Theological Seminary, Pasadena, CA.

Krug, S. E., & Ahadi, S. A. (1986). Personality characteristics of wives and husbands participating in marriage enrichment. *Multivariate Experimental Clinical Research, 8,* 149–159.

L'Abate, L. (1975). *Manual: Enrichment programs for the family life cycle.* Atlanta: Social Research Laboratories.

L'Abate, L. (1977). *Enrichment: Structured interventions with couples, families, and groups.* Washington, DC: University Press of America.

L'Abate, L. (1981). Skill training programs for couples and families. In A. S. Gurman & D. P. Kniskern (Eds.), *Handbook of family therapy* (Vol. 1, pp. 631–661). New York: Brunner/Mazel.

L'Abate, L. (1985a). *The handbook of family psychology and therapy* (Vols. 1–2). Homewood, IL: Dorsey Press.

L'Abate, L. (1985b). Structured enrichment (SE) with couples and families. *Family Relations, 34,* 169–175.

L'Abate, L. (1990). *Building family competence: Primary and secondary prevention strategies.* Newbury Park, CA: Sage.

L'Abate, L., Ganahl, G., & Hansen, J. (1986). *Methods of family therapy.* Englewood Cliffs, NJ: Prentice-Hall.

L'Abate, L., & McHenry, S. (1983). *Handbook of marital interventions.* New York: Grune & Stratton.

L'Abate, L., & O'Callaghan, J. B. (1977). Implications of the enrichment model for research and training. *Family Coordinator, 26,* 61–64.

L'Abate, L., & Rupp, G. (1981). *Enrichment: Skills training for family life*. Washington, DC: University Press of America.

L'Abate, L., & Weinstein, S. E. (1987). *Structured enrichment programs for couples and families*. New York: Brunner/Mazel.

L'Abate, L., & Young, L. (1987). *Casebook: Structured enrichment programs for couples and families*. New York: Brunner/Mazel.

Larsen, G. R. (1974). An evaluation of the Minnesota Couples Communication Program's influence on marital communication and self and mate perception. Unpublished doctoral dissertation, Arizona State University, Tempe, AZ.

Larson, D. B., Swyers, J. P., & Larson, S. S. (1997). *The costly consequences of divorce: Assessing the clinical, economic, and public health impact of marital disruption in the United States*. Rockville, MD: National Institute for Healthcare Research.

Larson, J. H., Wilson, S. M., & Beley, R. (1988). The assessment of family wellness in a university employee wellness program. *American Journal of Health Promotion, 2,* 20–30.

Lavee, Y., & Olson, D. H. (1993). Seven types of marriage: Empirical typology based on ENRICH. *Journal of Marital and Family Therapy, 19,* 325–340.

Lebow, J. L. (1983a). Client satisfaction with mental health treatment: Methodological considerations in assessment. *Evaluation Review, 7,* 729–752.

Lebow, J. L. (1983b). Research assessing consumer satisfaction with mental health treatment: A review of the findings. *Evaluation and Program Planning, 6,* 211–236.

Lederer, W. J., & Jackson, D. D. (1968). *The mirages of marriage*. New York: Norton.

Lee, E. (1989). Assessment and treatment of Chinese-American immigrant families. In G. W. Saba, B. M. Karrer, & K. V. Hardy (Eds.), *Minorities and family therapy* (pp. 99–122). New York: Haworth Press.

Lee, P. A., & Brage, D. G. (1989). Family life education and research: Toward a more positive approach. In M. J. Fine (Ed.), *The second handbook on parent education: Contemporary perspectives. Educational psychology* (pp. 347–378). San Diego, CA: Academic Press.

Leik, R. K., & Leik, S. A. (1977). Transition to interpersonal commitment. In R. L. Hamblin & J. H. Kunkel (Eds.), *Behavioral theory in sociology*. New Brunswick: Transition Books.

Lester, M. E., & Doherty, W. J. (1983). Couples' long-term evaluations of their Marriage Encounter experience. *Journal of Marital and Family Therapy, 9,* 183–188.

Levinson, D. J. (1978). *Season's of a man's life*. New York: Ballentine Books.

Liberman, R. P., Wheeler, E., & Sanders, N. (1976). Behavioral therapy for marital disharmony. *Journal of Marriage and Family Counseling, 2,* 383–395.

Lieberman, R. P., Yalom, I. D., & Miles, M. B. (1973). *Encounter groups: First facts*. New York: Basic Books.

Lief, H. I. (1977). Sensitivity to feelings. *Journal American Academic Psychoanalysis, 5,* 289–290.

Locke, H. J. (1951). *Predicting adjustments in marriage: A comparison of a divorced and a happily married group*. New York: Holt.

Locke, H. J., & Wallace, K. M. (1959). Short marital adjustment and prediction tests: Their reliability and validity. *Marriage and Family Living, 21,* 251–255.

Loew, P. (1990). *The development of an intentional ministry in a bilingual Chinese church in Brooklyn, New York*. Unpublished doctoral dissertation, Eastern Baptist Theological Seminary, Philadelphia, PA.

Lopez, F. G. (1993). Cognitive processes in close relationships: Recent findings and implications for counseling. *Journal of Counseling and Development, 71*, 310–315.

Love, P., & Robinson, J. (1994). *Hot monogamy*. NY: Penguin Books.

Lowman, J. (1984). *Mastering the techniques of teaching*. San Francisco: Jossey–Bass.

Luft, J. (1969). *Of human interaction*. Palo Alto, CA: Mayfield.

Luquet, W. (1996). *Short-term couples therapy: The Imago model in action*. New York: Brunner/Mazel.

Luthman, S. G., & Kirschenbaum, M. (1974). *The dynamic family*. Palo Alto, CA: Science and Behavior.

Mace, D. R. (1975a). Marriage enrichment concepts for research. *Family coordinator, 24*, 171–173.

Mace, D. R. (1975b). We call it ACME. *Small Group Behavior, 6*, 31–44.

Mace, D. (1981). The long trail from information giving to behavioral change. *Family Relations, 30*, 599–606.

Mace, D. R. (1987). Three ways of helping married couples. *Journal of Marital and Family Therapy, 13*, 179–185.

Mace, D. R., & Mace, V. C. (1974). *We can have better marriages if we really want them*. Nashville, TN: Abingdon Press.

Mace, D. R., & Mace, V. C. (1975). Marriage enrichment—Wave of the future? *The Family Coordinator, 24*, 131–135.

Mace, D. R., & Mace, V. C (1976). *Marriage enrichment in the church*. Nashville, TN: Broadman Press.

Mace, D. R., & Mace, V. C. (1977). *How to Have a Happy Marriage*. Nashville: Abingdon.

Mace, D. R., & Mace, V. C. (1978a). The marriage enrichment movement: Its history, its rationale, and its future prospects. In L. Hopkins, P. Hopkins, D. Mace, & V. Mace. *Toward better marriages*. Winston-Salem, NC: Association of Couples for Marriage Enrichment.

Mace, D. R., & Mace, V. C. (1978b). Measure your marriage potential: A simple test that tells couples where they are. *Family Coordinator, 27*, 63–67.

Mace, D. R., & Mace, V. C. (1982). *Marriage enrichment mini-retreat: A manual for leaders*. Winston-Salem, NC: Association for Couples in Marriage Enrichment.

Mace, D. R., & Mace, V. C. (1984). *Close companions: The marriage enrichment handbook*. New York: Continuum.

Mace, D. R., & Mace, V. C. (1986). The history and present status of the marriage and family enrichment movement. *Journal of Psychotherapy and the Family, 2*, 7–17.

Mak, Y. H. (1994). *Spousal disparity in cultural identity and marital quality among Chinese Americans*. Unpublished doctoral dissertation, School of Theology, Fuller Theological Seminary, Pasadena, CA.

Malcolm, K. D. (1992). Personal growth in marriage: An Adlerian unilateral marriage enrichment program [Special Issue: The process of aging and working with older adults]. *Individual Psychology Journal of Adlerian Theory, Research and Practice, 48*, 488–492.

Margolin, G. (1986). Ethical issues in marital therapy. In N. S. Jacobson & A. S. Gurman (Eds.), *Clinical handbook of marital therapy* (pp. 621–638). New York: Guilford Press.

Margolin, G., & Wampold, B. E. (1981). Sequential analysis of conflict and accord in distressed and nondistressed marital partners. *Journal of Consulting and Clinical Psychology, 49*, 554–567.

Markman, H. J. (1981). The prediction of marital distress: A five year follow-up. *Journal of Consulting and Clinical Psychology, 49*, 760–762.

Markman, H. J. (1984). The longitudinal study of couples' interactions: Implications for understanding and predicting the development of marital distress. In K. Hahlweg & N. Jacobson (Eds.), *Marital interaction: Analysis and modification* (pp. 253–281). New York: Guilford Press.

Markman, H. J., Floyd, F. J., Stanley, S. M., & Jamieson, K. (1984). A cognitive/behavioral program for the prevention of marital and family distress: Issues in program development and delivery. In K. Hahlweg & N. Jacobson (Eds.), *Marital interaction: Analysis and modification* (pp. 396–428). New York: Guilford Press.

Markman, H. J., Floyd, F. J., Stanley, S. M., & Lewis, H. C. (1986). *Prevention.* In N. S. Jacobson & A. S. Gurman (Eds.), *Clinical handbook of marital therapy* (pp. 173–195). New York: Guilford Press.

Markman, H. J., Floyd, F. J., Stanley, S. M., & Storaasli, R. (1988). Prevention of marital distress: A longitudinal investigation. *Journal of Consulting and Clinical Psychology, 56*, 210–217.

Markman, H. J., Renick, M. J., Floyd, F. J., Stanley, S. M., & Clements, M. (1993). Preventing marital distress through communication and conflict management training: A 4- and 5-year follow-up. *Journal of Consulting and Clinical Psychology, 61*, 70–77.

Markman, H. J., Stanley, S. M., & Blumberg, S. L. (1994). *Fighting for your marriage.* San Francisco: Jossey-Bass.

Mattson, D. L., Christensen, O. J., & England, J. T. (1990). The effectiveness of a specific marital enrichment program: TIME. *Individual Psychology, 46*, 88–92.

McFarlane, W. R. (1991). In A. S. Gurman & D. P. Kniskern (Eds.), *Handbook of family therapy* (Vol. 2, pp. 363–395). New York: Brunner/Mazel.

McGoldrick, M., & Gerson, R. (1985). *Genograms in family assessment.* New York: Norton.

McKeachie, W. J. (1994). *Teaching tips: Strategies, research, and theory for college and university teachers.* Lexington, MA: Heath.

McIntosh, D. M. (1975). *A comparison of the effects of highly structured, partially structured, and non-structured human relations training for married couples on the dependent variables of communication, marital adjustment, and personal adjustment.* Unpublished doctoral dissertation, North Texas State University, Denton, TX.

McLeish, J., Matheson, W., & Park, J. (1973). *Psychology of the learning group.* London: Hutchinson.

McManus, M. J. (1995). *Marriage Savers: Helping your friends and family avoid divorce* (Rev. ed.). Grand Rapids, MI: Zondervan Press.

Mendez, E. W. (1992). *Marital communication training using videotape self modeling.* Unpublished doctoral dissertation, Graduate School of Psychology, Fuller Theological Seminary, Pasadena, CA.

Miller, S. (1971). *The effects of communication training in small groups upon self-disclosure and openness in engaged couples' systems of interaction: A field experiment.* Unpublished doctoral dissertation, University of Minnesota, Minneapolis, MN.

Miller, S., Nunnally, E. W., & Wackman, D. B. (1975). *Alive and aware: Improving communication in relationships.* Minneapolis: Interpersonal Communication Programs.

Miller, S. (1997). *Great start instructor training.* Littleton, CO: Interpersonal Communication Programs.

Miller, S., Corrales, R., & Wackman, D. B. (1975). *Marriages and families: Enrichment through communication.* Beverly Hills, CA: Sage.

Miller, S., Miller, P., Nunnally, E. W., & Wackman, D. B. (1991). *Talking and listening together.* Littleton, CO: Interpersonal Communication Programs.

Miller, S., Nunnally, E. W., & Wackman, D. B. (1976). Minnesota Couples Communication Program (MCCP): Premarital and marital groups. In D. H. L. Olson (Ed.), *Treating relationships*. Lake Mills, IA: Graphic Publishing.

Miller, S., Wackman, D. B., Nunnally, E. W., & Miller, P. (1988). *Connecting with self and others*. Littleton, CO: Interpersonal Communication Programs.

Mirowsky, J., & Ross, C. E. (1986). Social patterns of distress. *Annual Review of Sociology, 12*, 23–45.

Murstein, B. I. (1974). Love, sex, and marriage throughout the ages. New York: Springer.

Murstein, B. L., & MacDonald, M. G. (1983). The relationship of "exchange-orientation" and "commitment" scales to marital adjustment. *International Journal of Psychology, 45*, 141–151.

Nadeau, K. G. (1971). An examination of some effects of the marital enrichment group. Unpublished doctoral dissertation, University of Florida, Gainesville, FL.

Navran, L. (1967). Communication and adjustment in marriage. *Family Process, 6*, 173–184.

Nelson, T. S., & Trepper, T. S. (Eds.). (1993). *101 Interventions in family therapy*. New York: Haworth Press.

Neville, W. G. (1971). *An analysis of personality types and their differential response to marital enrichment groups*. Unpublished doctoral dissertation, University of Florida, Gainesville, FL.

Niebuhr, H. R. (1954). *Christ and culture*. New York: Harper.

Nix-Early, V. (1984). A couples' workshop for college students. *Journal of College Student Personnel, 25*, 479–480.

Noller, P. (1984). *Nonverbal communication and marital interaction*. Oxford: Pergamon Press.

Nording, W. (1997, May). *To love and to charish*. Paper presented at the Coalition for Marriage, Family, and Couple Education Smart Marriages Conference, Washington, DC.

Noval, L. S., Combs, C. W., Winamaki, M., Bufford, R. K., & Halter, L. (1996). Cognitive-behavioral marital enrichment among church and non-church groups: Preliminary findings. *Journal of Psychology and Christianity, 24*, 47–53.

Nunnally, E. W. (1971). *Effects of communication training upon interaction awareness and empathic accuracy of engaged couples: A field experiment*. Unpublished doctoral dissertation, University of Minnesota, Minneapolis, MN.

O'Leary, K. D. (Ed.). (1987). *Assessment of marital discord: An integration for research and clinical practice*. Mahwah, NJ: Erlbaum.

O'Leary, K. D., & Smith, D. A. (1991). Marital interactions. *Annual Review of Psychology, 42*, 191–212.

Oliver, G. J., & Miller, S. (1994). Couple communication. *Journal of Psychology and Christianity, 13*, 151–157.

Oliver, R., Mattson, D. L., & Moore, J. (1993). Psychological reactance in marital enrichment training. *TCA Journal, 22*, 3–10.

Olson, D. H. (Ed.). (1976a). *Treating relationships*. Lake Mills, IA: Graphic Publishing Co.

Olson, D. H. (1976b). Bridging research, theory, and application: The triple threat in science. In Olson, D. H. (Ed.). *Treating relationships* (pp. 566–579). Lake Mills, IA: Graphic Publishing Co.

Olson, D. H. (1977). Insiders and outsiders' views of relationships: Research studies. In G. Levinger & H. Rausch (Eds.), *Close relationships*. Amherst, MA: University of Massachusetts Press.

Olson, D. H. (1990). Commentary: Marriage in perspective. In F. D. Fincham & T. N. Bradbury (Eds.), *The psychology of marriage* (pp. 402–419). New York: Guilford Press.

Olson, D. H., Fournier, D. G., & Druckman, J. M. (1996). *Manual for the Prepare/Enrich 2000.* Minneapolis, MN: Life Innovations.

Olson, D. H., & Fowers, B. J. (1986). Predicting marital success with PREPARE: A predictive validity study. *Journal of Marital and Family Therapy, 12,* 403–413.

Olson, D. H., Russell, C. S., & Sprenkle, D. H. (1988). Circumplex model: Systemic assessment and treatment of families [Special issue]. *Journal of Psychotherapy and the Family,* 4(1,2): 93–111.

Olson, E. (1990). Transitional couples. Unpublished doctoral dissertation, Graduate School of Psychology, Fuller Theological Seminary, Pasadena, CA.

Orling, R. A. (1976). *The efficacy of proactive marital communication training.* Unpublished doctoral dissertation, New Mexico State University, Las Cruces, NM.

Otto, H. (1969). *More joy in your marriage.* New York: Hawthorne.

Otto, H. A. (1972). *The utilization of family strengths in marriage and family counseling.* Beverly Hills: Holistic Press.

Otto, H. A. (1975). Marriage and family enrichment programs in North America: Report and analysis. *The Family Coordinator, 24,* 137–142.

Otto, H. (Ed.). (1976). *Marriage and family enrichment: New perspectives and programs.* Nashville: Abingdon Press.

Padgett, V. R. (1983). Videotape replay in marital therapy. *Psychotherapy: Theory, Research, and Practice, 20,* 232–242.

Parrott, L., III, & Parrott, L. (1995a). *The marriage mentor manual.* Grand Rapids, MI: Zondervan Press.

Parrott, L., III, & Parrott, L. (1995b). *Becoming soulmates: Cultivating spiritual intimacy in the early years of marriage.* Grand Rapids, MI: Zondervan Press.

Parrott, L., III, & Parrott, L. (1997). *Mentoring engaged and newly married couples.* Grand Rapids, MI: Zondervan Press. (Leader's Guide, Participant Guide, Video Curriculum kit, Questions couples ask).

Paul, N., & Paul, B. (1975). *A marital puzzle.* New York: Norton.

Piercy, F. P., & Sprenkle, D. H. (1986). *Family therapy sourcebook.* New York: Guilford.

Pilder, S. J. (1972). Some effects of laboratory training on married couples. Unpublished doctoral dissertation, United States International University, San Diego, CA.

Popenoe, D., Elshtain, J. B., & Blankenhorn, D. (1996). *Promises to keep: Decline and renewal of marriage in America.* Lanham, MD: Bowman & Littlefield.

Powell, G. S., & Wampler, K. S. (1982). Marriage enrichment participants: Levels of marital satisfaction. *Family Relations Journal of Applied Family and Child Studies, 31*(3), 389–393.

Rampage C. (1994). Power, gender, and marital intimacy. *Journal of Family Therapy, 16,* 125–137.

Rappaport, A. F. (1976). Conjugal Relationship Enhancement Program. In D. H. L. Olson (Ed.), *Treating relationships.* Lake Mills, IA: Graphic Publishing.

Rappaport, A. F., & Harrell, J. E. (1975). A behavioral exchange model for marital counseling. In A. S. Gurman & D. G. Rice (Eds.), *Couples in conflict.* New York: Aronson.

Reagan, M. C., Jr. (1996). Postmodern family law: Toward a new model of status. In D. Popenoe, J. B. Elshtain, and D. Blankenhorn (Eds.), *Promises to keep: Decline and renewal of marriage in America* (pp. 157–186). Lanham, MD: Bowman & Littlefield.

Regula, R. B. (1975). Marriage Encounter: What makes it work? *The Family Coordinator*, *24*, 153–159.

Renick, M. J., Blumberg, S., & Markman, H. J. (1992). The Prevention and Relationship Enhancement Program (PREP): An empirically based preventive intervention program for couples. *Family Relations*, *41*, 141–147.

Richardson, R. W. (1996). *Creating a healthier church: Family systems theory, leadership, and congregational life*. Minneapolis, MN: Fortress Press.

Ridley, C. A., & Bain, A. B. (1983). The effects of a premarital relationship enhancement program on self-disclosure. *Family Therapy*, *10*, 13–34.

Ridley, C. A., Jorgenson, S. R., Morgan, A. G., & Avery, A. W. (1982). Relationship Enhancement with premarital couples: An assessment of effects on relationship quality. *The American Journal of Family Therapy*, *10*(3), 41–48.

Roberts, P. V. (1975). *The effects on marital satisfaction of brief training in behavioral exchange negotiation mediated by differentially experienced trainers*. Unpublished doctoral dissertation, Fuller Theological Seminary, Pasadena, CA.

Robinson, L., & Blanton, P. (1993). Marital strengths in enduring marriages. *Family Relations*, *42*, 38–45.

Rohde, R. I., & Stockton, R. (1994). Group structure: A review. *Journal of Group Psychotherapy, Psychodrama, and Sociometry*, *46*, 151–158.

Romney, R., & Harrison, B. (1983). *Giving time a chance: The secret of a lasting marriage*. New York: Evans.

Rossi, P. H., & Freeman, H. E. (1989). *Evaluation: A systematic approach*. Newbury Park, CA: Sage.

Rusbult, C. E. (1980). Commitment and satisfaction in romantic associations: A test of the investment model. *Journal of Experimental Social Psychology*, *16*, 172–186.

Rusbult, C. E., & Drigotas, S. M. (1992). Should I stay or should I go? A dependence model of breakups. *Journal of Personality and Social Psychology*, *62*, 62–87.

Russell, C. S., Bagarozzi, K. A., Atilano, R. B., & Morris, J. E. (1984). A comparison of two approaches to marital enrichment and conjugal skills training: Minnesota couples communication program and structured behavioral exchange contracting. *The American Journal of Family Therapy*, *12*, 13–25.

Satir, V. (1967). *Conjoint family therapy* (Rev. ed.). Palo Alto, CA: Science and Behavior Books.

Satir, V. (1972). *Peoplemaking*. Palo Alto, CA: Science and Behavior Books.

Satir, V. (1988). *The new peoplemaking*. Mountain View, CA: Science and Behavior Books.

Sauber, S. R. (1974). Primary prevention and the marital enrichment group. *Journal of Family Counseling*, *2*, 39–44.

Sawyers, L. (Ed.). (1986). *Faith and families*. Philadelphia: Geneva Press.

Schaefer, R. T. (1993). *Racial and ethnic groups*. New York: Harper/Collins.

Schauble, P. G., and Hill, C. G. (1976). A laboratory approach to treatment in marriage counseling: Training in communication skills. *The Family Coordinator*, *25*, 277–284.

Schlien, S. R. (1971). Training dating couples in empathic and open communication: An experimental evaluation of a potential preventative mental health program. Unpublished doctoral dissertation, Pennsylvania State University, University Park, PA.

Schnarch, D. (1997). *Passionate marriage: Sex, love, and intimacy in emotionally committed relationships*. New York: Norton.

Schneider, C. E. (1996). The law and the stability of marriage: The family as a social institution. In D. Popenoe, J. B. Elshtain, and D. Blankenhorn (Eds.), *Promises to keep:*

Decline and renewal of marriage in America (pp. 187–214). Lanham, MD: Bowman & Littlefield.

Schwager, H. A., & Conrad, R. W. (1974). Impact of group counseling on self and other acceptance and persistence with rural disadvantaged student families (Counseling Services Report No. 15). Washington, DC: National Institute of Education.

Schultz, W. C. (1978). *FIRO (fundamental interpersonal relations orientation) awareness scales manual.* Palo Alto, CA: Consulting Psychologists Press.

Shelton, J. L., & Ackerman, M. (1974). *Homework in counseling and psychotherapy.* Springfield, IL: Charles C Thomas.

Sherman, R., & Dinkmeyer, D. (1987). *Systems of family therapy: An Adlerian integration.* New York: Brunner/Mazel.

Sherwood, J. J., & Scherer, J. J. (1975). A model for couples: How two can grow together. In S. Miller, R. Corrales, & D. B. Wackman, *Marriages and families: Enrichment through communication* (pp. 121–142). Beverly Hills, CA: Sage.

Shortz, J. L., Worthington, E. L., Jr., McCullough, M. E., DeVries, H., & Morrow, D. (1994). Published scholarship on marital therapy. *Journal of Marital and Family Therapy.* 20(2), 185–189.

Shostrom, E. L. (1967). *Caring relationship inventory.* San Diego: EDITS/Educational and Industrial Testing Service.

Skinner, B. F. (1953). *Science and human behavior.* New York: Macmillan.

Skinner, B. F. (1969). Contingencies of reinforcement. New York: Appleton Century Crofts.

Smalley, G. (1993). *Hidden keys of a loving and lasting marriage.* Grand Rapids, MI: Zondervan Press.

Smalley, G., & Trent, J. (1988). *The language of love.* Waco, TX: Word Books.

Smith, R. L., & Alexander, A. M. (1973). *Counseling couples in groups.* Springfield, IL: Thomas.

Smith, A., & Smith, L. (1981). *Growing love in Christian marriage* (Pastors book). Nashville, TN: United Methodist Publishing House.

Smith, R. C. (1995). *Assessing the impact of the "Love-Power Marriage Enrichment Seminar" on marital quality of couples in an African-American Seventh-Day Adventist Church.* Unpublished doctoral dissertation, Graduate School of Psychology, Fuller Theological Seminary, Pasadena, CA.

Spanier, G. B. (1976). Measuring dyadic adjustment: New scales for assessing the quality of marriage and similar dyads. *Journal of Marriage and the Family, 38,* 15–28.

Spanier, G. B. (1989). *Manual for the Dyadic Adjustment Scale (DAS).* North Tonawanda, NY: Multi-Health Systems.

Stahmann, R. F., & Salts, C. J. (1993). Educating for marriage and intimate relationships. In M. E. Arcus, J. D. Schvaneveldt, & J. J. Moss (Eds.), *Handbook of family life education: Vol. 1. Foundations of family life education* (pp. 33–61). Newbury Park, CA: Sage.

Stanley, S. M. (1986). *Commitment and the maintenance and enhancement of relationships.* Unpublished doctoral dissertation, University of Denver, Denver, CO.

Stanley, S. (1993). *Manual for Christian PREP.* Denver, CO: Author.

Stanley, S. M., & Markman, H. J. (1992). Assessing commitment in personal relationships. *Journal of Marriage and the Family, 54,* 595–608.

Stanley, S., Trathen, D. McCain, S. & Bryan, M. (1998). *A Lasting Promise.* San Francisco: Jossey-Bass.

Stein, E. V. (1975). MARDILAB: An experiment in marriage enrichment. *The Family Coordinator, 24,* 167–170.

Stevens, F. E., & L'Abate, L. (1986). Structured enrichment (SE) of a couple. *Journal of Psychotherapy and the Family, 2,* 59–67.

Straus, M. (1979). Measuring intrafamilial conflict and violence: The Conflict Tactics Scale. *Journal of Marriage and the Family, 41,* 75–88.

Strickland, J. H. (1982). *The effects of two marriage enrichment retreat models on marital satisfaction.* Unpublished doctoral dissertation, Texas Tech University, Lubbock, TX.

Strozier, A. M. (1981). *The effect of a selected marriage enrichment retreat upon relationship change, marital communication, and dyadic adjustment..* Unpublished doctoral dissertation, Southwestern Baptist Theological Seminary, Fort Worth, TX.

Strube, M. J., & Hartmann, D. P. (1983). Meta-analysis: Techniques, applications, and functions. *Journal of Consulting and Clinical Psychology, 51,* 14–27.

Stuart, R. B. (1980). *Helping couples change: A social learning approach to marital therapy.* New York: Guilford Press.

Stucky, F., Eggeman, K., Eggeman, B. S., & Moxley, V. (1986). Premarital counseling as perceived by newlywed couples: An exploratory study. *Journal of Sex and Marital Therapy, 12,* 221–228.

Swicegood, M. L. (1974). *An evaluative study of one approach to marriage enrichment.* Unpublished doctoral dissertation, University of North Carolina at Greensboro.

Tan, S. Y. (1991). *Lay counseling: Equipping Christians for a helping ministry.* Grand Rapids, MI: Zondervan.

Taylor, R. M., & Morrison, L. P. (1996). *Taylor-Johnson Temperament Analysis manual.* Thousand Oaks, CA: Psychological Publications.

Terman, L. M., Buttenweiser, P., Ferguson, L. W., Johnson, W. B., & Wilson, D. P. (1938). *Psychological factors in marital happiness.* New York: McGraw-Hill.

Terman, L. M., & Wallin, P. (1949). The validity of marriage prediction and marital adjustment tests. *American Sociological Review, 14,* 497–504.

Thielen, A., Hubner, H. O., & Schmook, C. (1976). *Studies of the effectiveness of the German revised version of the Minnesota Couples Communication Program on relationships between partners.* Heidelberg, Germany: University of Heidelberg, Institute of Psychology.

Thomas, C. C., & Tartell, R. (1991). Effective leadership: Evaluations of the next generation of workers. *Psychological Reports, 69,* 51–61.

Thompson, M. J. (1989). *Family: The forming center.* Nashville, TN: Upper Room Books.

Tolman, R. M., & Molidor, C. E. (1994). A decade of social group work research: Trends in methodology, theory, and program development. *Research on Social Work Practice,* 4(2), 142–159.

Touliatos, J., Perlmutter, B. F., & Straus, M. A. (Eds.). (1990). *Handbook of family measurement techniques.* Newbury Park, CA: Sage.

Travis, R. P., & Travis, P. Y. (1975). The Pairing Enrichment Program: Actualizing the Marriage. *The Family Coordinator, 24,* 161–165.

Travis, R. P., & Travis, P. V. (1976a). Self-actualization in marital enrichment. *Journal of Marriage and Family Counseling, 2,* 73–80.

Travis, R. P., & Travis, P. V. (1976b). A note on changes in the caring relationship following a marriage enrichment program and some preliminary findings. *Journal of Marriage and Family Counseling, 2,* 81–83.

Trower, P., & Kiely, B. (1983). Video feedback: Help or hindrance? A review and analysis. In P. W. Dowrick & S. J. Biggs (Eds.), *Using video: Psychological and social applications* (pp. 181–198). New York: Wiley.

Truax, C. B., & Carkhuff, R. R. (1967). *Toward effective counseling and psychotherapy.* Chicago: Aldine.

Ulriei, D., L'Abate, L., & Wagner, V. (1977). The E-R-A Model: A heuristic framework for classification of social skills training programs for couples and families. *Family Process, 16,* 46–48.

Van Zoost, B. (1973). Premarital communication skills education with university couples. *The Family Coordinator, 22,* 187–191.

Venema, H. B. (1976). *Marriage enrichment: A comparison of the behavior exchange negotiation and communication models.* Unpublished doctoral dissertation, Fuller Theological Seminary, Pasadena, CA.

Verseveldt, J. P. (1993). *The relation of therapy to marital adjustment, satisfaction, and commitment for couples who participate in a marital enrichment program.* Unpublished doctoral dissertation, Graduate School of Psychology, Fuller Theological Seminary, Pasadena, CA.

Vigeveno, H. S., & Claire, A. (1987). *No one gets divorced alone: How divorce affects moms, dads, kids, and grandparents.* Ventura, CA: Regal Books.

Vincent, C. E. (1973). *Sexual and marital health.* New York: McGraw-Hill.

Vincent, C. E. (1977). Barriers to the development of marital health as a health field, *Journal of Marriage and Family Counseling.* 3(3), 3–11.

Wampler, K. S., & Sprenkle, D. S. (1980). The Minnesota Couple Communication Program: A follow-up study. *Journal of Marriage and the Family, 42,* 577–584.

Waterman, J. A. (1990). *The assessment of marital communication, power, and model of marriage in relation to marital satisfaction.* Unpublished doctoral dissertation, Graduate School of Psychology, Fuller Theological Seminary, Pasadena, CA.

Watzlawick, P., Beavin, J., & Jackson, D. (1967). *Pragmatics of human communication.* New York: Norton.

Watzlawick, P., Weakland, J., & Fisch, R. (1974). *Change: Principles of problem formation and problem resolution.* New York: Norton.

Weeks, G. R. (Ed.). (1989). *Treating couples: The intersystem model of the Marriage Council of Philadelphia.* New York: Brunner/Mazel.

Weiner-Davis, M. (1992). *Divorce-busting: A step-by-step approach to making your marriage loving again.* New York: Fireside (Simon & Schuster).

Weinstein, C. G. (1975). *Differential change in self-actualizing and self-concept, and its effects on marital interaction, as an outcome of a selected growth group experience.* Unpublished doctoral dissertation, University of Southern California, Los Angeles, CA.

Weishaus, S., Marston, A. R., & Shieh, B. (1994). Long-term evaluation and divorce statistics for making marriage work: A Jewish marriage preparation program. *Journal of Jewish Communal Service,* 70(2–3), 207.

Weiss, R. L., & Heyman, R. E. (1990). Observation of marital interaction. In F. D. Fincham & T. N. Bradbury (Eds.), *The psychology of mariage* (pp. 87–117). New York: Guilford Press.

Weiss, R. L., Hops, H., & Patterson, G. R. (1973). A framework for conceptualizing marital conflict, a technology for altering it, some data for evaluating it. In E. J. Hamerlynck, L. C. Handy, & E. J. Mash (Eds.), *Behavior change: Methodology, concepts, and practice.* Champaign, IL: Research Press, 309–342.

Weitzman, L. J. (1981). *The marriage contract: A guide to living with lovers and spouses.* New York: The Free Press.

Wells, R. A., & Giannetti, V. J. (Eds.). (1990). *Handbook of brief psychotherapies: Applied clinical psychology.* New York: Plenum Press.

Whisman, M. A., & Jacobson, N. S. (1990). Brief behavioral marital therapy. In R. A. Wells & V. J. Giannetti (Eds.), *Handbook of brief psychotherapies: Applied clinical psychology* (pp. 325–349). New York: Plenum Press.

Whitaker, C. A., & Bumberry, W. M. (1988). *Dancing with the family.* New York: Brunner/Mazel.

White, G. T. (1995). *Relation between level of distress and couples' responses to structure of marriage enrichment programs.* Unpublished doctoral dissertation, Graduate School of Psychology, Fuller Theological Seminary, Pasadena, CA.

Whitehead, E. E., & Whitehead, J. D. (1981). *Marrying well: Stages on the journey of Christian marriage.* Garden City, NJ: Image/Doubleday.

Wieman, R. J. (1973). *Conjugal relationship modification and reciprocal reinforcement: A comparison of treatments for marital discord.* Unpublished doctoral dissertation, Pennsylvania State University, University Park, PA.

Williams, A. M. (1975). *Comparison of the effects of two marital enrichment programs on marital communication and adjustment.* Unpublished master's thesis, University of Florida, Gainesville, FL.

Wilson, D. A. (1980). *The effects of a partially structured Christian marriage enrichment program upon marital communication, general marital adjustment, and purpose in life.* Unpublished doctoral dissertation, North Texas State University, Denton, TX.

Witkin, S. (1977, December). *Communication training for couples: A comparative study.* Paper presented at the meeting of the Association for the Advancement of Behavior Therapy, Atlanta, GA.

Woodman, T. (1991). *The role of forgiveness in marriage and marital adjustment.* Unpublished doctoral dissertation, Graduate School of Psychology, Fuller Theological Seminary, Pasadena, CA.

Worthington, E. L., Jr. (1986). Client compliance with homework directives during counseling. *Journal of Counseling Psychology, 33,* 124–130.

Worthington, E. L., Jr. (1992). Strategic matching and tailoring of treatment to couples and families. *Topics in Family Psychology and Counseling, 1,* 21–32.

Worthington, E. L., Jr., Buston, B. G., & Hammonds, T. M. (1989). A component analysis of marriage enrichment: Information and treatment modality. *Journal for Counseling and Development, 67,* 555–560.

Wright, H. N. (1990). *Marital counseling: A biblical, behavioral, cognitive approach.* New York: Harper and Row.

Wright, L. & L'Abate, L. (1977). Four approaches to family facilitation. *The Family Coordinator, 26,* 176–181.

Yalom, I. D. (1970). *The theory and practice of group psychotherapy.* New York: Basic Books.

Zimpfer, D. G. (1986). The use of groups in religiously based helping relationships. *Counseling and Values, 30,* 154–168.

Zimpfer, D. G. (1988a). Marriage enrichment programs: A review. *Journal for Specialists in Group Work, 13,* 44–53.

FURTHER READING

Alexander, J. F., Holtzworth-Munroe, A., & Jameson, P. B. (1994). The process and outcome of marital and family therapy: Research review and evaluation. In A. E. Bergin & S. L. Garfield (Eds.), *Handbook of psychotherapy and behavior change* (4th ed., pp. 595–630). New York: Wiley.

Allen, J. L. (1984). *Love and conflict: A covenantal model of christian ethics.* Nashville, TN: Abingdon Press.

Burgess, E. W., & Cottrell, L. S. (1939). *Predicting success or failure in marriage.* New York: Prentice-Hall.

Carmody, D. L., & Carmody, J. T. (1984). *Becoming one flesh: Growth in Christian marriage.* Nashville, TN: Upper Room Press.

Carter, S. L. (1993). *The culture of disbelief: How American law and politics trivialize religious devotion.* New York: Basic Books.

Chia, D. S. K. (1996). *Reliability and validity of videotape ratings of couple functioning.* Unpublished doctoral dissertation, Graduate School of Psychology, Fuller Theological Seminary, Pasadena, CA.

Cole, C. L. (1985). Relationship quality in long-term marriages: A comparison of high quality and low quality marriages. *Lifestyles, 7,* 248–257.

Cooper, A., & Stoltenberg, C. D. (1987). Comparison of a sexual enhancement and a communication training program on sexual and marital satisfaction. *Journal of Counseling Psychology, 34,* 309–314.

Crabb, L. J., Jr., & Allender, D. (1984). *Encouragement: The key to caring.* Grand Rapids, MI: Zondervan.

Doherty, W. J., Lester, M. E. I., & Leigh, G. K. (1986). Marriage encounter weekends: Couples who win and couples who lose. *Journal of Marital and Family Therapy, 12,* 49–61.

Dreikus, R. (1945). *The Challenge of Marriage.* New York: Duell Sloane & Pearce.

Eggeman, K., Moxley, V., & Schumm, W. R. (1985). Assessing spouses' perceptions of Gottman's temporal form in marital conflict. *Psychological Reports, 57,* 171–181.

Filsinger, E. H. (Ed.). (1983). *Marriage and family assessment.* Beverly Hills, CA: Sage.

Finkelhor, D., Hotaling, G. T., & Yllo, K. (1988). *Stopping family violence: Research priorities for the coming decade.* Newbury Park, CA: Sage.

Gelles, R. J. (1987). *Family violence.* Newbury Park, CA: Sage.

Gelles, R. J., & Strauss, M. A. (1988). *Intimate violence: The causes and consequences of abuse in the American family.* New York: Simon & Schuster.

Gillespie, V. B. (1988). *The experience of faith.* Birmingham, AL: Religious Education Press.

Gingras, M., Adam, D., & Chagnon, G. J. (1983). Marriage enrichment: The contribution of sixteen process variables to the effectiveness of a program. *Journal of Sex and Marital Therapy, 9,* 121–134.

Gottman, J. M. (1979). *Marital interaction: Experimental investigations.* New York: Academic Press.

Gottman, J. M. (1993). The roles of conflict engagement, escalation, and avoidance in marital interaction: A longitudinal view of five types of couples. *Journal of Consulting and Clinical Psychology, 61,* 6–15.

Gottman, J. M. (1996). *What predicts divorce? The measures.* Mahwah, NJ: Erlbaum.

Gottman, J. M. (1997). *From the roots up: A research based marital therapy.* Seattle, WA: Seattle Marital and Family Institute.

Grant, B. W. (1986). *Reclaiming the dream: Marriage counseling in the parish context.* Nashville, TN: Abingdon Press.

Gurman, A. S. (1978). Contemporary marital therapies: A critique and comparative analysis of psychoanalytic, behavioral and systems theory approaches. In T. J. Paolino & B. S. Mc-Crady (Eds.), *Marriage and marital therapy* (pp. 445–566). New York: Brunner/Mazel.

Gurman, A. S., & Kniskern, D. P. (Eds.). (1991). *Handbook of family therapy* (Vol. 2). New York: Brunner/Mazel.

Guttman, H. A. (1991). Systems theory, cybernetics, and epistemology. In A. S. Gurman & D. P. Kniskern (Eds.), *Handbook of family therapy* (Vol. 2, pp. 41–62). New York: Brunner/Mazel.

Hahlweg, K., & Jacobson, N. S. (Eds.). (1984). *Marital interaction: Analysis and modification.* New York: Guilford Press.

Hamerlynck, E. J., Handy, L. C., & Mash, E. J. (Eds.). (1973). *Behavior change: Methodology, concepts, and practice.* Champaign, IL: Research Press.

Hawley, D. R., & Olson, D. H. (1995). Enriching newlyweds: An evaluation of three enrichment programs. *The American Journal of Family Therapy*, 23(2), 129–147.

Heyman, R. E., Sayers, S. L., & Bellack, A. S. (1994). Global marital satisfaction versus marital adjustment: An empirical comparison of three measures. *Journal of Family Psychology*, 8, 432–446.

Hinkle, J. S., & Wells, M. E. (1995). *Family counseling in the schools: Effective strategies and interventions for counselors, psychologists and therapists.* Greensboro, NC: ERIC/CASS.

Hunt, R. A. (1994). What research says about the five questions. *Journal of Psychology and Christianity, 13*, 133–142.

Hunt, R. A., & Hunt, J. A. F. (1995, April). *Christian LovePower for couples.* Paper presented at the Christian Association for Psychological Studies Conference, Virginia Beach, VA.

Institute for Relationship Therapy (1997). *Professional training programs in Imago Relationship Therapy.* Winter Park, FL: Author.

Karpel, M. A. (1994). *Evaluating couples: A handbook for practitioners.* New York: Norton.

Kasper, W. (1981). *Theology of Christian marriage.* New York: Crossroad.

Kelly, E. W., Jr. (1992). Religion in family therapy journals: A review and analysis. In L. A. Burton (Ed.), *Religion and the family: When God helps* (pp. 185–208). New York: Haworth Press.

Kerig, P. K. (1996). Assessing the links between interparental conflict and child adjustment: The conflicts and problem-solving scales. *Journal of Family Psychology*, 10, 454–473.

Kessler, M., & Goldston, S. E. (Eds.). (1986). *A decade of progress in primary prevention.* London: University Press of New England.

Kiecolt-Glaser, J. K., Fisher, L. D., Ogrocki, P., Stout, J. C., Speicher, C. E., & Glaser, R. (1987). Marital quality, marital disruption, and immune function. *Psychosomatic Medicine*, 49, 13–34.

L'Abate, L. (1986). *Systematic family therapy.* New York: Brunner/Mazel.

L'Abate, L., & Allison, M. Q. (1977). Planned change intervention: The enrichment model with couples, families and groups. *Transnational Mental Health Research Newsletter*, 19, 11–15.

L'Abate, L., & Weeks, G. (1976). Testing the limits of enrichment: When enrichment is not enough. *Journal of Marital and Family Therapy, 8,* 463–468.

Larson, D. B., & Larson, S. S. (1994). *The forgotten factor in physical and mental health: What does the research show?* Rockville, MD: Templeton Foundation.

Leigh, G. K., Loewen, I. R., & Lester, M. E. (1986). Caveat emptor: Values and ethics in family life education and enrichment. *Family Relations Journal of Applied Family and Child Studies, 35,* 573–580.

Lerner, H. G. (1983). *The dance of intimacy.* New York: Harper.

Lerner, H. G. (1984). *The dance of deception.* New York: Harper.

Lerner, H. G. (1985). *The dance of anger.* New York: Harper.

Levant, F. R. (1986). *Psychoeducational approaches to family therapy and counseling,* New York: Springer-Verlag.

Levinger, G., & Huston, T. L. (1990). The social psychology of marriage. In F. D. Fincham & T. N. Bradbury (Eds.), *The psychology of marriage* (pp. 19–58). New York: Guilford Press.

Levinson, D. J. (1986). A conception of adult development. *American Psychologist, 41,* 3–13.

Levinson, R. W., & Gottman, J. M. (1985). Physiological and affective predictors of change in relationship satisfaction. *Journal Personality & Social Psychology, 49,* 85–94.

Lund, M. (1985). The development of investment and commitment scales for predicting continuity of personal relationships. *Journal of Social and Personal Relationships, 2,* 3–23.

Malony, H. N., & Hunt, R. A. (1991). *The psychology of clergy.* Harrisburg, PA: Morehouse.

Matthews, D. A., Larson, D. B., & Barry, C. P. (1993) *The faith factor: An annotated bibliography of clinical research on spiritual subjects.* Rockville, MD: National Institute for Healthcare Research.

McCullough, M. E., & Worthington, E. L., Jr. (1992). Encouraging clients to forgive people who have hurt them: Review, critique, and research prospectus.

Mead, D. E., Vatcher, G. M., Wyne, B. A., & Roberts, S. L. (1990). The comprehensive areas of change questionnaire: Assessing marital couples' presenting complaints. *American Journal of Family Therapy, 18,* 65–78.

Most, R., & Guerney, B. G., Jr. (1983). An empirical evaluation of the training of lay volunteer leaders for premarital relationship enhancement. *Family Relations, 32,* 239–251.

Nathan, E. P., & Joanning, H. H. (1985). Enhancing marital sexuality: An evaluation of a program for the sexual enrichment of normal couples. *Journal of Sex and Marital Therapy, 11,* 157–164.

Nelson, J. B. (1978). *Embodiment: An approach to sexuality and Christian theology.* Minneapolis: Augsburg Press.

Noller, P., & Fitzpatrick, M. A. (Eds.). (1988). *Perspectives on marital interaction.* Clevedon: Clevedon, Avon, England: Multilingual Matters.

Olson, D. H., McCubbin, H., Barnes, H., Larsen, A., Muxen, M., & Wilson, M. (1983). *Families: What makes them work.* Beverly Hills, CA: Sage.

Palmer, P. J. (1983). *To know as we are known: Education as a spiritual journey.* San Francisco: Harper.

Paolino, T. J., & McCrady, B. S. (Eds.). (1978). *Marriage and marital therapy.* New York: Brunner/Mazel.

Parrott, L., III, & Parrott, L. (1995). *Saving your marriage before it starts (SYMBIS)*. Grand Rapids, MI: Zondervan Press.

Patton, D., & Waring, E. M. (1991). Criterion validity of two methods of evaluating marital relationships. *Journal of Sex and Marital Therapy, 17*, 22–26.

Phillips, E. L., & Wiener, D. N. (1966). *Short-term psychotherapy and structured behavioral change*. New York: McGraw-Hill.

Piercy, F., & Sprenkle, D. (1986). Family therapy theory building: An integrated approach. *Journal of Psychotherapy and the Family, 1*, 5–14.

Pinsof, W. M., & Wynne, L. C. (1995). The efficacy of marital and family therapy: An empirical overview, conclusions, and recommendations. *Journal of Marital and Family Therapy, 21*, 585–610.

Sager, C. J. (1976). *Marriage contracts and couple therapy: Hidden forces in intimate relationships*. New York: Brunner/Mazel.

Sabourin, S., Lussier, Y., & Wright, J. (1991). The effects of measurement strategy on attributions for marital problems and behaviors. *Journal of Applied Social Psychology, 21*, 734–746.

Schmaling, K. B., Fruzzetti, A. E., & Jacobson, N. S. (1989). Marital problems. In K. Hawton, P. M. Salkovskis, J. Kirk, & D. M. Clark (Eds.), *Cognitive behavior therapy for psychiatric problems: A practical guide* (pp. 339–369). Oxford, England: Oxford University Press.

Smith, L., & Smith, A. (1976). Developing a national marriage communication lab training program. In H. A. Otto (Ed.), *Marriage and family enrichment: New perspective and program*. Nashville, TN: Abingdon Press.

von Bertalanffy, L. (1968). General systems theory. New York: Braziller.

Waldo, M. (1988). Relationship enhancement counseling groups for wife abusers. *Journal of Mental Health Counseling, 10*(1), 37–45.

Wallerstein, J. S. (1991). The long-term effects of divorce on children: A review. *Journal of the American Academy of Child Adolescent Psychiatry, 30*, 349–360.

Wampler, K. S. (1982a). Bringing the review of literature into the age of quantification: Meta-analysis as a strategy for integrating research findings in family studies. *Journal of Marriage and the Family, 44*, 1009–1023.

Wampler, K. S. (1982b). The effectiveness of the Minnesota couple communication program: A review of research. *Journal of Marital and Family Therapy, 8*, 345–355.

Waterman, J. A. (1989). *Communication ability and marital satisfaction of egalitarian versus hierarchical couples*. Unpublished master's thesis, Graduate School of Psychology, Fuller Theological Seminary, Pasadena, CA.

Weiss, R. L. (1980). Strategic behavioral marital therapy: Toward a model for assessment and intervention. In J. P. Vincent (Ed.), Advances in family intervention, assessment, and theory (Vol. 1, pp. 229–271). Greenwich, CT: JAI Press.

Worthington, E. L., Jr. (1991). Marriage counseling with Christian couples. In G. R. Collins, (Ed.), *Case studies in Christian counseling* (pp. 72–97). Dallas, TX: Word Books.

Worthington, E. L., Jr. (1993). *Hope for troubled marriages*. Downers Grove, IL: InterVarsity Press.

Worthington, E. L. (1995, April). *New directions in helping marriages and families*. Paper presented at Christian Association for Psychological Studies Conference, Virginia Beach.

Worthington, E. L., Jr. (1996). *Christian marital counseling: Eight approaches.* Grand Rapids, MI: Baker Book House.

Worthington, E. L., Jr., Shortz, J. L., & McCullough, M. E. (1993). A call for emphasis on scholarship on Christian marriage and marriage counseling. *Journal of Psychology and Christianity, 12,* 13–23.

Wright, H. N. (1994). Marital counseling. *Journal of Psychology and Christianity, 13,* 174–181.

Young, J. J. (1985). New Testament perspectives on divorce ministry. *Pastoral Psychology, 33,* 205–216.

Index

Duke Center for Living, 203
Dyad, marital, family and, 188
Dyadic Adjustment Scale (DAS),
    104, 105
Dynamic view, 16–17
Dysfunction, marital
    needs with, 175–176

Education, 5
Educational approach, 101–102
Educational communities, 60
Educational model, 18–19
Effectiveness, program, 131–144. *See
    also* Research
    improving measures of, 143–144
    long-term change monitoring in,
        133–138 (*See also* Change
        monitoring, long-term)
    marital status and quality in,
        138–142
    preevent to postevent changes in,
        142–143
    theory, research, and application in,
        131–132
Elements, essential, 76–77, 145–161
    couple commitment as, 147–150
    couples therapy as, 159–161
    homework as, 152–156
    leader qualities as, 156–159 (*See
        also* Leaders, program)
    ME team research design as,
        145–147
    program structure as, 150–152
Employee assistance programs,
    201–203
ENRICH inventory, 105–106, 135,
    136, 137
Enrichment, 5, 6
    definition of, 14
Epstein, N., 46
Ethnic couples, 179–184
    African-Americans, 179–181
    Chinese Americans, 181–184

Event characteristics, 69–70
    size of event, 69–70
    types of programs, 69

Faith, 60
Family(ies)
    adults in, 7
    dysfunctional, 7
    marriage and, 51–52
Family structure, 51
Family therapy, 32
Family Wellness Associations, 228
Fatherhood, as male role, 58
Feedback
    couple group formats for, 32
    video, 108–109
Five steps, intervention, 171–172
Floor exercise, 100
Follow-up, 39–40, 82–83
    in PREP, 133
Format, 77–82. *See also* Schedule and
    format
Foundations, theoretical, 35–39
Four Horsemen of the Apocalypse, 13,
    139
Fournier, David, 92
Fraenkel, Peter, 92
Fulfillment, individual, 21
Fun deck, 100
Fundamental interpersonal relationship
    organizations (FIRO) theory, 88

Gallagher, Father Chuck, 26
Gay couples, 10
Generalizability, 117
Getting the Love You Want, 10, 29,
    88–89, 228. *See also* Imago
    Relationship Therapy
    exercises in, 101
    research on, 142
GIFT, 201, 228
Gifts, three, 102
Goals, 12, 14, 100